Understanding
Britain

For my Parents

Understanding Britain

A History of
the British People
and their Culture

JOHN RANDLE

Basil Blackwell · Oxford

© *John Randle 1981*

First published in 1981 by
Basil Blackwell Ltd
108 Cowley Road
Oxford OX4 1JF
England
Reprinted with corrections 1981; 1983, 1985

British Library Cataloguing in Publication Data

Randle, John
    Understanding Britain.
    1. English language − Text-books for foreigners
    2. Great Britain − Social life and customs
    I. Title
    428'.2'4   PE1128

ISBN 0-631-12471-3
      0-631-12883-2 pbk

Filmset in Monophoto Times New Roman by
Latimer Trend & Company Ltd, Plymouth.
Printed and bound in Great Britain
by Billings & Sons Limited, Worcester.

Contents

Preface

This book has been written for all people interested in extending their knowledge of Britain. In addition to the many British who may wish to look at the development of their society at this time of national self-examination, there are now millions of foreign students of the English language who want to know about the country that produced the language they are learning.

Britain can never be understood if our attention is confined to contemporary affairs. The British Isles are made up of old countries whose institutions and structure are the product of that history. Unashamedly this book begins with the roots of British history and presents a survey of the past before going on to deal with the twentieth century in greater detail.

I have tried to present the material here as clearly and simply as possible to aid general readers. It is my hope that their enthusiasm will be roused and that they will carry on to read more specialised works, visit churches, galleries and museums and give some thought to the many questions posed by the study of the history of these island peoples.

Acknowledgements

I am most grateful to Professor Peter Marshall and Mr Ashley Aasheim for patiently reading through the modern sections of this book at draft stage and offering many useful suggestions. My thanks also go to Mr John Steven for his help and encouragement while I was teaching at Pitmans.

The publishers are grateful to the following for their help in providing illustrations:

Aerofilms: pages 48, 55, 204; BBC Hulton Picture Library: pages 120, 137, 143, 146, 149, 150, 151, 160; BL Cars Limited: page 201; Janet and Colin Bord: pages 2, 39, 104; British Library: pages 21 (Harley MS. 5102, f. 32), 35 (Add. MS. 5141, f. 1); Trustees of the British Museum: page 9; Syndics of Cambridge University Library: page 34; Camera Press: pages 122, 171 (photo: Alan Cowell), 176 (photos: Alan Clifton and Michael Evans), 193, 197 (photo: Lionel Cherruault), 209 (photo: A. Ashwood); Information Canada Phototheque: page 124 (photo: Hans Blohm); Cosway Estate Offices: page 147; The Dean and Chapter of Durham Cathedral: page 33; Edinburgh City Libraries: page 108; Department of the Environment, Crown Copyright – reproduced with permission of the Controller of Her Majesty's Stationery Office: page 5; Fox Photographs: pages 177, 187, 206; Her Majesty's Stationery Office, Edinburgh, Crown Copyright Reserved: page 46; Dezo Hoffman: page 205; Trustees of the Imperial War Museum: page 138; Keystone Press: page 196 (top); Mansell Collection: pages 25, 63, 77, 81, 91, 93, 114, 130; Roger Mayne: page 161; Trustees, the National Gallery, London: page 28; National Library of Ireland: page 99; National Portrait Gallery: pages 53, 60, 67, 76, 87, 96, 109, 118, 127, 139, 148; National Trust: page 64; Phaidon Press: page 15; George Philip and Son Ltd for maps from *Muir's Historical Atlas* (1969, London): pages 12, 41; Popperfoto: page 208 (three photos); RAF Museum, Hendon: page 165; Routledge and Kegan Paul Ltd for a map from Lloyd and Jennifer Laing, *Anglo-Saxon England* (1979, London): page

9; Syndication International: page 176 (Harold Wilson); Thomas Photos, Oxford: page 84; *The Times:* pages 172, 196 (bottom); Topix: page 181; Board of Trinity College, Dublin: page 10; University Tutorial Press for maps from B. Nixon, *The British Isles* (1978, Cambridge): pages 174, 199, 201; Wales Tourist Board: page 186; Warwickshire County Libraries (Rugby Collection): page 128; Woodspring Museum, Weston-super-Mare: page 132.

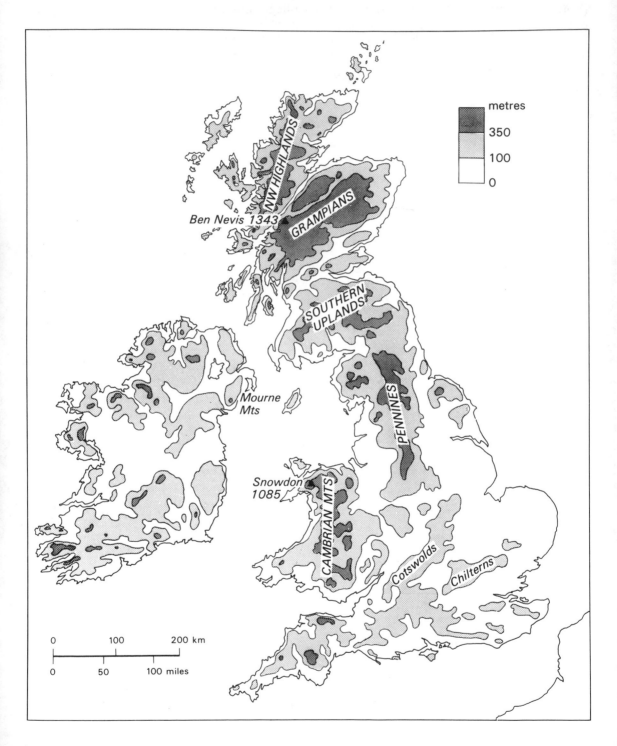

metres

350

100

0

NW HIGHLANDS

GRAMPIANS

Ben Nevis 1343

SOUTHERN UPLANDS

Mourne Mts

PENNINES

Snowdon 1085

CAMBRIAN MTS

Cotswolds

Chilterns

0   100   200 km

0   50   100 miles

Relief map of Britain and Ireland

1

The Founding of Britain

Prehistory

Until 8300 BC Britain, for several hundred thousand years, experienced alternating periods of intense cold, when ice sheets covered much of the country, and periods at least as warm as the present. During the glacial periods Britain was connected to the Continent by broad stretches of land in the present Channel and North Sea areas, and animals and human groups were able to move between Britain and the Continent. It is from the middle inter-glacial stage (200,000–125,000 BC) that firm evidence for human occupation in Britain comes.

Palaeolithic man hunted, and doubtless collected, whatever food was available. As a number of Palaeolithic settlements have been discovered at the edge of lakes, there is speculation that he slaughtered animals when they came to drink. Early man must have been a brave and skilled hunter, for during the glacial periods there were animals such as the mammoth and woolly rhinoceros and, in the inter-glacial times, similarly formidable specimens such as the wild boar and straight-tusked elephant.

In the Mesolithic period which followed the Palaeolithic, man had to adapt to post-glacial conditions, in which a spread in forest and a big drop in the food supply occurred. The discovery of axes from this time perhaps indicates his effort to make clearings. Some of the best artefacts come from settlements on the western coast of Scotland and Yorkshire.

Around 4000 BC a new people joined the scanty Mesolithic population. The newcomers, the Neolithic people, were knowledgeable about forest clearance. Additionally, Neolithic man sowed corn, kept animals and knew how to make pottery. In the next 2000 years much of southern Britain at least saw widespread farming. Tools, though still of flint and stone, were more sophisticated, as they were made, for the first time, by groups of specialists.

The most spectacular achievement of the Neolithic people was their monumental architecture. They have left behind remains of their causewayed camps, burial mounds known as barrows, chambered tombs and enormous ritual centres called henges. Many of the first Neolithic monuments are found in Wiltshire, in the south-west of Britain. At Silbury Hill there is the largest man-made mound in Europe. Stonehenge dates from before 2000 BC and is one of the most mysterious and complex archaeological sites in the world. It took several centuries for Stonehenge to be completed, and it remained a ritual centre for 2000 years.

Over four thousand years ago the Neolithic peoples of Britain began the construction of Stonehenge on Salisbury Plain. It is one of the world's most mysterious and complex archaeological sites.

At the other end of Britain, in Orkney and Caithness, there are also astonishing Neolithic remains. The availability of flagstones helped in the construction of chambered tombs, or cairns, which were covered over with massive mounds of earth. The chambers inside the cairns were used (or re-used) continuously for the burial of large numbers of people, perhaps families or tribal groups.

Neolithic society was transformed, before 2000 BC, by the arrival of a vigorous people known as Beaker folk because of a characteristic drinking vessel, a beaker, which was generally buried with their dead. These people knew how to extract and work metal. They made copper at first and, later, bronze. The use of bronze made possible the manufacture of stronger tools and weapons, more splendid decorative objects and utensils and even musical instruments. The Bronze Age seems to have been warmer than now, and Britain possibly supported a larger population then than during the Middle Ages. The Beaker people seem to have dominated, and then merged with, the local population. They continued to use and elaborate Neolithic ritual centres (for example, Stonehenge), but they did not follow the Neolithic burial practices of burying numbers of people in collective tombs; the dead were buried in single, shallow graves, together with personal possessions, including the beaker. Some of the graves in the Early Bronze Age have yielded great riches, including gold work, which indicates that there was a more defined aristocracy than in Neolithic times. Later Bronze Age society (1400–700 BC) seems to have developed more slowly, and this together with the practice of cremation, which was adopted during this period, has meant that fewer artefacts are available for archaeological examination.

There seems to have been a quickening of tempo from the eighth century BC, which stemmed from greatly increased trade with the Continent. This, combined with the possible settlement in Britain of new peoples from the Continent, gradually introduced Iron Age cultures into Britain. Iron Age or Celtic culture had certainly spread through lowland Britain by the sixth century BC, though pastoral Bronze Age lifestyles persisted in much of the north and west until the arrival of the Romans some 500 years later.

At the end of the second century BC Celtic invaders, the Belgic tribes, arrived and settled in areas of southern England, despite fierce resistance from the indigenous Celtic population. Settled Celtic ways of life were upset, and kingdoms led by a martial aristocracy emerged across the country. These warriors were renowned fighters, charging into battle in chariots and fighting on foot with their long iron swords when they had broken through the enemy lines. Sometimes they went into battle naked or painted in a blue dye called woad. They wore massive gold jewellery and had splendidly ornamented shields. Equal in power at least to this secular aristocracy was a priestly class, the Druids, who supervised worship of supernatural and magical forces, which required frequent human sacrifices.

Throughout Britain the Celts have left remains of their massive hillforts, which, it is thought, were not only defensive positions but also places where the community could assemble for social and religious functions. In this respect these forts were similar to the causewayed camps of the Neolithic period. The forts were formidable strongholds, containing buildings to house the population, ample space for their herds and stores for their grain. Normally these hillforts gave great security to the population in times of danger. However, the next group of invaders, the Romans, had a military technology superior to Celtic defences – just as the discipline of the Roman legionaries was more effective than the dash and bravado of the Celtic warriors.

The Romans

The aim of the Romans when they first landed in Britain in 55 BC was to assess the wealth of the country with a view to absorbing it later into the Empire. The Roman commander, the famed Julius Caesar, had an easy victory over the Britons, but he was forced to retire, as storms in the Channel prevented his cavalry from arriving from Gaul (France). In 54 BC Caesar returned and marched through southern Britain. The Britons were divided, but Cassivellaunus, king of the Catuvellauni, mounted stiff opposition. Finally Cassivellaunus' stronghold was taken and the king himself captured. The Romans took hostages and obtained promises that tribes friendly to the Romans would not be punished when Caesar and his army left. The Romans also arranged for the Britons to pay an annual tribute to Rome.

The Romans gained first-hand knowledge of Britain and noted its agricultural and mineral wealth. After they departed trade between Britain and the Empire increased, and schemes to annex such a potentially rich country to the rest of the Empire were continually forwarded by Roman planners.

The conquest of most of Britain came in AD 43, when Aulus Plautius, acting on the instructions of the emperor, Claudius, invaded Britain with an army of some 40,000 men. After the army had established control of the south-east, Claudius himself arrived with an impressive retinue, including elephants. The emperor received the submission of a number of the British kings and then left. The annexation was duly celebrated in Rome, and Claudius' son was named Britannicus (Britannia being the Roman name for the island). But there was a lot of hard fighting to be done before Britain was conquered. British hillforts had to be stormed systematically, and not until AD 51 was Caratacus, the principal British leader opposed to Rome, in Roman custody.

The last serious resistance of the Celts in the south came in AD 61, when Boudicca, queen of the Iceni, led her people in revolt. The Iceni had been harshly treated by the Romans, and their revenge was terrible. Three Roman centres, Colchester, London and St Albans, were destroyed and some 70,000 people killed. The revolt was suppressed, and the queen took poison. However, revenge against the Iceni was checked, and the governors, with the backing of Rome, took a conciliatory line. Southern Britain settled down to peace and rapid Romanisation. Where possible, the Romans ruled through the existing upper class, which was encouraged to adopt Roman dress, a luxurious lifestyle and the Latin language.

There was no part of the country which the Romans could not have conquered if they wished, but some areas had such difficult terrain and, from the Roman point of view, such un-co-operative peoples, that garrisoning would have been extremely costly after conquest. Thus, the north of Scotland, peopled by the fierce Celtic people known as the Picts, or Caledonians, was not occupied by the Romans. Rome exercised sovereignty over the lowlands of Scotland, but with the Picts to the north Roman civilisation could not take root there. Between AD 122 and 127 the Romans undertook the stupendous task of constructing a wall from the Tyne to the Solway. This was manned by 10,000 men and, together with the great fortresses at York, Chester and Caerleon, marked a massive military presence in the north. Hadrian's Wall was intended to divide two tribes, the Brigantes and the Selgovae, and to prevent them from forming an alliance against Rome. It was also meant to protect the population to the south from the Picts and their allies.

The fiercest allies of the Picts were the Scotti, a Celtic people so named by the Romans. They had lived in Ireland until the third century, but they then moved to the western coast of

Hadrian's Wall was built by the Romans as a defence against invasion from the north. It still sweeps majestically over the desolate landscape of Northumberland.

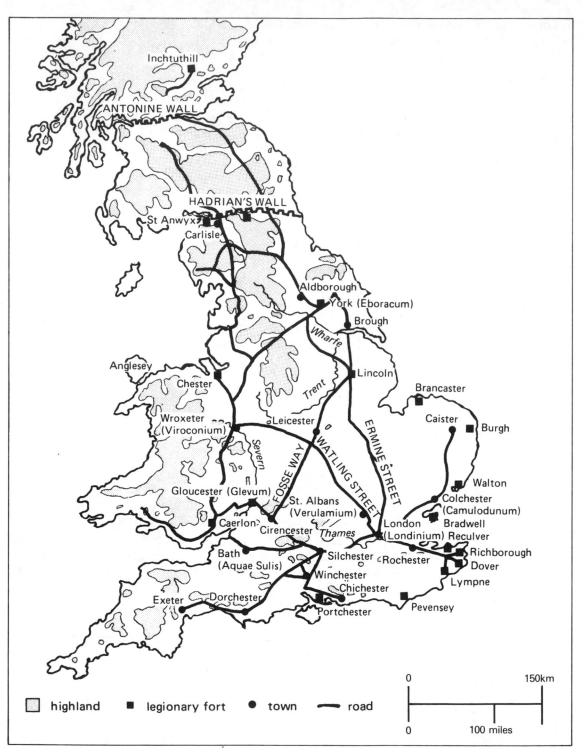

Roman forts, towns and roads

Scotland, giving that country their name. Ireland itself was divided into warlike principalities enjoying a Celtic or Iron Age culture. Though the Romans boasted that it would only take one legion, or about 5000 men, to conquer Ireland, the Romans left Ireland completely alone.

The Romans established a flourishing province in Britain. They founded the first cities, and though some of these were later abandoned by the Saxons, they often became the sites of medieval towns and cities. Londinium (London), founded by the Romans where it was convenient to bridge the Thames, became the provincial capital and a major trading centre in northern Europe. Britain became a big exporter of corn, lead and tin. From London a network of roads radiated across the country, and not until the eighteenth century was there any road building in Britain which could begin to match the Roman achievement. Villas, the characteristic Roman establishment in the countryside, which combined a gracious country residence with a large estate, were founded throughout Britain. The south, warmer and more civilised, naturally saw the greatest density of villas. At Bath the Romans used a British site to establish a remarkable series of baths and temples. The baths, fed by underground springs, have to a great extent survived until the present day.

In the fourth century Roman Britain was threatened not only by Picts and Scots from the North but also, more menacingly, by the Saxons, a loose term used to describe a number of peoples living in present-day Denmark, north-west Germany and the Netherlands. The Roman fleet was unable to prevent Saxon raids and piracy, and there had to be a rapid acceleration in the building of defences along the east and south coasts. In 367 there was a combined attack on Britain by Picts, Scots and Saxons. Confidence in the province never recovered. When Rome itself was directly threatened by enemies the Roman armies had to abandon the outlying parts of the empire. In 410 the Roman army withdrew, and the Romano-British population had to look after its own defences. Without Roman military might, Roman civilisation in Britain disintegrated.

Perhaps Roman Britain disappeared because it failed to make much impact on the ordinary people. They had certainly enjoyed peace and good government, tremendous assets in any age. Yet most of the population lived in the countryside, and farming techniques do not seem to have changed much under the Romans, though new vegetables like cabbages, peas and root crops, and fruits like plums, apples and cherries, were introduced. The British population seems to have retained its Celtic languages, Latin being confined to the upper sections of society. The marvellous buildings and public facilities like sanitation systems were found in the towns, where only a minority of the population lived. But Celtic culture was submerged by the incoming Saxons, and survived only in present-day Cornwall, north Wales, Scotland and Ireland, which saw neither Roman nor Saxon.

The Saxons and Vikings

The Picts and Scots, who might have been expected to take full advantage of the Roman army's withdrawal, chose instead to war with each other until the ninth century. There were, however, no such quarrels to hold back the Saxons, who came across the North Sea and attacked the east and south-east coasts of Britain. Vortigern, a British leader in the south-east, employed two Saxon warriors, Hengist and Horsa, to defend the country, but with little success; instead, they appropriated parts of the south-east for themselves, and the invasions continued. By 450 Essex, Kent and Sussex were held by the Saxons. The invaders experienced a temporary check in the west, where the British rallied under the legendary King Arthur; some time between 490 and 503 he won a great victory over the Saxons at Mount Badon. The west remained British, though intermarriage with Saxons and, later, conversion to Christianity must have lessened the differences between the two peoples.

The rest of England, now so called after one of the invading groups, the Angles, fell to the invaders, as did the lowlands of Scotland. By the early seventh century Saxon Britain was divided into seven kingdoms – the Heptarchy. There were the comparatively small kingdoms of East Anglia, Kent, Essex and Sussex, and three superpowers – Northumbria, Mercia and Wessex. These three, mutually hostile, in turn dominated English politics until the peace of Saxon England was shattered by the Vikings some 200 years later.

The abandonment by the Saxons of the towns and villas signalled the abandonment of the Roman way of life. But the Saxon settlement in villages and homesteads marked a great forward step in the countryside. The Saxons were excellent farmers. They cleared much of the forest, which had in Roman times stretched in a broad swathe from the south coast to the base of the Pennine Hills. The Saxons used a heavy plough, which worked much more effectively on English soils than anything used before and which remained basically unchanged until the Agricultural Revolution in the eighteenth century. Indeed, the Saxon villages have largely survived and evolved until the present day – an indication of their clever siting.

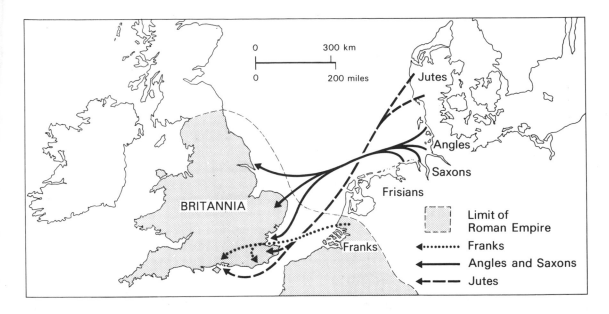

The Saxons lived in strong family and tribal units, the most prominent feature of which was intense loyalty to a man's king or chief. There were features of Saxon civilisation which we might admire. An example is *wergild*, a custom which dictated that a man who committed a murder should pay suitable compensation to the bereaved family rather than be executed. There is also, however, unsavoury evidence of burials of living people, probably a wife or servants, at the funeral of a great person. Indeed, Saxon graves in the period 400–650 provide much of our information about Saxon England. The Sutton Hoo treasure (now in the British Museum) is one of the most spectacular hoards to have come to light anywhere in Europe. In all probability it belonged to King Raedwald of East Anglia, who died in 625.

Many colourful stories are told about the arrival of Christianity in England, one being the tale of Pope Gregory's alleged comment on seeing English slaves in Rome: 'Non Angli sed angeli' (They are not Angles but angels'), and his vow that these angelic people should be converted to Christianity. Certainly, Rome was interested in bringing England into the Christian fold. St Augustine, who was sent to England by Gregory, arrived in Kent in 597 and, not being able to enter London, established the ecclesiastical capital at Canterbury, where it has remained until the present day. Conversion was carried out with the support of the Saxon kings, who were receptive to the idea that Christianity would support their authority and would produce a supply of educated administrators and advisers.

The treasure found at Sutton Hoo in Suffolk, now displayed at the British Museum, comes from the grave of a Saxon king of the seventh century. Despite its forbidding appearance, this reconstructed helmet was probably never worn in battle but used on ceremonial occasions.

9

While Southern Britain was converted to Roman Christianity, the north was converted by monks from Ireland and Scotland. Christianity had been brought to Ireland in 432 by St Patrick, a slave of the Irish who had escaped to Rome and who had determined to take the faith back to his former captors. Ireland had rapidly become Christian and the Irish became vigorous missionaries abroad. They reinforced the Christianity of Wales and Scotland which had survived in scattered communities. The most famous missionary to Scotland was St Columba, and a great religious centre grew up on the island of Iona.

The Celtic Church now established in the north of England was in some ways different from the Roman Church. Easter, for example, was celebrated at a different time, and monasticism took a different and more austere form. The differences were sufficient to cause a split between the northern and southern Churches. The two religious parties met at the Synod of

The masterpiece of Celtic art in the eighth century was the Book of Kells, an illuminated manuscript of the Gospels.

10

Whitby in 663, and the English Church as a whole resolved to follow the Roman model, although Celtic Christianity persisted in Scotland, Wales and Ireland.

Christianity inspired great works of art. Northumbria had a Golden Age in the seventh century, when the great monasteries produced copies of the scriptures, wonderfully enriched by paintings. The monks were influenced by the craftsmanship of Celtic Ireland as well as by current trends on the Continent. The copies of the Gospels made around 700 at the monastery of Lindisfarne are among the treasures of the period. In the eighth century the centre of English manuscript illumination decoration moved to Canterbury. In Ireland and Scotland, too, manuscripts were exquisitely illuminated. The Book of Kells, probably written at Iona, is one of the masterpieces of the Irish Celtic Church.

The great Northumbrian monastery of Monkwearmouth was the home of a famed scholar, the Venerable Bede, who in 731 completed his 'Ecclesiastical History of the English People' and numerous other works which gave English scholarship a European reputation. Bede gives an invaluable outline of English history from the end of Roman rule in Britain, and at the same time takes the opportunity to avenge the Church for the harm it suffered at the hands of the Saxon invaders.

In the eighth century to the litanies of the monks was added: 'A furore Normanorum, libera nos, Domine!' ('From the fury of the Norsemen, Lord deliver us!'). Known variously as Norsemen, Viking or Danes, these new invaders were a heathen people from present-day Norway, Sweden and Denmark, highly skilled in sailing and fighting. They sailed south and west from their homeland and attacked every coast which offered the opportunity of plunder. A great shock to Britain, and indeed to Christendom, was the destruction in 793 of the great monastery of Lindisfarne and the murder of the monks there.

The Vikings increased their raids on the coast of England and in 865 began a great invasion of Northumbria and East Anglia, where they established settlements. Scotland was similarly attacked, and Orkney, Shetland, the Western Isles and the extreme north of the mainland (modern Caithness and Sutherland) were conquered. The Isle of Man in the Irish Sea was taken, and Ireland, which had suffered neither Roman nor Saxon invasions, was attacked. From settlements at the mouths of rivers, later to be great cities like Dublin, the Vikings raided the whole of Ireland.

Divided as it was between Picts and Scots, Britons with their kingdom in Strathclyde and Angles (English) in Lothian,

The Viking invasions

Scotland could not hope to throw out the Norsemen. Ireland was also divided, and Danish settlement in Ireland was a recognised fact even after the Irish won a great victory over the Danes at the Battle of Clontarf in 1014.

Just as the resistance to the Saxons in the fifth century had come from the west, so the Danes encountered effective opposition in Wessex, which was ruled by King Alfred. A warrior and scholar, Alfred's strategy of combining guerrilla warfare and open pitched battle with the enemy eventually led to the defeat of the Danes. In 878, by the terms of the Peace of Edington, England was partitioned between Saxons and Vikings. East Anglia and part of Northumbria formed the Viking sector, the Danelaw. Also the Danish Prince, Guthrum, agreed to become a Christian. How seriously Guthrum regarded his conversion is open to question, but the steady Christianisation of the Vikings had begun. This would inevitably lead in time to their fusion with the local population. They were basically of the same stock as the Saxons, and their language was Germanic, as Saxon was. Together their tongues would later form the basis of English.

Alfred's dynasty, the House of Wessex, became the rulers of Saxon England and gradually took the Danelaw back from the Vikings. Alfred's grandson, Edgar, was crowned king of a united England in 973, at a ceremony in Bath which has formed the basis of the coronation service up to the present day. Scotland, too, was achieving a measure of loose unity (see Chapter 3). Ethelred II, the second son of Edgar, failed to stem renewed Viking attacks, and he had to pay Danegeld. Ethelred, popularly known as 'the Unready', died in 1016, and his son, Edmund II, lived only a few months longer. Saxon resistance collapsed, and Canute, king of the Vikings, became the ruler of the whole of England, Viking Scotland, Denmark and Scandinavia. Canute provided strong, wise rule and, as a devoted Christian, fully supported the Church. Only a person of Canute's stature could have ruled such a diverse empire, and it fell to pieces on his death in 1035. His two sons, Harold 'Harefoot' (reigned 1035–40) and Hardicanute (reigned 1040–43) ruled England in succession.

Neither Harold nor Hardicanute had any children, and the son of Ethelred 'the Unready' and Emma of Normandy succeeded to the throne. This son, Edward, though of the House of Wessex had been brought up in Normandy. Edward faced severe political problems and was occasionally dominated by the greatest nobleman of the kingdom, Earl Godwin, who was the real ruler of England. Godwin cemented his family's tie with the throne by marrying his daughter to Edward. King Edward, known as 'the Confessor', had no children, and

Godwin's son, Harold Godwinson, by virtue of his great power in the country and the fact that he was Edward's brother-in-law, believed that he should be king on Edward's death.

Harold was not the only claimant to the throne of England, however. Duke William of Normandy, whose father, Robert, had been the brother of Emma, the wife of Ethelred and Canute, also believed he should succeed Edward. His claims were reinforced when, in 1064, Harold was shipwrecked off the Norman coast. William took Harold prisoner and obliged him to swear an oath recognising William as Edward's rightful heir. Neither Harold Godwinson nor William, Duke of Normandy, was the natural heir to Edward; rather, each man believed that he should rule. They were ambitious and determined to get their way. In January 1066 Edward died. Harold was crowned king in London; William immediately began to make preparations to invade England, which he believed was rightly his and not Harold's.

The Normans

King Harold faced two threats in 1066. Not only was Duke William of Normandy intent on taking the throne which he believed was his, but Harold's half brother, Earl Tostig, whom Harold had previously dispossessed and driven out of the country, was planning invasion and revenge. Tostig's threat was serious, as he was allied to the powerful king of Norway, Harold 'Hardrada' ('the Severe'), who commanded a huge Viking fleet and army. Tostig and Harold 'Hardrada' enjoyed the friendship of the king of the Scots, and the English could accordingly expect a fearsome attack from the north.

In September 1066 Tostig and the Norwegian king landed in the north of England. King Harold was in the south, awaiting Duke William's invasion; he had to march rapidly north to meet the Scandinavian invaders. At a great battle at Stamford Bridge in Yorkshire on the 25 September Harold defeated and killed Tostig and Harold 'Hardrada'. Though the Vikings continued to be a presence in Scottish and Irish life for another 200 years, they never menaced England again, and the Viking king's plan to revive Canute's great northern empire was abandoned.

Meanwhile, on the 28 September, Duke William landed at Pevensey Bay on the Sussex coast with an army of about 8000 men. Though the Normans were descendants of Viking settlers in northern France, they fought quite differently from the Scandinavians (and the English). The basis of their army was the knight, who fought on horseback; both rider and horse were covered in chain-mail. Harold's men were foot soldiers armed with axes and spears. The Bayeux tapestry, which was made soon after the Norman Conquest to record the events of 1066, shows the English army without any horses whatsoever.

The Battle of Hastings in 1066 is graphically depicted in the Bayeux Tapestry. This section shows the victorious Normans, on horseback; the numerous corpses at the bottom indicate that the battle is drawing to its bloody close. The tapestry, which is in fact embroidery, is 70.34 metres long and 50 cm high and is housed in the former Bishop's Palace in Bayeux, Normandy.

The men who came with William hoped that victory would bring them great rewards – land and treasure. Harold, perhaps mistakenly, marched quickly south to confront William. Though he had an army roughly the same size as William's, he could have commanded a much bigger force had he travelled more slowly. Harold's army was tired after fighting and marching, but its morale was high after having won its great victory over Tostig.

The two armies met at Hastings on 14 October. After a long and hard battle William and the Normans won. Harold died on the battlefield after an arrow hit him in the eye. William then marched north and took London. He was crowned king of England at Westminster Abbey by the Archbishop of York on Christmas Day 1066. William (known as 'the Conqueror') then set about subduing England. The English had no natural leader to succeed Harold, and they were disunited. William ruthlessly suppressed opposition to Norman rule.

The north of England, always a distant, turbulent part of the kingdom, accepted William's rule and then, in 1069, revolted against him. Between 1069 and 1070 William set out to destroy the most fertile and populous areas of Yorkshire. For years afterwards this part of the country lay wasted and empty. In

1071 William finally put down the last serious English rebellion. The opposition came from the fen district – a watery, marshy part of East Anglia – which was ideally suited to warfare conducted by a resistance movement. The leader was Hereward the Wake, whom later Englishmen were to class with Arthur and Alfred as a great English hero.

Hastings is rightly regarded as a turning point in English history. The native English aristocracy was replaced by a French aristocracy. Language separated the new rulers of the country from their subjects. Clearly defined classes appeared in English society. At the top of society was the king, who was surrounded by great nobles or barons; these looked upon the king as a near-equal. After the great barons came lesser lords, who lived in manors or castles in villages and to whom the ordinary people or peasants owed their services. The peasantry was Saxon (that is, English). The people could not move from their land or village without the permission of their lord. This system of dependence and hierarchy is known as the feudal system. Though it would be wrong to say that feudalism was unknown in Saxon England, the rigid system imposed by the Normans was an innovation which brought England into line with the rest of western Europe.

The Normans needed to maintain a large standing army in England – between 4000 and 7000 knights. A lord would supply his overlord or baron with a fixed number of knights, and the baron, in turn, would supply the king with a quota of knights. In this way the king could, in times of trouble, raise a strong professional army. But the feudal system also created a warrior aristocracy, which could, with its armed knights, cause trouble for a king in a weak position. England, like western Europe, was to experience for centuries the problems associated with an armed nobility, or baronage, which disturbed the peace of the country. The barons on the borders of Scotland and Wales were particularly independent as, in return for their guarding of the English frontiers against the Scots and Welsh, they were granted extraordinary privileges by successive monarchs. In each county the king's authority was upheld by the sheriff.

Around the king was the royal curia, or court, which was made up of advisers and officials. In 1086 the king's officials compiled a remarkable book called the Domesday Book. It is a record of England's population and wealth. The Domesday Book was used by William and his successors for taxation purposes. It is of tremendous value to English historians, as it presents a description of Norman England, village by village.

The Norman Conquest brought the English Church into the mainstream of reform directed by the papacy. William the

16

Conqueror had fought under a papal banner at Hastings. In 1070 an Italian, Lanfranc, who had been an abbot in Normandy, became archbishop of Canterbury. In 1073 Hildebrand became Pope Gregory VII. He was a great pope, and his reforms helped to establish the authority of the medieval church, particularly in England.

William died in Rouen in Normandy in 1087. He had ruled both Normandy and England. This control of land in both France and England was to establish a pattern until the sixteenth century. It created great problems, as kings of England were obliged to divide their attention between their widely scattered and diverse possessions. Kings of France became increasingly annoyed by the fact that English monarchs controlled land in France which, they believed, should belong to the French monarchy. As a consequence, wars between England and France became a common feature throughout history from this time on.

2

Medieval England

Norman and Plantagenet, 1086–1199

William had three sons. The eldest, Robert, became duke of Normandy. William, the second son, became king of England. William, because of his shock of red hair, was known as William 'Rufus'. Relations between William the Conqueror's sons were bad. From 1089 to 1096 there was war in Normandy between Duke Robert and William II. William was successful and believed that he should rule all his father's possessions. The Conqueror's strict policies of subjugation and centralisation were pursued in England by his son. There was little remorse when King William was killed by a stray arrow in a hunting accident in 1100. Henry succeeded his brother as king of England.

From the outset Henry I had trouble with his brother, Duke Robert of Normandy. The two brothers met in battle at Tinchebrai in 1106. Robert was decisively beaten and condemned to perpetual imprisonment in England until his death in 1134. At Tinchebrai Englishmen fought for Henry; this is the first sign of an identification of interests between the English people and their Norman kings. Henry was the master of both England and Normandy as a result of his victory at Tinchebrai.

Henry was a powerful ruler. He enforced the law with the help of a team of judges, who each toured a region of England, holding court in the main towns they came to. This circuit system is still in operation today. Henry also set up the Exchequer to supervise monetary and fiscal matters. This it still does. England had the most centrally organised government in Europe.

Henry had one son, William. He was drowned in the winter of 1120, on his way from Normandy to England. This tragedy meant that the succession to the crown was in dispute. Henry had a daughter, Matilda, popularly known as Maud. She had married Henry V, the Holy Roman Emperor, in 1109. On his death in 1125 Matilda married Geoffrey, count of Anjou. She was hard and capable but, as a woman, was unacceptable to the barons as their ruler.

In 1135, when Henry I died, Matilda was pushed aside by Stephen, son of Adela, the daughter of William the Conqueror. She was out of the country at the time of Henry's death, and Stephen's brother, Henry, bishop of Winchester, rallied Church opinion to the cause of Stephen. Stephen was king from 1135–54, but throughout that time he was opposed by Matilda, who wanted the throne first for herself and then for her son, Henry. There was civil war until 1153, when by the Treaty of Winchester it was agreed that Stephen should rule until his death, taking counsel from Prince Henry. On the death of Stephen it was agreed that Henry should become king.

Henry II, who came to the throne in 1154, was master of a great empire. In 1150 he had become duke of Normandy. In 1151 he became count of Anjou, Touraine and Maine. In 1152 Eleanor of Aquitaine, queen of Louis VII of France, obtained a divorce and remarried Henry. To Henry she brought large parts of the south of France. In 1154, on Stephen's death, Henry became master of England. Henry's emblem was a plant called *Planta genesta*; hence his dynasty was to be called the Plantagenet dynasty.

Henry held his great empire together by his ability and energy. In England he re-established the authority of the centre after the weak government of Stephen's reign. He created the common law system, according to which every freeman had a right to plead in royal courts, even against his feudal lord. Henry also remodelled the Exchequer, which, being responsible for the collection of taxes, was at the centre of royal government. (The system of common law and the Exchequer exist today, and they serve many of the same functions as in Henry's reign.)

Henry's power was challenged by the kings of France, who were alarmed to see the major part of France in English hands Royal authority was also challenged by the Church. In the Middle Ages there was continuous conflict between the monarchs and the Church. The Church claimed that the appointment of bishops was its own exclusive right. Kings, however, believed that they should have some say in the appointment of Church leaders, as these men exercised a great deal of authority in the state.

In 1162 Henry decided to appoint his personal friend, the Chancellor Thomas Becket, to the vacant archbishopric of Canterbury. In this way Henry believed that he would have a good and peaceful relationship with the Church. Becket at once put his loyalty to the Church before his loyalty to Henry. Becket condemned Henry for his action against the Church, and in 1164 Henry exiled Becket. The archbishop did not return to England until 1170, when Becket immediately condemned the archbishop of York and six other bishops, who had, in Becket's absence, crowned Prince Henry, the heir

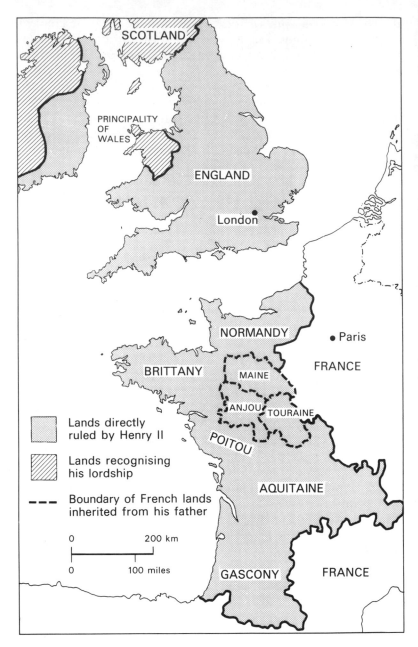

The empire of Henry II

apparent, at Henry II's request. The archbishop of York and the six bishops fled to Henry in Normandy and told him of Becket's actions. The king was furious with Becket and asked who could rid him of this troublesome archbishop. Four knights heard Henry's words and immediately went to Canterbury, where they cut down the archbishop as he was standing at the high altar in the cathedral.

The long conflict between Thomas Becket, Archbishop of Canterbury, and the king, Henry II, ended in the gruesome murder of Becket in his own cathedral in 1170. His death is imminent in this Latin psalter of about 1200, now in the British Library.

The murder of Becket in 1170 shook the whole of Christendom. Henry was faced with an angry Church and an angry people. The king was obliged to do penance in public for Becket's death. In 1172 the feud between Henry and the Church was settled at Avranches. It was agreed that the Church would invest the bishops, but the king would have to be consulted on the choice of candidates. The king and the English Church continued to work together until the Reformation in the 1530s.

In 1171 Henry assumed the lordship of Ireland (see Chapter 3). War with France continued. Henry also had to fight his four sons, Henry, Richard, Geoffrey and John. Prince Henry died in 1183, and when Henry II died in 1189 he was succeeded as king by his second son, Richard.

Richard I was a great soldier. Almost immediately on becoming king he set off for the Holy Land, the modern Middle East, to join the third Crusade against the Moslems.

Richard entrusted the government of England to William Longchamp, bishop of Ely. Prince John, Richard's brother, was given six counties in England, virtually a separate kingdom within England. John was deeply jealous of Richard and of the power of Longchamp. John and the French king Philip Augustus agreed to work together against King Richard.

In 1192 Richard was shipwrecked in the Adriatic on his way back from the Holy Land. He became a prisoner of the duke of Austria. John declared that Richard was dead and made himself king. The news that Richard was still alive spread, however, and John fled in panic to France. Richard's captor demanded an enormous ransom of 150,000 marks for the king's freedom. The English paid the ransom, as they were proud of their great and brave king, and it would have been dishonourable to let a crusader end his life in prison. Richard arrived back in England in February 1194. The rest of Richard's reign was spent abroad, principally in defending his possessions in France. He was killed in this struggle in 1199.

Magna Carta and Parliament, 1199–1272

Richard was succeeded by his brother, John. History has branded John a tyrant and an enemy of the Church, but modern opinion has a more favourable view of him. John may have been ill-tempered, vicious and jealous, but he was also at times brave, energetic and resourceful. In short, he was rather typical of the Plantagenet family. John was faced with three main problems. The power of the English nobility was increasing; the possessions of the English kings in France were daily becoming more difficult to defend; and the Church was still eager to gather into its hands as much power as possible. In Innocent III the papacy had one of its strongest and most militant popes in history.

Geoffrey, John's elder brother, had died in 1186. He had left a son, Arthur, prince of Brittany. The French king, Philip Augustus, at once supported Arthur against John. Philip invaded Normandy in 1202, and John was obliged to go to France to defend his French possessions. In 1203 John captured Arthur and, in all probability, had him murdered; certainly, no more is heard of Arthur after this date. War with Philip continued, and in 1204 the English lost Normandy.

In 1206 Pope Innocent III rejected John's candidate for the vacant see of Canterbury and instead chose his own man, Stephen Langton. John in turn rejected Innocent's choice, and the pope retaliated by placing England under an interdict from 1206 until 1212 (this meant that church ceremonies were suspended). In 1209 Innocent excommunicated John. Philip Augustus and the pope formed an alliance, and in 1215 John was obliged to give in to the papacy. But John, staging something of a diplomatic coup, offered England to the pope as a fief (in other words, John became the vassal of the pope). Innocent was delighted and now became John's firm friend. The pope's alliance with the king of France immediately came to an end. But John's campaign in France in 1214 finally ended in defeat at the Battle of Bouvines.

Meanwhile, the English nobility had become tired of the demands King John had been making on them. The war with the papacy and the French war had meant that John had increased taxation and had used every available means of collecting the money. The Church had been angry, first at the war with the papacy, and secondly at the king's surrender to the pope. After John's concordat with Innocent the English Church was flooded with appointees of the pope. Thus in 1215 the richest and most powerful sections of English society – the aristocracy, the Church and the merchants – formed a coalition against the king. At Runnymede, a small island in the Thames, near Windsor, John's opponents obliged him to agree to the terms of Magna Carta, or the Great Charter. 1215 is one of the most important dates in English history: it rivals 1066 in fame.

Magna Carta was a document which laid down the rules that a feudal king had to follow. It listed the abuses the king had committed and the remedies to rectify the ills. Magna Carta signified the increased importance of the barons (the feudal aristocracy) and the need for the king to work with them if his government of the country were to succeed. From 1215 until the accession of the Tudors in 1485 the feudal aristocracy was to be one of the mainsprings of national life. Rich and powerful, the barons could cause infinite trouble in the country through their fights with each other and with the king. Until the advent of gunpowder in warfare, a baron could shut himself up in a great castle and defy besiegers for months (and sometimes years) on end.

John had no intention of agreeing to Magna Carta without a fight. The war with the barons continued. Some of the barons invited Philip Augustus of France to England to be their liege and lord. When John died in 1216 England was deep in war.

The death of John did something to abate the warfare. In 1216 his son, Henry, was only nine and obviously not implicated in the misdeeds of his father. Also the French were the traditional enemies, and their presence in England harmed the baronial cause. Further, the Church strongly supported Henry.

By 1217 Henry III's guardians had triumphed and the

French withdrew. Magna Carta was reissued and regents were appointed to look after the kingdom. Henry was dominated by the regents until 1234. From 1234 until 1258 Henry III ruled on his own, without depending on any single counsellor. Henry surrounded himself with favourites, men who flattered rather than advised him. The barons took offence at their exclusion from membership of the royal councils.

Henry married Eleanor of Provence in 1236. Many of her relatives came to England and held high office. The king's young sister (another Eleanor) married a Frenchman, Simon de Montfort. The favouritism shown to foreigners greatly angered the English nobility. In 1252 Henry withdrew his brother-in-law, Simon, from Gascony, where he had been the royal commissioner. Simon had been charged with mis-government by the Gascons, and Henry upheld the Gascon charges. At a stroke Henry made a life-long enemy of Simon. The barons, who were increasingly opposed to the king, found a leader in Simon. Ironically, Simon de Montfort, originally chief of the foreign favourites, became leader of the baronial cause.

Since his childhood Henry had depended on papal advisers, and so in 1254 he accepted the crown of Sicily from the pope. For an English king to defend his claim to a distant country required vast expenditure of money. Henry raised enormous sums through the Church. There were bad harvests in the three years following 1255 and hence economic hardship in the country. The taxes were bitterly resented, and the king's actions aroused great anger in the country.

At Easter 1258 a group of barons rebelled. Henry was obliged to abandon the Sicilian crown and to consent to the Provisions of Oxford. These proposals were intended to remedy the abuses of Henry's government. A panel of four knights was set up in each county to supervise local government. The king's chief official in the county, the sheriff, was to be appointed for only one year at a time. At the royal court 'traditional' offices were to be restored and their positions more clearly defined. In addition, in 1259 the Provisions of Westminster were passed by the gentlemen, or knights. These demanded reforms in baronial administration which were similar to the reforms that had been undertaken at the royal court.

A council of fifteen people was appointed to direct the government of the country. Increasingly, however, it became difficult to rule through this council and the panels in the counties. The pope condemned the barons and gentry and supported Henry. St Louis, king of France, also strongly backed Henry, his fellow sovereign, in this time of crisis.

PARLIAMENT

OF EDWARD I.

Parliament became of increasing importance in the reign of Edward I (1272–1307). In this eighteenth-century print which reconstructs the Parliament of those times, Edward is flanked by the King of Scotland and the Archbishop of Canterbury on his right and by the Prince of Wales and the Archbishop of York on his left. As the left-hand side of the picture shows, churchmen played a significant part in Parliament.

Inevitably, there was war. Henry and his son, Prince Edward, commanded the royalist forces, and Simon de Montfort led the barons. In April 1264 the king and Edward were badly defeated by Simon at Lewes, and they were taken prisoner by the barons. Simon was effectively ruler of England.

To help him in the task of government, Simon summoned knights and burgesses to his parliaments in June 1264 and January 1265. Parliaments had first been established as a regular form of government by the Provisions of Oxford in 1258. Parliaments were meetings of the most important men in the country to exchange views and offer advice. Parliament's origins are unclear but the calling together of barons and prelates to exchange views and give advice to the monarch was not a great departure from the king's traditional practice of consulting the great men of the kingdom. The inclusion of two knights from each shire and two burgesses from each town in the parliaments of 1264 and 1265 may have helped to give his regime more popular support. Certainly support for the new regime came increasingly from the middle classes and the clergy. The barons disliked the great power Simon wielded. Simon was defeated and killed at the battle of Evesham in 1265.

Henry's energies were devoted to directing the rebuilding of Westminster Abbey, where he was buried when he died in 1272. The Abbey remains his best memorial.

The thirteenth century saw not only the emergence of parliaments but also the establishment of universities at Oxford and Cambridge. In practice, these were independent institutions; the Chancellor of each University granted degrees. This independence has remained an important feature of English university life. Students in the Middle Ages (young men only, of course) went to university at a much earlier age than they do now, perhaps in their early teens. Colleges were founded, each governed by a master, to accommodate the young students, to look after their welfare and to help direct their studies. The collegiate system has remained a distinct feature of the universities of Oxford and Cambridge, though it has been copied to some degree by other universities as they have appeared from the beginning of the last century. Simi-

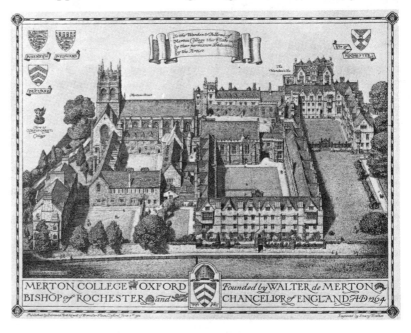

This is one of Oxford's oldest colleges, Merton, founded in 1264. The picture illustrates the arrangement of the college in quadrangles, typical of the architectural plan of Oxford and Cambridge colleges, and later of many public schools.

larly, Inns of Court were established in London in the thirteenth century, to teach and look after law students. More lawyers were needed to serve an increasingly complex society. Secular lawyers were useful servants and officials for the king.

Late Medieval England

The energies of Edward I (reigned 1272–1307) were principally engaged by his Welsh and Scottish campaigns (see Chapter 3), though he had to mount a series of defensive operations in France to safeguard English possessions from French attacks.

His son, Edward II, who ruled from 1307 until 1327, ran into severe difficulties with the barons. He relied greatly on his favourites, in particular a young Frenchman, Piers Gaveston. The barons rose against Edward in 1311 and beheaded Gaveston. The Battle of Bannockburn in 1314 (see Chapter 3), which ensured the continuance of an independent Scottish kingdom, saw the final disgrace of Edward. In 1327 Edward's queen, Isabella, with the Earl Mortimer, gained custody of the heir apparent, Prince Edward, and then took over the government from Edward II. The king was brutally murdered.

Rule by the queen mother and Mortimer came to an end in 1330, when Edward III firmly took over the government of the country. Like his grandfather, he was a great and popular soldier. Edward III's war was wholly with France. In 1337 Edward refused any longer to pay homage to Philip and claimed the throne of France through his mother. Thus began the Hundred Years' War. English sovereigns did not formally renounce their claim to the French throne until the Peace of Amiens in 1802.

In 1304 the French and English navies met at the Battle of Sluys, which ended in a decisive victory for the English. Thereafter the English controlled the Channel. In 1346 Edward invaded France. The English were trapped by the French at Crécy, but the English archers were equipped with the longbow, and this proved a deadly weapon. The English archers cut down the French knights, and the outcome of the Battle of Crécy (1346) was another great English victory. Edward went on to take the important coastal city of Calais.

In 1355 war was renewed. At the Battle of Poitiers in 1355 Edward's son, Edward, the Black Prince, defeated the French decisively, and John, king of France, was taken prisoner. In May 1360 England and France concluded the Treaty of Bretigny, by which England's ownership of Gascony was confirmed and England was also granted Aquitaine. John was returned to France on the payment of the gigantic ransom

Richard II (1377–99) was very young when he ascended the throne to face the problems of the Peasants' Revolt, Lollardy and the war with France. The Wilton Diptych, which is one of the treasures of the National Gallery, London, shows him kneeling in prayer attended by his patron saints. Richard was dethroned by Henry of Lancaster, imprisoned and eventually murdered.

of £500,000. The most significant point to emerge from the first phase of the Hundred Years' War was that the French army could not beat the English; at the same time, however, England could never conquer France.

In 1376 the Black Prince died. In 1377 Edward III was succeeded by his young grandson, Richard, son of the Black Prince.

Richard was just ten years old, and power was therefore exercised by a regency council headed by the Black Prince's younger brother, the powerful John of Gaunt, duke of Lancaster. A period of regency is never good for strong government. It was particularly difficult at that time, as England was suffering from the horrific consequences of the Plague.

In 1348–50 plague (sometimes called the 'Black Death') swept over the country, killing about one-third of the population. Feudalism was already breaking down before the arrival of the Plague. The reduction of the work-force to between two-thirds and half of what it had been meant that there was a severe shortage of labour. It was not possible to keep peasants on one estate when a neighbouring lord was willing to offer employment at higher wages. The feudal system, which had obliged each labourer to stay in the village where he was born, was upheld by the Statute of Labourers, passed in 1351. Enforcement of the Statute was sporadic but harsh. The Act was detested by the peasantry, which also suffered from terribly heavy taxes, which the government imposed to pay for the costs of the war and for an increasingly expensive administration.

The grievances of the peasantry came to a head in 1381. Led by Wat Tyler, angry peasants marched to London, where they beheaded Simon Sudbury, the archbishop of Canterbury and Chancellor, and Sir Robert Hales, the Treasurer. At Smithfield the young King Richard II met the rebel leaders. They demanded the repeal of oppressive statutes, the abolition of villeinage (serfdom) and the division of Church property. Thinking Wat Tyler was going to kill the king, the mayor of London struck Tyler down and killed him. Richard II took charge of the situation, riding forward and putting himself at the head of the rebels. The crowds dispersed quietly. Richard had no intention of giving way to rebel demands, and all who had rebelled were punished.

In addition, the monarchy and the aristocracy undertook a campaign against the followers of a religious reformer, John Wyclif. He wished to cleanse the Church of corruption and to reform it. Wyclif's followers were known as Lollards. Their policy of reform seemed to be turning into revolution, and they were therefore persecuted by both Church and state.

Richard II tried to build a party round himself. The great nobility, led by the earls of Gloucester, Arundel and Warwick, disliked the royal policy of excluding them from influence, and they struck against the king's party in 1386. Robert de Vere, the earl of Oxford, Richard's favourite, was defeated in battle in 1387 and had to flee abroad. Leaders of Richard's party, among them, the Chief Justice, Tresilian, were hanged, drawn and quartered. Richard himself only just escaped death.

In 1389 Richard declared himself of age. In 1396, after the death of his first wife, Anne of Bohemia, Richard married Isabelle, the daughter of Charles VI of France. Richard made peace with France, thus reducing his expenditure, in an effort to make himself independent of Parliament and nobility. In

1397 Richard struck at his enemies. He had Gloucester murdered and Warwick exiled. In 1398 Richard also exiled Henry, his cousin, the son of John of Gaunt. In February 1399, on the death of John of Gaunt, Richard disinherited his cousin and seized his estates.

In July 1399 Henry of Lancaster came back to England and defeated and captured Richard. Henry had himself declared king in 1399. In 1400 Henry ordered the murder of Richard, who had been kept in prison since his overthrow.

Richard's ruthless behaviour began a bloody period in English history. After Henry's seizure of the crown, the House of Lancaster, to which Henry IV belonged, was not allowed to rule in peace. The House of Lancaster sprang from John of Gaunt, son of Edward III. But Edward III had had eleven children, and the House of York, through the House of Mortimer, had a stronger claim to the crown. The battles between the Houses of Lancaster and York, which lasted from 1455 till 1485, are known as the Wars of the Roses. The emblem of the House of Lancaster was a red rose, and that of the House of York was a white rose.

Henry IV, who ruled from 1399 to 1413, was a capable administrator and a fine soldier. He was succeeded as king by his son, Henry, who became the famous Henry V.

In an attempt to seal the divisions in the ruling class, Henry had Richard II's body brought to London and reinterred in Westminster Abbey. Partly to occupy the nobility and partly to enlarge England's French empire, Henry reopened war with France. In 1415 Henry crushed a generally superior French army at Agincourt. In 1420, by the Treaty of Troyes, Henry was recognised as heir to Charles VI, the French king. But Henry died suddenly in 1422, just two months before King Charles VI. Thus by two months Henry's ambition to rule both England and France was thwarted.

Prince Henry was just nine months old when his father, Henry V died. In France there was a new king, Charles VII, who was determined to expel the English from France. He was helped by a peasant girl, Joan of Arc, whom the French claimed to be a saint. Although Joan was burnt to death by the English in 1431, the luck she had brought the French persisted. The English empire in France was finished.

Henry VI was a gentle and pious man, but weak both physically and mentally. Richard, duke of York, emerged as a rival to Henry VI. He was the great-grandson of Edward III and had a double claim to the throne, in that he was descended from both Lionel, duke of Clarence, and Edward, duke of York, both sons of Edward III. In 1458 there was a Yorkist revolt against Henry. Initially the Yorkists were successful, but in 1460 the Lancastrians defeated the Yorkists. The duke of York and other Yorkist leaders were executed, and their heads were displayed on the city walls of York. Richard of York's son, Edward, became the new duke of York and leader of the Yorkist cause.

In 1461 Edward marched on London at the head of an army. Henry VI was put in the Tower of London and Edward had himself crowned king.

Edward ruled, with only one interruption, until 1483. In 1470 the Lancastrians revolted against Edward IV, and Henry VI was briefly reinstated as king. The Lancastrians were totally defeated in battle, and Henry, a pathetic figure, was murdered in 1471. Henry's only son, Prince Edward, was killed in battle.

Edward IV was succeeded by his twelve-year-old son, Edward V. Edward IV's brother, Richard, duke of Gloucester, seized Edward V and his younger brother, Richard, and put them in the Tower. The duke claimed that Edward's marriage had been unlawful and that the two princes were bastards. The princes were doubtless murdered by the duke's men, though no conclusive evidence has ever been produced to prove that Richard was guilty. In 1674 the skeletons of two children were discovered during alterations in the Tower, and they were subsequently buried at Westminster Abbey.

Richard's only son died in 1484. The heir to the throne was a Lancastrian, Henry Tudor, earl of Richmond. Henry struck against Richard in 1485. At the Battle of Bosworth in Leicestershire Henry defeated and killed Richard III. The earl of Richmond became Henry VII. The Wars of the Roses came to an end. England now had a new dynasty, the Tudors.

English Architecture, 1066–1556

In England a magnificent architectural heritage survives from the Middle Ages. England has some of the finest cathedrals, churches and castles in Europe. In terms of quantity, the number of England's medieval buildings is equalled only by Italy's.

An important reason for the survival of so many buildings is that virtually all great buildings of the Middle Ages were constructed in stone, which has proved very durable. Despite periods of upheaval in the sixteenth and seventeenth centuries, when much damage was done to ecclesiastical buildings, England has also enjoyed peace and stability.

The Normans conquered England and governed a hostile population with the help of castles. These were simple in design. A stone tower, or keep, was built on a hill, with a wall surrounding the castle area. Between 1066 and 1100 the Normans built about eighty-five castles. The Tower of London was built by William both to protect and to subdue his new capital.

Castle building was continually refined. The keeps became larger; extra walls and towers were added; and 'towns' were built within the precincts of castles to house offices. After Edward I's conquest of Wales a series of splendid castles was built to control the populace (see Chapter 3). From 1350 onwards castle building declined, as the increasing use of gunpowder changed the nature of warfare. Castles were increasingly 'domesticated' in the period 1350–1550. Between 1350 and 1377 Edward III spent £50,000 on the conversion of Windsor from a barracks to a palace. New castles were built primarily as residences and only marginally as defences.

But it is England's cathedrals and churches that are particularly famous. Some Saxon churches survive, but they are few in number. The great start to medieval church building was made by the Normans. Norman or Romanesque cathedrals were heavy and solid. They were dark inside, as there were only a few windows, placed high up. Columns were thick and numerous. Windows and arches were rounded, after the Roman style. Decoration was simple but effective. There is some fine carving in Norman buildings (but one suspects that Saxon craftsmen, who were renowned sculptors, decorated the cathedrals of their new masters).

Durham is the most perfect of Norman cathedrals. The typical, grand zig-zag decoration can be seen on the columns in the nave. The naves at Gloucester, Tewkesbury, Peterborough and Southwell are also magnificent. There is a grand Norman doorway at Rochester Cathedral, and Peterborough Cathedral has the largest painted Romanesque wooden roof in Europe.

The Norman style in church architecture lasted from about 1066 until 1150 (though, of course, it would be absurd to try to give precise dates to the Norman, as to other architectural styles). The Romanesque style began to be replaced by the first of the English Gothic styles when the pointed arch was found to span a much greater distance than the Norman rounded arch. Thus buildings could have fewer arches and appear higher and more graceful. The Gothic style (the name 'Gothic' was applied to the Middle Ages in the eighteenth century) also made use of buttresses (supports built against walls) to take the weight of the roof. This in its turn meant that there could be thinner walls and bigger windows filled with the great triumph of the Middle Ages – stained glass.

Durham Cathedral is the finest English example of Norman or Romanesque church architecture. This view of the nave highlights its massive columns and rounded arches and shows the bold simplicity of its decoration.

The first Gothic style is named 'Early English' and lasted from 1150 to about 1250. It has acutely pointed arches. Sometimes a number of slim columns were clustered together to form one big column. Among the finest examples of Early English are Salisbury, Lincoln, Wells and Worcester cathedrals. Salisbury was built between 1220 and 1289. The main body of the church has great unity of design, but the spire, which at 123 metres is the highest in Britain, was added between 1330 and 1375. Lincoln is a brilliant example of Early English. It stands on a hill, dominating the surrounding countryside. It has many fine carvings. It also has a rather long, low profile with a double transept, a characteristic of English cathedrals. Wells is particularly famous for its sculptured west front, added between 1230 and 1250. This front has 400 figures, standing row upon row, and it is the finest collection of medieval sculpture in Europe. Worcester is classically Early English, with a fine nave.

Canterbury Cathedral had to be rebuilt after a fire devastated the cathedral in 1174. Its choir is the first building in the Early English style. But, in common with other English cathedrals, the building was designed by French architects. Canterbury has a distinctively French feature, a 'chevet' (that is, a curved east end, or apse, with small chapels opening off it). Westminster Abbey, rebuilt by Henry III (1216–72) was also influenced by French ideas. As a result, the nave looks Early English but is exceptionally high – a French, and not an English, characteristic.

Following the Early English style came the Decorated Gothic. This lasted from approximately 1250 to 1370. As the name would suggest, this architectural style was characterised by its carving and ornamentation. Arches and windows were more intricately divided and filled with increasingly sumptuous stained glass. There is wonderful medieval glass at Canterbury, York, Lincoln and Gloucester. The carving was particularly

Late Gothic architecture reached its most inspired in King's College Chapel, Cambridge, completed in the early sixteenth century. The Chapel is shown flanked by eighteenth-century college buildings in a typical idyllic Cambridge riverside scene.

elaborate on the capitals at the top of the columns; the designs were often inspired by plants and leaves. Exeter has the most carving inside, though York Minster is the largest decorated cathedral and has the most stained glass. The Decorated style made use of flying buttresses (arches which support walls and are themselves supported by buttresses proper) to take the greater weight of the roof and walls, and spires to make towers appear more graceful. Salisbury and Norwich cathedrals have beautiful spires.

The last period of the Gothic, from about 1370 to 1550, was dominated by the Perpendicular style. Builders were then so accomplished that their churches could be filled with large windows, with the minimum of wall in between. Inside few columns were needed to support the lofty roof. Thus an overwhelming impression of light and graciousness was given. The delicate quality of the interior was enhanced by the use of fan vaulting. This appeared for the first time at Gloucester Cathedral in 1331. The most brilliant use of fan vaulting, however, is at King's College Chapel, Cambridge. This building can be regarded as the climax of the Perpendicular style. Other fine examples of the Perpendicular are to be found in Bath Abbey and in Henry VII's King's Chapel at Westminster Abbey.

England's flourishing wool trade furnished much of the money for church building in the fourteenth and fifteenth centuries. The money came directly from wool merchants, and the Church itself also owned great sheep farms. Monasteries, in particular, were able to finance their building from the wool trade. Kings and the nobility were the greatest of patrons, and the tombs of the powerful line English cathedrals and chur ches.

The Church was the centre of life in the Middle Ages (and, of course, later). Holidays were religious festivals and journeys away from home could well be pilgrimages to a famous shrine. 'The Canterbury Tales', a collection of tales in verse written by Geoffrey Chaucer in the fourteenth century, depicts one such pilgrimage by a mixed group of travellers to the most famous shrine in Britain, that of St Thomas Becket at Canterbury. The tales are told by the pilgrims to while away the time on the four-day journey from London to Canterbury. They form not only a work of literature and entertainment in a recognisable form of English (Middle English) but also a portrait of Chaucer's England. The Church receives both praise and criticism from Chaucer. There is the parish priest, poor and devoted to his flock – but there is also the pardoner, unpleasant and unscrupulous in his sale of pardons for sins. The great church buildings of the Middle Ages testify to the wealth

The greatest English writer of the Middle Ages was Geoffrey Chaucer. The humour and insight of his *Canterbury Tales* have ensured their widespread popularity to this day. Chaucer is shown here in an illuminated manuscript preserved in the British Library.

of talent and spirituality of the period, but Chaucer reminds us of the strengths and frailties of the institution of the Church itself, made up as it was of mortal beings.

3

Medieval Ireland, Wales and Scotland

Ireland and Wales in the Middle Ages

Both Ireland and Wales lacked unified government under one monarch, an advantage enjoyed by England and, to a great extent, by Scotland.

Ireland was ruled by a number of kings, not one of whom had managed to establish supremacy as the House of Wessex, and more definitely the Normans, had done in England. Ireland had, unlike England, no Romanised Church which believed its interests were best served by the creation of a strong monarchy. Rather, the Church was ruled by great abbots interested mainly in preserving their own and other local freedoms. Ireland also had a body of law which made it difficult for an Irish ruler to change society in the way that English kings had done. Irish law was interpreted by the chief *brehon*, whose authority was placed on the same footing as that of abbots and the king.

In the twelfth century there was a bitter power struggle between the Irish kings. Dermot MacMurrough, king of Leinster, looked for outside help and gained the service of a number of Norman lords from England. The most prominent was Richard, whose family had been earls of Pembroke on the Welsh frontier. He was popularly known as Richard Strongbow. He was spectacularly successful and drove Dermot's enemies out of Leinster. He married Dermot's daughter, as the king had promised, but claimed that he should be king on Dermot's death. In 1171 Strongbow won a great victory over the king of Connacht, who had invaded Leinster. At this point Henry II intervened to prevent Strongbow from becoming dangerously powerful and independent.

Henry II let Strongbow and other Norman lords keep their lands, but as his vassals. He also reserved key castles and ports as centres of royal authority. Rory O'Connor, king of Connacht, was recognised as overlord of the rest of Ireland. By the end of Henry's reign part of Ireland – Leinster, Munster and Meath – had been given to Norman lords. The rest of Ireland was ruled by native Irish kings, who acknowledged

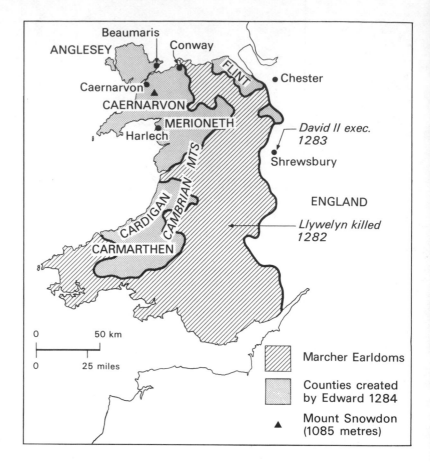

Edward I (1272–1307) and Wales

the power (and sometimes the authority) of the king of England. Henry became lord of Ireland. Henry had hoped for a simple solution to the problems in Ireland: he had wanted his son John to become king of Ireland as a whole, ruling strongly and directly from Dublin, but John was too young and untalented for this task.

Henry's policy resulted in the division of the land into Norman Ireland and Irish Ireland, the first of many splits between peoples in Ireland that would make the country's history a sad one. The area under royal administration from Dublin, which fluctuated in size, came to be called the Pale. Poyning's Law of 1495 decreed that no Bill could be initiated in Ireland until it was approved by the king and his council in London. Ireland was thus prevented from enjoying any growth in parliamentary power and initiative, such as that which emerged in England.

Wales had been penetrated by Norman lords at the time of the Conquest. The rich southern coastal plain was under their control, as was a little of the northern coastal strip. But the

38

poor mountainous area in between, covering most of Wales, was ruled by native Celtic princes. The kings of England were obliged to grant great powers to the 'marcher lords' on the border, who protected England from Welsh raiders. English kings did not welcome this delegation of authority, but a conquest of Wales would have been difficult and expensive. They were satisfied with a recognition by the native princes of the sovereignty of the English monarchy.

Unwisely, Llywelyn ap Gruffydd, prince of Wales, who had loose authority over much of central and north Wales, refused to do homage to Edward in 1275. When it appeared that Llywelyn could not be persuaded to recognise English over-lordship, a state of affairs which could lead to the emergence of a dangerous and ambitious neighbour on England's border, Edward resolved on war. Edward marched into North Wales in 1277, supported by the English navy which blockaded the Welsh coast. Llywelyn, cut off from the food supplies of Anglesey, had to surrender. He remained prince of Wales but lost much of his power over lesser lords. Edward then began

Harlech remains one of the most imposing castles built by Edward I to secure his conquest of Wales. The geography and people that had hitherto defied the ambitions of English kings finally succumbed to permanent conquest when a string of castles were built throughout North Wales.

to build a series of spectacular castles in Wales, which would serve as bases for any expeditions he might have to undertake against the Welsh in the future.

Llywelyn did not like the new settlement, and he and his brother, David, rose in revolt again. However, Llywelyn was killed by an English soldier as he rode unattended through the countryside. With the death of their leader, Welsh resistance collapsed. David was captured and executed. By the Statute of Wales (1284) the whole of Wales was made subject to the English crown. Edward's son, Prince Edward, who was born in 1284, was declared prince of Wales in 1301.

Edward's castle building continued after the conquest of 1284. His castles include such military masterpieces as Conway, Caernarvon, Harlech, and Beaumaris in Anglesey. Next to each castle Edward founded a 'free borough' of English colonists, who were granted many privileges. Thus Edward hoped to stimulate urban expansion and commercial growth as well as to establish peace through military might in Wales. English settlement in mid- and north Wales was not extensive, however, as economic prospects were not attractive enough. The native Welsh population, therefore, remained in the majority. It retained both its Welsh or Celtic language and its own culture. The earliest recorded *eisteddfod*, or great festival for the performance of music and the recitation of Welsh poetry, was held in 1176. This independent tradition of music and poetry has continued to the present day. South Wales, by contrast, is richer and more accessible to England, and so it has been much more open to English cultural influences.

Scotland: The Unification of the Kingdom

Scotland, in contrast to Ireland and Wales, was a success story. Though composed of several peoples living in diverse landscapes, Scotland was unified under a single monarchy. England was a rich and powerful neighbour, but to overcome Scotland's size and geography – not to mention the resistance of its peoples – would have required greater determination and more resources than even the most powerful English monarch could muster.

The unification of Scotland is traditionally dated to 843, when Kenneth MacAlpin, king of the Scots, defeated the Picts and absorbed their territory to form the kingdom of Scotia, which covered the mountainous area north of the Forth. In about 1016 a descendant of MacAlpin's, Malcolm II, defeated the Angles and brought Lothian under Scottish rule. The Angles (the English in Lothian) were the northern inhabitants

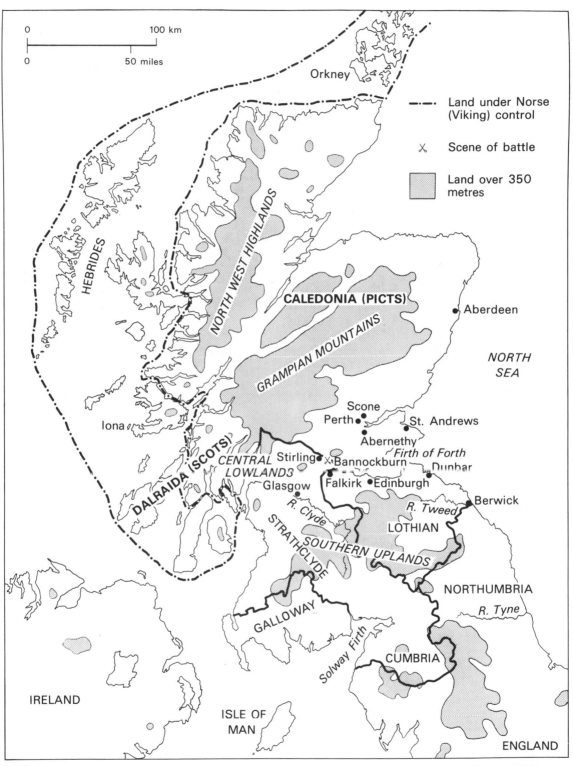

Scotland in the Middle Ages

of the old kingdom of Northumbria, and for many years ambitious Scottish kings saw no reason why they should not extend their kingdom to the Tyne, to absorb the whole of Northumbria. This aim was an obvious source of friction between Scotland and England.

In 1018 Malcolm's grandson, Duncan, while still heir to the Scottish throne, became king of the British kingdom of Strathclyde by virtue of a claim through the female line. Strathclyde stretched from Dumbarton (just north of Glasgow) to the present-day English Lake District (Cumbria). Though predominantly British, there were other peoples in Strathclyde: Northumbrians, Vikings and Gaels. Galloway, which came under the Scottish monarchy at this time, was peopled by Britons. The Scottish king's authority over Strathclyde was weak, but over Galloway, for many years, it was at best nominal. The Vikings continued to control the islands off the western and northern coasts of the Scottish mainland, the last of which did not pass to the Scottish kingdom until the mid fifteenth century. Their allegiance was to the king of Norway.

In the eleventh century, recognising that English thought and ways, rather than Celtic, tended to make for a strong central monarchy, Malcolm III, or Malcolm Ceann Mor ('Bighead'), moved the centre of Scottish national life to English Lothian and southern Scotia, away from Celtic Scotia to the north. English settlers fleeing from William the Conqueror added to the English element in Scotland. The king's marriage, in about 1070 to Margaret (of the old royal House of Wessex) was of paramount importance. Her energies were devoted principally to bringing the Scottish Church into line with developments in the rest of western Europe, and to shaking off Celtic ideas of a loosely organised Church with hereditary leaders, who were eager to maintain their families' power within the Church. Margaret herself was revered as a saint.

Malcolm's relations with England were not peaceful. He mounted five invasions in all. He was so brutal in Northumbria that people there learned to their cost that a Scottish king would treat them no better than the Conqueror. William invaded Scotland in 1071 and forced Malcolm to pay him homage at Abernethy (Perthshire). Malcolm III was killed during his last invasion of England in 1093, and Margaret died of grief three days later.

Malcolm and Margaret had tried to establish the English custom of primogeniture, by which the eldest son succeeded the father. But when, at their deaths, Malcolm's brother, Donald Ban ('the Fair'), took the throne, there was a strong reaction against the Anglo-Norman influences of Malcolm's reign, and a number of the English at court were expelled. Significantly, the fourth of Malcolm's and Margaret's sons, Edgar, secured the throne from Donald with the help of the English king, William Rufus. The main political event of Edgar's reign (1097–1107) was the understanding reached with the king of Norway in 1098, through which Norwegian rule over Shetland, Orkney, the Hebrides and Man was recognised. Clearly, though, Scottish kings would alter this arrangement when they had the power. Edgar was succeeded by his brother, Alexander I (reigned 1107–24), and the close ties with England were confirmed by Alexander's marriage to Sibylla, an illegitimate daughter of Henry I of England.

David I (reigned 1124–53) brought great skill and energy to the rule of Scotland. He set about a major reform of the Church, which was ill organised and out of step with the European model, despite Queen Margaret's efforts. He founded more bishoprics, so that the whole of Scotland was covered by episcopal authority, and a string of monasteries, which had a major impact on religious and economic life. He did not obtain archiepiscopal status for St Andrew's which many churchmen in Scotland considered important.

In David's reign more Anglo-Norman lords settled in Scotland and helped to give the country a feudal structure like that of the rest of Europe. David encouraged a more vigorous administration of justice. The first Scottish coins were minted in his reign, and a standard system of weights and measures was set up. A great achievement was the establishment of the custom of primogeniture in the royal succession once and for all. As a testimony to his success in this matter, on his death in 1153 his grandson, Malcolm IV (known as 'the Maiden'), succeeded to the throne at only eleven years of age.

Malcolm IV was in no position to resist Henry II of England's redrawing of the border between the two countries at the Solway–Tweed line, by which the English gained Northumbria. Malcolm died in 1165 and was succeeded by his brother, William the Lion. The new king resented the loss of Northumbria and concluded an alliance with France in 1174, which was to endure for centuries and was, accordingly, to be known as the 'Auld Alliance'. But Henry II heavily defeated William and the Scots, and the Treaty of Falaise (1174) put Scotland under the authority of the English king. The main castles of southern Scotland were also taken over by the English. William was able to cancel the Treaty of Falaise in 1189, when the English monarch, Richard Coeur de Lion, eager for funds for a crusade, agreed to renounce his feudal superiority over Scotland and hand back the castles occupied by the English in return for 10,000 marks.

There were reasonably good relations with England for the next century. Alexander II (reigned 1214–49), the son of William the Lion, aspired to rule Northumbria but eventually gave up the idea. Ties with the English monarchy were strengthened. Alexander married Henry III's sister, Joan, and, though his remarriage to a French lady (after Joan's death in 1238) introduced French influence into the Scottish court, his young son, the future Alexander III (reigned 1249–86), married Henry III's young daughter, Margaret. Harmony was no doubt helped by the fact that in the thirteenth century the English monarchy was preoccupied with both constitutional problems and wars in France.

In 1263 King Hakon of Norway led a great army and fleet to Scotland to make the point that the islands lying off the north and west Scottish coasts were Viking territory. The Vikings were defeated by storms and by the forces of Alexander III. The Treaty of Perth (1266), which was concluded between Alexander III and Hakon's son, King Magnus, surrendered Viking control over Man and the Hebrides to the Scottish king. The peace at Perth marked the beginning of friendly relations between Scots and Vikings; Orkney and Shetland, the two remaining Viking possessions off the Scottish coast, went to Scotland in 1469.

The Scottish War of Independence

The death of Alexander III in 1286 precipitated a grave political crisis, which was, ultimately, to lead to full-scale war with England to preserve the country's independence. Alexander was succeeded by his granddaughter, Margaret, the only child of Margaret of Scotland and King Eric II of Norway. 'The Maid of Norway', as she was known, was only three years old and sickly. It was arranged, by the Treaty of Birgham in 1290, that Edward's son should marry Margaret. Though this would result in a union of the crowns, Scotland was to remain a separate and independent kingdom. The arrangement was never put to the test; Margaret died on her way to Scotland from Norway.

A dispute then broke out over the succession to the crown. The two competitors with the strongest claims were John Balliol and Robert Bruce. Their claims were evenly balanced, and though Bruce had more support among men of influence in Scotland, this was not enough to decide the issue. The king of England, Edward I, was called upon to arbitrate in the matter, which he did at Berwick in 1291 and 1292. Balliol and Bruce were in no position to refuse to do homage to the English king; Edward was recognised as the 'superior lord' of whomever was chosen to be king.

Edward chose Balliol and at once attempted to interfere in Scottish affairs to a much greater extent than either Balliol or Bruce had agreed to. King John (who was given the unflattering nickname of 'Toom Tabard', or 'Empty Coat') was in a difficult position. To refuse Edward's claims would bring certain retaliation from England, but John's compliance would reduce his own authority as king of Scotland and would be greatly resented in Scotland. Finally, John decided to defy Edward and fight a war.

Edward invaded Scotland in 1296 – with complete success. The Scottish army was heavily defeated at Dunbar, and Balliol was taken prisoner. The Stone of Destiny, on which Scottish kings were enthroned, was removed from Scone to Westminster Abbey (where it can still be seen, built into the English coronation chair), together with the 'Black Rood' of St Margaret, Scotland's most precious relic. An English administration was installed in Scotland.

But in the midst of defeat a Scottish hero arose. William Wallace, a knight, rallied the Scots, and at Stirling, on 10 September 1297, the Scottish forces inflicted a crushing defeat on the English. Wallace became the guardian of the realm of Scotland. But in 1298 Edward invaded the country again and defeated the Scots at Falkirk. The defeat was not convincing, however, and Edward had to gather a new army and invade Scotland again in May 1303. In 1304 Edward captured Wallace, who was taken to London and executed. In 1305 Edward imposed a new order of government on Scotland.

No matter how statesmanlike Edward's settlement was, Scottish feeling was hostile. Robert Bruce, grandson of the contestant for the throne in 1290, claimed the crown in 1306 after murdering his rival. He lost the first battle against the English forces in Scotland and fled the country. When he returned Edward prepared to defeat him, but the English king died in Scotland in the summer of 1307. Without Edward's military genius and determination, England failed to maintain its hold on Scotland. By 1314 only Stirling Castle remained in English hands.

Edward II marched into Scotland in 1314 with an impressive army. At Bannockburn the English were severely defeated. The English knights were not able to penetrate the Scottish ranks and, on withdrawal, became bogged down in the marshy meadows bordering the burn (stream). Edward, who had fought bravely, fled from this scene of confusion. Bannockburn is the most famous victory in Scottish history, but it did not end the war, which lasted until 1328, when Scotland was recognised as an independent kingdom and Robert was acknowledged as king.

The Scots had defeated the English because the nation had been united by a feudal monarchy backed by a Romanised Church. In 1320 the clergy of Scotland had produced the Declaration of Arbroath, to which the nobility had assented. Addressed to Pope John XXII, it expressed defiant nationalism: 'For so long as there shall but one hundred of us remain alive, we will never consent to subject ourselves to the dominion of the English.'

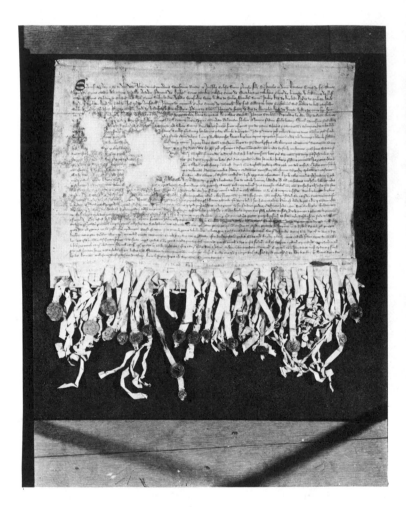

The Declaration of Arbroath, sent by the clergy and nobles of Scotland to the Pope in 1320, maintained their implacable resistance to the erosion of Scottish independence. The cause triumphed in 1328 when the English finally recognised Robert Bruce as King of Scotland, thus according him the fruits of his victory at Bannockburn.

Late Medieval Scotland

In 1329 Bruce died, leaving an only son, David, aged five. Edward Balliol, son of John Balliol ('Toom Tabard'), backed by Edward III of England, claimed the throne and invaded Scotland. David II went to France for safety in 1334. When he returned to Scotland as a young man he answered the appeal of his ally, the king of France, who had been defeated at the Battle of Crécy by the English. But the Scots were also badly beaten by the English at Neville's Cross, near Durham, in 1346. David II was captured and spent eleven years in captivity in England, until he was returned to Scotland in exchange for the enormous ransom of £160,000. Over half of the ransom was actually paid, a considerable drain on the resources of the country.

David II did not have children and despite an arrangement he had made by which the Scottish throne was to pass to Edward III's younger son, in 1371 the crown went to Robert 'the Stewart', his nephew and former regent. Robert II, the first Stuart king, ruled until 1390. The Scottish monarchy proved incapable of curbing the power and independence of the great aristocrats. The lords who defended the border on both the Scottish and the English side were particularly powerful and difficult for their kings to control. In 1388 there was the Battle of Otterburn, or Chevy, between the Douglases of Scotland and the Percys of Northumberland. This was a confrontation between large private armies. The problems of the Scottish monarchy were increased by the fact that after the death of Robert II no adult ascended the Scottish throne for over 200 years.

Robert III proved to be a weak king. As he was irresolute and crippled, his younger brother, the duke of Albany, exercised virtual control over the kingdom. Robert's son, James, was captured by English pirates while on his way to France. He was handed over to the English king and remained a prisoner in England for eighteen years. The news of his capture caused the death of Robert III in 1406.

James I was proclaimed king in his absence. When James and his English wife, Joan Beaufort, came to Scotland in 1424 the king decided to take drastic action to restore the authority of the crown. He executed the duke of Albany and others who had been governing Scotland. He led expeditions against the western clans in the highlands. He imprisoned the head of the Douglas family and exiled the earl of March.

James encouraged the growth of the Scottish Parliament to counter the power of the nobility. But James, who had used

In the rugged landscape of Scotland, the nobility depended heavily on their numerous, though often quite small, castles and fortified places to preserve their power. The photograph shows Dunnoltar castle on the east coast.

brutality to enforce royal authority, was himself the victim of the sword. In 1437 he was stabbed to death in the presence of the queen. His son, now James II, was only six years old, and another regency followed.

James II (reigned 1437–60) continued to confront the power of the Douglas family. In 1452 he personally stabbed to death the earl of Douglas, a guest at his dinner table, and with parliament's connivance confiscated much of the Douglas family's property. Like his father, James tried to give Parliament more prominence in national life. By the Act of Annexation in 1455 he endeavoured to put royal finances on a firm footing by declaring that the crown had a right to certain funds (in particular, revenue from customs). James died during the siege of Roxburgh Castle in 1460.

James III, who came to the throne after the customary minority, married Margaret, daughter of the king of Denmark and Norway. When her father was unable to produce the money which should have formed part of her dowry, the islands of Orkney and Shetland passed to the Scottish kingdom. James III was intelligent and as committed to the policy of enhancing royal authority as the first two Jameses had been. But he failed to appeal much to the nobility. He was too interested in architecture and archaelogy for their liking, and he relied too much on the advice of low-born favourites. Above all, however, he seemed suspicious and contemptuous of many of the great nobles. He was killed at the Battle of Sauchieburn by Scots nobles who were opposed to him, and he was succeeded by his young son, James IV.

The dominance of Scottish politics by the crown's attempts to assert its authority over the nobility should not obscure other developments in Scottish society. Commerce was growing. Between 1450 and 1516 fifty-one new burghs (towns) were founded, and the monarchy looked for support from the urban middle class in its struggle with the mighty nobility. But society was still very poor and overwhelmingly rural. Those who worked on the land enjoyed a standard of living not far above survival level, and their lifestyle was in marked contrast to the quality of life enjoyed by English labourers, particularly in the south of England. Many Scots sought employment as mercenary soldiers in Europe.

The fourteenth century saw the foundation of St Andrew's University, and in the fifteenth century the universities of Aberdeen and Glasgow were founded. This was, perhaps, an over-generous provision. (England had only two universities, Oxford and Cambridge, until the early nineteenth century.) The late fifteenth century also witnessed the flourishing of a large group of Scottish poets, the most famous of whom was William Dunbar.

By late medieval times the lowlands (south) of Scotland had been English-speaking for more than a hundred years. However, Gaelic, a Celtic tongue, continued to be the language of the highlands and western islands. A cultural split had developed between the richer and more settled lowlands and the poorer highlands. This was reflected in politics too. At the end of the fifteenth century the highlands were still only nominally under the rule of the crown; the lord of the western islands had made a series of treaties with the English kings, and he was obedient to the Scottish king only because he was given a free hand in his part of Scotland.

The people of the highlands (and some parts of the border country) lived in clans – families or tribes of people with the same name. The head of each clan was the chieftain. Frequently he also had a feudal title – an earldom or a lordship. He exercised complete control over his people. Property was shared in principle by the clan, but in reality owned by the chieftain. The clan system derives from Gaelic–Celtic tradition, and many of the clans traced their origins back to ancient Celtic mythologies.

49

The highlands, because they were remote and independent, had become a problem for any king (and later administration) wanting to impose a system of tidy central government. Clearly, the highlands would remain autonomous until the king's power became much greater than it was in the late Middle Ages.

4

The Tudors

Henry VII

Henry VII came to the throne in 1485, after a period of weak monarchy and civil war. His considerable achievement was threefold: he made the monarchy strong; he brought stability to England; and he earned the respect, if not the affection, of his subjects.

Henry Tudor helped to establish his claim to the throne with greater certainty by marrying the Yorkist heiress, Elizabeth, in 1486. But the symbolic uniting of the red rose of Lancaster and the white rose of York did not end Yorkist attempts to take the throne. The Yorkists persuaded a young man, Lambert Simnel, to impersonate Richard of York and then the earl of Warwick (Richard was dead and Warwick imprisoned). His claim ended in an unsuccessful rebellion in 1487. Perkin Warbeck also pretended to be Prince Richard of York, and his claim was taken seriously by ardent Yorkists until his final capture and execution in 1499. The earl of Warwick, though an innocent party in the plot against Henry VII, was also executed in 1499. Warwick's was only the first of a series of executions of leading Yorkists which were undertaken by Henry VII and Henry VIII in order to ensure the succession of the Tudor family.

The major obstacle to strong monarchy in the fifteenth century was the willingness of the nobility to take advantage of weak kingship, although in Henry VII and Elizabeth the nobility faced clever and determined rulers. The power of the nobility had been weakened by loss of life and property in the Wars of the Roses, but it was still considerable. Henry VII was able to combine financial and political policies. During the course of his reign about two-thirds of the great nobility found themselves dependent on the king's mercy for misdeeds they had committed. At best, if these great families offended Henry Tudor, he could force them to pay heavy fines, and Henry was also able to enforce the Statute of Livery and Maintenance, according to which the nobility were forbidden to keep private armies. Such laws had existed before, but it needed a strong king to enforce them.

Henry was determined to make the monarchy rich and

therefore strong. He reclaimed royal lands that had been lost since the reign of Henry VI and seized the estates of men who had opposed him in war or had died without heirs. Henry saw to it that all the feudal revenues due to him were paid. In this he was aided by ministers who were unyielding in their demands for money (two of Henry's principal tax collectors, Empsom and Dudley, were executed by Henry VIII at the beginning of his reign, a move which gained the new king instant and widespread popularity); but it was Henry VII himself who personally supervised finance. The avoidance of wars also spared the king much unnecessary expense. By the end of his reign Henry had a great fortune in jewels and plate and an income which exceeded revenue.

Henry VII's dynasty was sufficiently respected in Europe for his eldest son, Arthur, to marry the Spanish princess, Katharine of Aragon. When Arthur died in 1502 the Spanish royal family was keen that Katharine should remarry the younger of Henry's sons, the future Henry VIII. Henry VII's daughter married King James IV of Scotland, a traditional means of attempting to secure good relations between England and Scotland. Despite Henry VII's desire for wealth, particularly in the last years of his reign, he maintained a splendid court to indicate to the nobility at home and rulers abroad that the Tudor dynasty was the established royal house of England. Henry VII's Chapel in Westminster Abbey was a sumptuous mausoleum for the Tudor family. Above all, Henry Tudor's peaceful government earned his family the general approval and loyalty of the English people.

Henry VIII

Henry was eighteen when he succeeded his father in 1509. He was handsome and accomplished and very extravagant, in marked contrast to his father. His first move away from Henry VII's cautious policies was his revival of the historic and expensive wars with France. Henry invaded France and won the Battle of the Spurs. His commander also defeated the Scots, the allies of France; James IV, king of Scotland, Henry's brother-in-law, was killed in the Battle of Flodden.

Henry was bored with the routine of government and was quite willing to leave the affairs of state to his Chancellor, Cardinal Wolsey, who was a remarkable man. Although of humble birth he had quickly risen through the hierarchy of the Church to become archbishop of York, cardinal, and ultimately legate *a Latere* (the permanent representative of the pope in England), a position which gave him complete control of the English Church.

Wolsey's supremacy over the Church left it weaker and less able to face the attack which would soon be mounted against it. Wolsey did not give the Church either reform or uniformity, and his personal extravagance and worldliness were a vivid example of the corruption rife in the Church. Wolsey's immense energies and talents were mainly consumed by foreign affairs. He cherished the ambition of becoming pope and bent English foreign policy to this unrealistic end.

However, Wolsey failed to find a solution to the supreme crisis of the reign, when in 1525 the king decided to divorce his queen, Katharine of Aragon. The queen was forty, five years older than Henry, and she had only had one child, the Princess Mary, born in 1516. Henry considered it essential to have a son to succeed him, fearing that a female succession would bring the return of civil war. After the divorce Henry hoped to marry the attractive Anne Boleyn, whose beauty and liveliness contrasted with Katharine's plainness and piety.

Henry did not at first think that the divorce would present serious problems, as the Church had consented to the separation of royal couples in the past and his own relations with the Church were good. But difficulties soon arose. Katharine was opposed to any suggestion of divorce, and in this she was supported by her family, the Habsburgs, who were the most powerful royal house in Europe, controlling both the empire and Spain.

Henry and Katharine both presented their cases to European opinion. The king argued that his marriage to Katharine was unlawful, as the Bible forbade the marriage of a man to his brother's widow (Prince Arthur, Henry's older brother, had been married to Katharine). The queen claimed that her marriage to Arthur had never been consummated. Henry received the backing of influential universities, but his case was far from convincing, and public sympathy in England was on Katharine's side.

Henry's hopes that the pope would grant a divorce were dashed in 1527, when Rome was captured by the armies of the Habsburg emperor, Charles V. The pope became a virtual prisoner of Charles, who, as a nephew of Katharine's, would never have agreed to the pope's granting a divorce. Cardinal Wolsey had failed to obtain what the king wanted, and Henry turned against him. Wolsey was stripped of all his offices of state and allowed to keep only one of his many former ecclesiastical offices. In 1529 Henry had Wolsey charged with treason, and if he had not died on his way to London, Wolsey would almost certainly have been executed.

The ease with which Henry removed the Church's leading servant in England illustrated the immensity of royal power.

Cardinal Wolsey became supremely powerful in church and state under Henry VIII. Yet when he failed to secure for the king a divorce from Katharine of Aragon, nothing could save him. This portrait now hangs in the National Portrait Gallery, London.

It was also one example of Henry's complete lack of loyalty and mercy to servants who had failed him.

Henry's diplomatic efforts to secure a divorce failed, and he turned to a policy of force against the Church, which ended in a complete break with Rome. The enormous task of carrying out the Reformation in England was accomplished by Thomas Cromwell who, from 1531 until his disgrace and execution in 1540, was the most powerful of the king's ministers. He arranged for Parliament (which sat from 1529 until 1536 and is called the 'Reformation Parliament') to pass statutes which swept away the power of the papacy in England and vested it in the crown instead. Cromwell then nationalised the monastic lands and was a moving force in the creation of the bureaucracy which was needed to manage the revenues now at the monarchy's disposal. Cromwell's actions resulted in a great strengthening of the House of Commons, which was asked to endorse not only one of the greatest religious changes in English national life but also a new succession to the crown. A new bureaucratic system emerged, which resulted in a permanent change from administration through the royal household on an informal and personal basis to administration through government departments, which continued to manage the affairs of the country despite changes of ministers or monarch.

In 1532 the archbishop of Canterbury died and was replaced by Thomas Cranmer, a man of great learning, who aimed at Church reform and showed complete devotion to the king. In January 1533 he married Henry and Anne Boleyn, and in May he pronounced Henry's first marriage to Katharine null. On 1 June Cranmer crowned Anne queen of England. But the king was bitterly disappointed at the birth, in September 1533, of the long-awaited child, the Princess Elizabeth.

Since 1532 Parliament and the king had prevented substantial revenue from the Church in England from going to Rome. In 1534 the pope's right to tax the English Church was abolished. Judicial appeals to the pope were stopped in 1533, and finally, and most important, in 1534 the Act of Supremacy declared Henry to be the supreme head of the Church in England. In the same year an Act of Succession vested the succession in Anne's heir, Elizabeth. In 1536 a second Act of Succession allowed Henry an extraordinary and unprecedented freedom: to name his own heir. The pope's excommunication of Henry in 1533 meant little, as the great Catholic powers, the empire and France, preferred Henry's friendship to his hostility.

The reformation of the Church was intended to be political and not religious. Henry was a Catholic; in 1521 he had earned

One of the consequences of the reformation in England was the dissolution of the monasteries. The great wealth of the church was diverted into Henry's coffers, where it was quickly spent to finance an expensive court and government in an age of high inflation. Until that time, Fountains Abbey in Yorkshire, now fallen into ruins, had been one of the most magnificent religious houses in Europe.

the title of *Fidei Defensor* ('Defender of the Faith') from the pope for writing a denunciation of the German Protestant reformer, Martin Luther. In 1539 Henry had the Six Acts passed, which demanded complete conformity to Catholic doctrine and practice. Those who refused to obey were to be punished savagely. But few could have expected conservative religious practice to continue after such a successful attack had been made on the traditional organisation of the Church. This certainly did not happen. The publication of the Bible in English, which was followed in 1538 by its placing in every church in England, could only serve to encourage Protestantism, for the Protestant faith was based on the authority of the Scriptures, on the belief that the truth about the Christian religion was to be found in the Bible, particularly in the New Testament, and that any man could discover the truths of religion for himself. According to Protestant doctrine, salvation was personal and could not be achieved through the Sacraments, as the Roman Catholic Church taught.

Between 1536 and 1539 Henry mounted an attack on the monasteries, as they owned vast wealth, certainly more than one-fifth of the land in the country. Cromwell had a scheme to use the monastic lands as a source of income on which the monarchy could live forever, but the king desperately needed the money from the quick sale of monastic property to pay for government expenditure. The land went both to old landowners and to new men with money, who were establishing themselves for the first time. Their ownership of this property gave landowners an interest in maintaining the Reformation settlement. When England re-entered the Church of Rome in Mary's reign (1553–8) it was impossible for the Church to reclaim this land. The suppression of the monasteries meant the destruction of much of the artistic heritage of the Middle Ages.

The reputation of the Church was at a low ebb, and all agreed that some reform of the Church was needed. However, the hierarchy of the Church was dominated by one of the strongest rulers in English history, who enjoyed devoted loyalty even from people who were deeply offended by his policies. This was illustrated late in 1536, when the most serious rebellion of the king's reign, the Pilgrimage of Grace (which demanded a return to the Church of Rome and was supported widely in the north of England) failed because its leaders believed the king when he promised that he would reverse his religious policies. Henry had no intention of keeping his promise, but the rebellion was abandoned.

Thomas Cromwell reformed the financial administration of the country and established six courts, or departments, each responsible for collecting a particular sort of revenue. Cromwell chose to be Principal Secretary rather than Chancellor, as Wolsey had been; he thus elevated the Secretaryship to new importance in government, which position was retained until the nineteenth century. Most important, he made the Privy Council the greatest of the king's councils. It became the centre of government under the Tudors and Stuarts and later developed into the modern Cabinet. Cromwell's reforms laid the foundation for the machinery of government of the modern state.

The north, which was always the wildest and most remote part of the country, was brought more directly under central control by Cromwell, who abolished the judicial liberties which some areas enjoyed. Wales was incorporated into the English state when, in 1536 and 1543, it was divided into shires (counties), as England was. In Ireland royal policy encouraged the native Irish lords to accept titles from Henry and even spend time at court. In 1540 Henry exchanged his title of lord of Ireland for that of king of Ireland. But the attempt to bring Ireland closer to English rule had very limited success. The Irish Church was reformed along Henrician lines, but when later English monarchs attempted to make more fundamental changes they faced the opposition of the people, who remained loyal to Roman Catholicism, as many have done to the present day. Henry's attempts to control the whole of the British Isles signally failed with his policy towards the Scots.

Henry was cruel and egotistical. For reasons of state, in 1535 he executed Thomas More, the leading humanist scholar of the day and, later, a saint of the Roman Catholic Church (though it must be said that More was the only leading figure to object to the religious changes). Henry underwent six Christian marriages in pursuit of happiness and a son to succeed him. He dispensed with his two great ministers, Wolsey and Cromwell, without regret.

Yet Henry's authority was supreme, even though he had no permanent army or local bureaucracy. He had great presence. He was a king to his fingertips. He struck at the Roman Church when it was weak and without friends, and his unwitting creation of a national Church provoked a favourable response from a nationalistic people. From 1534 we can refer to the Church of England instead of the Church in England.

Edward VI and Mary Tudor

Edward was only nine when, in 1547, he succeeded his father, Henry, as king. The regency council set up by Henry before his death to rule during Edward's minority was dominated by Protestants, and the guardians quickly set about advancing the Reformation. In 1549 Archbishop Cranmer wrote the *Book of Common Prayer* (in English), which gave the Church of England a very moderate Protestant form of worship. However, by 1552 extreme Protestant thinking had prevailed and Cranmer wrote a Second prayer book, together with forty-two articles stating Church doctrine. This was the high point of radical Protestantism in the Church of England's history.

Henry VIII had excluded a number of powerful men from the regency council to prevent any one man from assuming complete control, but this very thing happened almost at once. The duke of Somerset became the effective head of government, and when a deteriorating economy led to a serious peasants' rebellion in 1549, the duke of Northumberland took advantage of the situation and seized power. Somerset was an idealist who became a martyr in the eyes of the ordinary people after his execution in 1552. But his lack of firm government deeply alarmed the ruling classes. Northumberland was an unattractive power-seeker, but he restored a measure of strong government. He had the complete confidence of the young king, but, unfortunately for Northumberland, Edward was a sickly boy, and in 1552 it was clear that he would not live much longer. Northumberland had good reason to be afraid of the succession of Edward's half-sister, Mary, the daughter of Katharine of Aragon. Northumberland had forced through the change to extreme Protestantism, while Mary remained an ardent Catholic.

Northumberland persuaded the king to name Lady Jane Grey heir to the throne. She was the daughter of Mary, the younger daughter of Henry VII. She was also the wife of Northumberland's son, and it was clear that her succession to the throne was a means to allow her father-in-law to retain control of government. When Edward died in 1553 Jane was proclaimed queen, but she received barely any support, and Mary Tudor took the throne with little trouble. Lady Jane, an innocent and tragic figure, was executed, as were her husband and the duke of Northumberland. Edward VI has not impressed history; the indications are that he would have been a cruel and arrogant ruler.

Mary devoted herself to the restoration of the Catholic religion in England. It was not difficult to restore the old services and doctrines, but it was impossible for the Church to regain the property it had lost during the Reformation. A number of Protestants refused to change their religion, and those who openly defied Mary were executed. Among those burnt at the stake were the bishops of London and Oxford and, most important, Thomas Cranmer, the archbishop of Canterbury. This harsh policy did not stamp out Protestantism; it only served to nourish it, and the Queen earned the title of 'Bloody Mary'.

In 1553, when she was thirty-seven, Mary married Philip II of Spain. Mary hoped that Philip would bring the resources of Spain and of the Habsburg family to her aid in the difficult task of Catholicising England. Philip in turn looked for the support of English military and sea power. He was troubled by discontent in the Netherlands, which at that time was part of the Spanish empire, and he was engaged in war with France. Philip had little liking for England and the English. They also disliked him and saw in the connection with Spain only trouble and expense.

English fears were realised when war was declared on France

in support of Spain. The English were no match for the French, who in 1557 took Calais, the only English possession left in France. Mary was deeply moved by the loss, but in fact England was better off without Calais, for English possessions in France only served as a source of friction between the two countries.

Both Mary and Philip wanted a son, and when, fourteen months after their marriage, it was quite clear that Mary was not going to have any children Philip went back to Spain, never to return to England nor to see Mary again. For Mary this was the severest of many blows in her reign. She was faced with the unpleasant fact that when she died she would be succeeded by her half-sister, Elizabeth. Mary was deeply suspicious of Elizabeth's hasty conversion to Catholicism, and feared – as it turned out, with justification – that on her death Elizabeth, and England with her, would abandon Rome.

Elizabeth I

It is not clear where Elizabeth stood theologically, but she judged that if a religious settlement were not quickly reached, England, like other European countries, could be consumed by religious wars. Elizabeth aimed to accommodate the views of as many people as possible in a national Church. Continued adherence to Rome was impossible. The Roman Catholic Church had condemned the marriage of her mother, Anne Boleyn, to Henry VIII, and Elizabeth was their offspring. Elizabeth had indicated at the beginning of her reign that the Catholic service was not to her liking. She took the title of Supreme Governor of the Church rather than Supreme Head, as Henry VIII had done, hoping that Catholics would be able to accept their monarch's lesser claim to governorship of the church.

Elizabeth was obliged by the House of Commons and pressure from within the Church to adopt a prayer book similar to that of 1552. This was distinctly Protestant, as were the Thirty-nine Articles, which set out Church doctrine. She hoped that Catholics might in time come to prefer the national Anglican Church service to the Latin mass. Elizabeth enjoyed a long reprieve before being excommunicated in 1570; even then her excommunication was clumsily handled and Elizabeth appeared to be the aggrieved party. The Roman Catholic Church did not, in fact, launch a serious missionary programme in England until the 1580s, by which time the Catholic cause was lost.

Serious opposition to Elizabeth's settlement came from the

Elizabeth I (1558–1603), seen here resplendent in one of her many gowns and standing on a map of England, established Protestantism in the country once and for all. Elizabeth's religious settlement and English independence were guaranteed by the defeat of the Spanish Armada in 1588. Her reign brought a magnificent flowering of the arts.

Puritans. These were Protestants who wished to 'purify' the Church of all Roman Catholic ideas. At first, English Puritans were concerned to get rid of vestments (garments worn by priests during the service) and what they considered to be unnecessary ceremonial. Elizabeth would make no concessions on these issues; neither would she accept the later Puritan demands for a reform of Church government, which envisaged the abolition of bishops and the Church hierarchy. The queen's refusal to give way led to an important development: the Puritans launched their attacks on the Elizabethan Church in the House of Commons.

Elizabeth believed that it was a royal prerogative to decide Church matters. The Commons, which had been involved in all the major questions of religion since 1529, believed otherwise. Though Puritan opposition had abated by the end of the 1580s, the Puritan party remained a strong minority in the Church, in Parliament and among men of influence. Parliament's habit of questioning matters of royal prerogative extended to matters like proposed marriages for the queen and foreign affairs. Elizabeth could not dispense with Parliament, no matter how irritating its intervention was. The monarchy was bankrupt, and the queen needed Parliament's help in collecting money.

The Commons was concerned for the queen to marry and to secure the succession. Marriage never came. Elizabeth used marriage as a diplomatic weapon, gaining the friendship of countries whose rulers thought she would be a good match. Marriage with an English noble house was impossible, as the Tudors considered themselves ordained by God to rule and therefore very distant from even the noblest house. Elizabeth had a succession of affairs, most notably with the earls of Leicester and Essex. The earl of Essex led a rebellion against Elizabeth, which led to his execution and contributed to the queen's deep melancholia at the end of her reign.

Elizabeth realised that Catholic Europe – and in particular Spain, the leading Catholic nation – could never be expected to support her religious settlement. Her foreign policy was designed to ensure that Spain's many problems were never solved. She helped the Dutch, who were in rebellion against Philip II of Spain, and on the whole maintained a policy of friendship toward France, Spain's great rival in Europe.

The strongest reason for not executing Mary, Queen of Scots, who fled to England in 1568 and was the centre of Catholic conspiracies while she was in Elizabeth's custody, was that she was the recognised Catholic claimant to the English throne. On her death this claim would pass not to her son, who was being brought up a Protestant, but to Philip II of Spain. Mary's part in the Babington Plot to kill the queen in 1587 persuaded Elizabeth to agree to the House of Commons's demand for Mary's execution. Elizabeth tried to rescind the order, but to prevent the queen from changing her mind, it had been arranged for the execution order to be delivered at full speed. Mary's claim duly passed to Philip.

In 1588 Philip launched the Spanish Armada against England. It comprised 130 ships and 8000 seamen, and it was intended to transport a Spanish army from the Netherlands to England. But though the Spanish fleet was larger than the English one, its ships were less manoeuvrable and less effective in northern waters. The English were at home off their own coast, and they were ably led by Lord Howard of Effingham and Sir Francis Drake. In July the English defeated the Spanish fleet, and the remaining Spanish ships limped home after being further savaged by storms. The defeat of the Armada was hailed as a great victory in England. Both Elizabeth and Protestantism had been saved. However, the war with Spain continued, and English successes thereafter were infrequent and often unspectacular. Of great concern to Elizabeth was the fact that the war, like all other ventures in foreign policy, was costing a lot of money.

It was financial considerations that held up Elizabeth's conquest of Ireland, which was not completed until 1603, the year of her death. The English controlled the Pale, the area around Dublin, but felt that the rest of Ireland should be under their control, if only to stop Irish attacks on their territory and to prevent Ireland from being used as a base for enemy attacks against England. The English presence in Ireland served to consolidate Irish support for Roman Catholicism. On the other hand, Elizabeth had considerable success with Scotland. The two countries shared the same religion, and, most important, King James hoped to succeed Elizabeth and did not wish to endanger his inheritance by anti-English moves.

Elizabeth was confronted with serious economic problems. First there was her own financial weakness, which was caused by a reliance on a fixed income at a time of high inflation. Perpetual meanness and a willingness to increase royal funds by whatever means available, from parliamentary grants to shares in pirate ventures, saved the monarchy from bankruptcy. But it was a hard job, and it is amazing that Elizabeth's government achieved what it did on an income of about £200,000 a year (Philip of Spain must have had at least four times as much). The gentry and merchants who did well out of speculation in monastic lands and foreign trade were often, as Members of Parliament, the least sympathetic to royal demands for increased revenues, believing the monarchy should live on its traditional sources of income. Nobody clearly understands the reasons for inflation in Tudor England, but Elizabeth's stabilisation of the currency by refusing to debase the coinage any further (as Henry VIII and Northumberland had done) eased inflation considerably.

Some of the distress in the countryside among the poor (at least 90 per cent of the population lived in the country) was caused by the consolidation (enclosure) of land under the ownership of one man or a group of landowners in each district, a measure designed to improve arable farming or to introduce sheep farming. The results of enclosure were a drop in employment in the countryside and the drift of men to towns which could not absorb the surplus labour. Enclosures happened throughout the Tudor period and continued until the eighteenth century, when they were most numerous. Although Elizabeth's government took a strong line against enclosures, in practice the momentum of the enclosure movement was little affected.

Elizabeth's government instituted two social measures of great importance. In 1563 the Statute of Artificers made masters responsible for the welfare and education of their apprentices for a period of seven years. The Poor Laws of 1597 and 1601 obliged the parishes to provide for the sick and unemployed. These were attempts by the government to regularise conditions in the craft industries and to look after the poor who could not help themselves. The state did not pity those who were considered able-bodied and idle, and often men who were unemployed as a result of the general state of the economy were harshly treated. As with all Tudor and later legislation, the responsibility for enforcing it was laid on the parishes, which were controlled by the local landowners and merchants. As (virtually) unpaid Justices of the Peace, they were responsible for law, order, welfare and adherence to the true religion in their locality. If the Justices did not co-operate, there was little that could be done about it.

Elizabeth's reign saw the founding, out of local funds, of many grammar schools, hospitals and alms houses to look after the aged. The Christian conscience has demanded in all ages that the rich should help the poor, but the need was sharper after the dissolution of the monasteries, which had for centuries helped both the local community and travellers. Some of the money available as a consequence of the confiscation of Church property was used to found professorships at the universities of Oxford and Cambridge and for other educational purposes, but the sum was a tiny fraction of the whole.

Elizabeth's reign was fraught with religious tensions and serious economic problems, but the achievements of a religious settlement which avoided warfare and the defeat of Spain were considerable. Elizabeth was well served by her principal minister, William Cecil, Lord Burghley, but her own talents, intelligence and charm were ultimately responsible for the success of her monarchy.

There was an effervescent spirit in Elizabethan England.

The greatest English dramatist of this or indeed any period was William Shakespeare (1564–1616). The picture shows his memorial in Westminster Abbey.

Half-timbered buildings are a distinctive feature of Tudor architecture. One of the finest examples is Little Moreton Hall in Cheshire, which also demonstrates that by the sixteenth century English houses, even of this size, were designed more for comfort and refinement than for defence.

London was a lively, though insanitary, city of 200,000 people. Oxford and Cambridge universities were great centres of Classical and theological study (Cambridge inclined to Puritanism). Elizabeth's reign coincided with a highly productive phase in English literature, which was to continue throughout James I's reign. Edmund Spenser, for example, wrote the lyric poem 'The Faerie Queene' in honour of Elizabeth. In the theatres that sprang up just outside London (to escape the jurisdiction of the City) plays by Shakespeare, Marlowe and Ben Jonson were performed. William Shakespeare (1564–1616) dominated the theatre. Though little is known about his life, he received the patronage of both Elizabeth and James I.

The growing wealth of Tudor England was reflected in a vast building programme. Defence considerations were minimal, except on the Scottish borders, and windows were therefore large, looking out on to the estates of property owners. Often monasteries were converted into local great houses or local churches. Elizabeth's reign saw a flourishing of the half-timbered style of building; a manor house like Morton in Cheshire must have been typical. Ideas from Italy had a marked influence on English building. The Gate of Honour at Gonville and Caius College (1575) was an elaborate combination of Classical orders (styles) and motifs. Cardinal Wolsey's palace at Hampton Court was a beautiful but homely creation in brick. Longleat House, which was also built in Elizabeth's reign, has the elegance and lightness of a Loire *château*.

Elizabeth's reign produced a crop of adventurers, who continued the exploration of the New World. From 1577 to 1580 Sir Francis Drake completed the circumnavigation of the globe – the first by an Englishman. By Elizabeth's reign the territory of Newfoundland, claimed during Henry VII's reign for England, was recognised as one of the world's great fisheries. Attempts to establish colonies in America failed, despite the efforts of, among others, Sir Walter Raleigh. It was he who perpetuated his sovereign's name by calling his proposed colony Virginia, in honour of the Virgin Queen.

Scotland in the Sixteenth Century

James IV was fifteen when his father died in battle. After a brief regency he took over government with enthusiasm. He made a number of journeys to the highlands and learned the Gaelic language in an attempt to understand that part of his kingdom. James's solution to the highlands was to prove highly unsatisfactory, however. He suppressed the lordship of the Isles and distributed its power among the heads of clans of his own choosing. Without a single source of authority, warfare between the clans became more intense, and royal control of the Highlands was no easier to exercise.

In 1503 James married Margaret Tudor, the eldest daughter of Henry VII. The marriage was intended to stabilise relations between the two countries. But James IV and Henry VIII, who had succeeded his father to the English throne in 1509, were in different alliances. James backed Scotland's old ally, France, and England supported the Holy Roman Empire. There was war between Scotland and England in 1513, in support of their respective Continental partners, and at Flodden the Scottish army was heavily defeated by the English commander, the Earl of Surrey. James IV was killed.

When the next king, James V, assumed power in his teens he proved ambitious, assertive and energetic. He spent lavishly, as his father had. He exploited the Church's funds shamelessly, knowing that, with Protestantism on the attack, the Church would not wish to give up his friendship. James V's second marriage was to Marie de Guise. Her family was one of the most powerful in France and would shortly be the leaders of the Catholic cause in that country. James foolishly embarked on war with Henry VIII, just as his father had done. The Scots were defeated at Solway Moss in 1542, and James died in the same year. Both of James's sons had died at birth, and the new monarch was his one-week-old daughter, Mary, Queen of Scots. The war with England continued, as the regency (headed by the extremely capable queen mother, Marie de Guise) would not assent to Henry's demands for custody of the queen, her marriage to his son Edward or the ultimate control of Scotland by the English. Rather, the queen mother preferred to send Mary to France, to contract a French marriage for her and to maintain Scotland's alliance with France.

Scotland had remained within the Roman Catholic Church while Henry VIII broke ties with Rome. But it was impossible for the Scottish Church to prevent Protestant literature and ideas from crossing the border, particularly when, after Henry VIII's death in 1547, England became a fully Protestant country. The head of the Church in Scotland, Cardinal Beaton, spasmodically persecuted heretics. In 1546 he was himself assassinated by a group of Protestants. The Scottish Church, under the leadership of Archbishop Hamilton, Beaton's successor, attempted reform, but the Church was in a bad state. Its funds had been largely diverted from the parishes, where the real work of the Church was done; consequently, the parish clergy were poor and ignorant, and the ordinary people were badly served by their priests.

One of Beaton's assassins was John Knox. After serving a sentence in the French galleys, Knox continued his work, which he saw as the task of converting Scotland to Protestantism. He was tough and determined. He preached Calvinism, the most severe form of Protestantism. It placed great emphasis on the authority of the Bible and on extreme simplicity in church services. Two tenets of Calvinism were predestination and assurance: according to Calvinist doctrine, there was a group of the faithful which was foreordained (predestined) to be saved by God, and this predestined elite knew, or was assured, that its members were the 'elect', or the 'chosen'. In practical terms Calvinism gave its followers a tough, fighting creed and an absolute certainty that they were right.

Calvinism spread like fire through Scotland, and the queen mother, Marie de Guise, was obliged to call in a French army to confront the Protestants. Queen Elizabeth of England intervened at this point to prevent a French victory and the defeat of her co-religionists. In 1560 an English fleet and army was sent to support the Scottish Protestant rebels. The French were defeated and withdrew, and in June Marie de Guise died. The Scottish Parliament, meeting in August 1560, abolished the authority of the pope in Scotland, and the Latin mass was outlawed. Decisions about the details of worship were left to a group of reformers led by John Knox, who agreed on a strictly Calvinist doctrinal settlement. The severity of Calvinism extended to moral and social life. It gave piety and purpose to the Scottish people – but it also robbed them of what would now be considered innocent pleasures, like organ music in church and Christmas celebrations. However, Catholicism continued to be a major religious force in the highlands, just as it endured in the poorer and wilder north of England after the English Reformation.

Mary, Queen of Scots, had married the Dauphin Francis (the heir to the French throne) in 1558 and was queen of France during his brief reign from April 1559 to December 1560. After Francis II's death there was no place for Mary at the French court, and she returned to Scotland in August 1561. Mary was, of course, Catholic, but she wisely accepted the fact that Protestantism was the religion of most of the Scots.

In 1565 Mary married her cousin, Henry Stewart, Lord Darnley, who was also a Catholic. The marriage quickly ran into trouble, principally because Darnley wanted the authority of kingship, which Mary could not and would not give him. In 1566 Darnley and others murdered the queen's secretary, David Riccio, who, as a confidant of Mary's, had aroused

Mary Queen of Scots posed considerable security problems for Elizabeth. Mary was forced to flee her own land but, as the Catholic claimant to the English throne, she presented too grave a threat to be welcomed by Elizabeth, who imprisoned her for much of her life and finally executed her in 1587.

Darnley's intense jealousy. In 1567 Darnley's house in Edinburgh was blown up; he was killed. It was common knowledge that this was the work of James Hepburn, earl of Bothwell. Two months later Mary married Bothwell, according to the rites of the Protestant church. The nobility had been alarmed, as first Darnley and then Bothwell grabbed power by marrying Mary, and they decided to force Mary to abdicate in favour of her baby son, whose regency could be arranged to their satisfaction. Mary's conduct had outraged the Scottish nation, and she could have expected no popular support.

Mary escaped from captivity in 1568, fought a battle and lost, and then fled to England, where she became a prisoner of Queen Elizabeth. Her son, James VI, remained in Scotland and finally proclaimed himself king in 1583. He had found the regency very irksome and was determined not to let himself be controlled by the nobility again. His main aim was to secure his succession to the English throne. When Mary was executed in 1587 for complicity in the Babington plot James kept quiet. He ensured that Scotland remained neutral during the attack of the Spanish Armada in the following year. In 1589 James married Princess Anne of Denmark – a solidly Protestant marriage. But James was not a Calvinist. He liked the rule of bishops in the Church and a moderate form of Protestant service. When he was king of England he would make moves to impose some of his ideas on the Scottish Church (or 'kirk', as it was more commonly called). In 1603 James went to England to become king on Elizabeth's death. He was very eager to possess his new inheritance, which was vastly rich compared with Scotland.

5

The Stuarts

Growing Protest, 1603–1640

James, Elizabeth's successor in 1603, was king of both England and Scotland, though the union of the two crowns did not go as far as James wanted. The administrations, Parliaments and courts of the two countries continued to function separately, and differences in culture and religion between England and Scotland were pronounced. The union of the crowns did, however, solve the problem of the border; the warlords on each side lost their *raison d'être*.

James was learned, warm and sincere, but he was disagreeably argumentative and tended to become pedantic. Though he had done well in Scotland, he saw too clearly the attractions of England and at first underestimated the problems of ruling the country. The difficulties were great – conceivably, beyond the solution of any ruler at that time. The Tudors had created an autocracy in Church and state but without the financial means to sustain it. For the monarchy to become financially independent, it would have been necessary to impose greater taxes on the ruling classes both in town and country. Their representatives in the House of Commons would not consent to this, particularly when they began to have serious doubts about the policies and methods of Stuart government and were deeply suspicious of the advisers who surrounded the king. James was criticised but, on the whole, liked. His son Charles was aloof and widely distrusted. To save themselves from what they saw as an approaching state of ruinous taxation imposed at royal will, restrictions on economic activities, a bad foreign policy and the encouragement of Catholicism at home (all imposed on the country, if need be, by a foreign army), large sections of the ruling classes revolted against the king in 1640. The legislation their Parliament passed in 1641 was intended to make it impossible for a king to rule without Parliament. Though it was not aware of the new political theory that it was advancing, Parliament was stating that sovereignty should reside not in the king alone but in the king in Parliament.

At this momentous period the affairs of England and Scotland were bound together. Ironically, the initiative in the revolution came from Scotland, which was smaller and poorer than England and distant from the king in London.

Religious problems faced James. The king readily adopted the Anglicanism of Elizabeth's Church, and at a great conference held at Hampton Court in 1604 James made it clear that he would make no changes in religion. He condemned the Puritans. They could either conform to James's wishes, protest or leave the country. Many men had Puritan sympathies but obeyed the laws as they stood. Other Puritans mounted criticism of royal policy in the House of Commons and outside. A small number of Puritans left to establish colonies in North America, where they could worship as they wished. The voyage of the *Mayflower* in 1620 is the most celebrated of the Puritan exoduses. (By 1640 there were five colonies in North America, which were sufficiently independent in their approach to religion and government for Charles I, James's heir, to consider sending an expedition against them. But domestic problems obliged Charles I to abandon this scheme.)

The one positive result of the Hampton Court Conference was the setting up of a commission to make a new translation of the Bible. This, when completed in 1611, was known as the Authorised Version, or King James's Bible; its beautiful language has endeared it to generations of readers.

Catholics, too, hoped for favours from James (his mother, Mary, Queen of Scots, had been the Catholic claimant to the English throne). Disappointed with the new monarch, a group of Catholic extremists decided to blow up the king and Parliament when James opened the new session of Parliament in November 1605. One conspirator, Guy Fawkes, placed gunpowder in the cellars beneath the Houses of Parliament, but the plot was discovered, and Fawkes and the other plotters were arrested and later executed. Since then the deliverance of the king, Parliament and Protestantism has been celebrated each year on 5 November.

Whether Puritan or not, there was widespread discontent among the members of the House of Commons, and among those whom they represented, with the methods James's government adopted to increase revenues. The sale of titles and the manipulation of feudal rights caused widespread irritation. Most resented was the sale of monopolies, which often went to court favourites. (Monopolies allowed the holder to control the sales and distribution of a product.) In 1621 there were 700 monopolies and some were highly lucrative: for example, the earl of Salisbury and government ministers were receiving £7000 a year from the silk monopoly in 1612. The most controversial court decision of James's reign was made in 1605, when the judges (appointed by the king) decreed that the king could fix customs duties as he thought fit. Merchants and gentlemen complained that they would be ruined, and James did not implement the court's decision. But there was deep suspicion of the government's financial policies, which were seen as a potential threat to the liberties of the king's subjects.

One source of friction between the king and the House of Commons was foreign policy. Peace was made with Spain in 1604, but this was unpopular. The Commons, particularly the Puritan element, urged England's intervention to support Protestantism on the Continent. In 1621 the Commons defied James and discussed foreign affairs – hitherto an area which came under exclusively royal control. Enraged at the Commons' action, the king entered the Commons chamber and tore out the pages recording the debate from the Commons journal. However, James finally conceded to his critics and declared war on Spain in 1624. When France and Spain formed an alliance in 1626 England declared war on France. The English navy did badly, and the Commons were bitterly critical of the government. James died in 1625, but his son, Charles, inherited the Commons' wrath at England's military failures.

In the eyes of the Commons, the king's chief adviser, George Villiers, the duke of Buckingham, was responsible first for James's and then for Charles's failures abroad and misguided policies at home. Villiers had risen from nothing to become almost the sole adviser of royal father and son, and this was resented. He was handsome and arrogant and clearly did not deserve the complete confidence which James and Charles placed in him. When Buckingham was murdered in 1627 Parliament and London openly rejoiced. This attitude shocked and appalled Charles, who regarded Buckingham as a close personal friend as well as a trusted adviser.

When Charles I succeeded his father in 1625 the House of Commons had clearly greatly increased in confidence since Elizabeth's reign. An Opposition had formed, which had seized the initiative in debates and now dominated proceedings. In 1625 Parliament refused to grant Charles the traditional taxes of tunnage and poundage for life, as was customary. Charles dissolved Parliament in anger. A second Parliament was also dissolved quickly, in the face of debates dominated by foreign affairs and the attempted impeachment of Buckingham.

Charles hoped that his third Parliament would be more co-operative, but it went further in its opposition to the king than any Parliament had done before. It passed the Petition of

Right in 1628, which reminded the king that there could be no taxation without the consent of Parliament, that imprisonment without proper trial was illegal, that military law should not be applied to civilians and that billeting on private citizens should not be allowed. The House of Commons believed that it was protecting personal liberty and property against royal encroachment. When Charles went on collecting tunnage and poundage without parliamentary authorisation a revolutionary scene occurred in the Commons. The Speaker (chairman) of the Commons was held down in his seat and not allowed to adjourn proceedings, while the Members passed resolutions on taxation and religion. They spoke of people who paid taxes without Parliament's consent as 'a capital enemy to the kingdom and people'. Charles arrested the leaders of the Opposition, dissolved Parliament and determined never to call another.

From 1629 until 1640 Charles ruled without a Parliament; this period has been variously called the 'Personal Rule' and the 'Eleven Years' Tyranny'. Opposition to the king continued. In 1637 a former member of Parliament, John Hampden, obliged Charles to take him to the courts over his objections to paying a tax called 'ship money'. This, Hampden claimed, was an unlawful imposition, as the tax could only be levied from counties bordering the sea, in order to provide for the navy in times of war. Hampden protested that he lived in an inland county and that the country was not at war. The judges appointed by the king were aware of the importance Charles attached to the case, as ship money could restore royal finances, but decided in the king's favour by only seven votes to five. Hampden and the Opposition had clearly won a great moral victory.

Charles's archbishop of Canterbury, William Laud, mounted a fierce campaign to make the Puritans conform to his interpretation of the state religion, Anglicanism. The campaign was resented beyond the ranks of the Puritans, as punishments normally reserved for the lower classes were inflicted on gentlemen, as in 1637, when three leading Puritans were publicly whipped and branded in the streets of London. Also, the punishments were imposed by Church courts under the direct control of the monarchy and outside the common law. Charles was a fervent believer in Anglicanism, which, he believed, combined Protestant theology with Catholic tradition and ceremony. But the king's court was under a cloud of suspicion for being a centre of Catholicism, generally regarded in England as a totally alien and subversive creed. The truth was, however, that Charles's queen, Henrietta Maria, the daughter of Henry IV of France, was allowed to practise the

Catholic religion, which gave the impression that everyone around the king was Catholic.

The most hated of Charles's ministers was Thomas Wentworth, the earl of Strafford, who was president of the Council of the North and Lord Deputy of Ireland. He was loyal and coldly efficient. Parliament's great fear was that Strafford, who had collected together a large Catholic army in Ireland, intended to use it to suppress opposition to royal authority in England.

The chain of events which led to the calling of Parliament started in Scotland in 1637, when Charles imposed a new liturgy on the Scottish kirk. This followed gradual pressure by James and Charles to make the Scottish Calvinist Church more like the Church of England, but the new liturgy at once united all classes throughout Scotland against Charles. The Scottish army expelled Charles's forces from Scotland. Charles asked the nobility for money to fight the war, but none was forthcoming. In April 1640 he called the Short Parliament, but it would only grant money on terms unacceptable to Charles. In August the Scots invaded England and occupied the important city of Newcastle. At the end of 1640 Charles was obliged to call the Long Parliament – one of the most famous Parliaments in English history – which undertook sweeping reforms of Church and state. The Scottish leaders were in touch with the English Parliament throughout this time, and their close co-operation brought about King Charles's submission.

War and Republic, 1640 1660

The Long Parliament at once impeached Strafford and Laud. Strafford was executed in May 1641 and Archbishop Laud in 1645. The king was obliged to summon regular parliaments by the Triennial Act, and the Long Parliament itself, under a separate measure, could only be adjourned, prorogued or dissolved with its own consent. Charles was thereafter powerless to prevent the Commons from dismantling royal autocracy. Non-parliamentary taxes were declared illegal. Prerogative courts in which the king or his councillors judged cases directly and without appeal were abolished. (The most famous such court was Star Chamber.) Leading Puritans who had been imprisoned during the Personal Rule were released and compensated.

This was welcomed by most Members of Parliament, but by the end of 1641 there had been a significant rallying of support for the king. When Parliament indicted the monarchy and advanced proposals for complete reform of the Church, just under half of the Members of Parliament turned to Charles. The situation deteriorated; Parliament attempted to take custody of the royal family, and Charles endeavoured to arrest the leaders of the Commons. Throughout the country there was a taking of sides, and in August 1642 the Civil War began.

The country divided broadly into two. The economically advanced south and east, and nearly all major commercial and manufacturing cities, including London, sided with Parliament. The poorer north, the west and Wales fought for the king. It was a war which divided the traditional ruling classes of the country. Most of the aristocracy fought for the king, but some supported Parliament. The parliamentary army was commanded by great nobles until 1644. The gentry or country landowners, who were the Justices of the Peace and upholders of law and order in the countryside, divided according to their consciences. Country gentlemen who were committed to the Church of England or were loyal to Charles Stuart fought for the king. Puritans and those who had not forgiven the king for his methods of government fought for Parliament. Merchants who had been restricted by Stuart economic measures fought mainly for Parliament. Catholics who could not expect anything from a Puritan Commons fought for the king. Many men remained neutral, and life in the country went on relatively smoothly, despite the war.

Though the war was fought in the interests of the property-owning section of society who paid the taxes and had the vote (no more than 10 per cent of the population), the struggle obviously involved ordinary people working in the countryside and towns. Particularly in the parliamentary armies, ideas grew up about the nature of government and society which were far more radical than the great majority of parliamentary gentlemen found acceptable. The removal of bishops and the lifting of censorship presented an opportunity for the circulation of ideas and literature that would not have been tolerated before. There were the Levellers, who wanted the franchise extended to small property owners and artisans. There were Diggers, who advocated rural communism and the common ownership of land. The Civil War produced an amazing ferment of ideas, and the vast pamphlet literature which has survived testifies to this.

Initially, the king had the advantage, as he commanded the only army and alone had any clear idea of what he wanted. The parliamentary side was a collection of interests which at first did not know how seriously to fight the war. The long-term advantages all lay with Parliament, however. Parliament

The Civil War – England at the end of 1643

controlled most of the money, the productive capacity of the country and the seas, isolating the king and keeping trade under its control. In September 1643 the English Parliament formed an alliance with the Scots (who had been neutral since the beginning of the war), under the terms of which the English agreed to adopt the Scottish form of worship in return

Charles I (1625–49) faced a conflict with Parliament which culminated in the Civil War and his own execution. This portrait is in the style of Sir Anthony Van Dyck, the principal painter at the court at that time.

for the services of a large Scottish army. The arrangement did not take account of the fact that only one section of the parliamentary side (let alone the English nation at large) liked the Scottish religious model. Scottish and English troops defeated the Royalists at Marston Moor, Yorkshire, in July 1644, and the king's army was finally and decisively defeated at Naseby, in Northamptonshire, by an English army in June 1645.

With the end of fighting, Charles surrendered to the Scots, who in January 1647 handed him over to the English Parliament for £200,000. But a serious division grew up between Parliament and the army. Members of Parliament were afraid of the power of the army and suspicious of the generals' intentions. The army in turn felt that as it had won the war, it should have some say in the ordering of affairs in peacetime.

The army was needed anyway, for peace could not be guaranteed without the soldiers.

Oliver Cromwell was the leader of the army. He was primarily a brilliant soldier who responded to events with speed and determination. These qualities enabled him to win battles. They helped him less in politics. He had been a Member of Parliament and a leading Puritan critic of Charles Stuart, but he had no ideas about how he wanted the country ruled. He was loyal to the army but impatient of idealists and subtle politicians in Parliaments, who seemed intent on taking power for themselves and disregarded the interests of those who had fought the king. Cromwell had to secure the parliamentary victory in Ireland and Scotland. He subdued Ireland with such brutality in 1649 that his name has been associated there with curses to the present day. The Scots accepted Charles after he escaped from captivity in 1648. He agreed to the Scottish line in religion but not, one imagines, with any sincerity. The Scottish army was decisively beaten by Cromwell, and the captured king was brought to trial. Cromwell was determined that Charles should die, as he was convinced that if the king's life was spared, plots and war would continue. In January 1649 Charles was executed, the first European monarch to be executed after a formal trial and to be found guilty of crimes against his people. European political thinking had been profoundly, albeit harshly, advanced.

Cromwell demonstrated that he was well able to maintain order throughout Britain. Sporadic Royalist uprisings were easily crushed. When the Scots raised an army in favour of Charles I's son, Charles (II), they were decisively beaten on 3 September 1650 and 3 September 1651. Scotland was put under English rule and controlled by an army big enough to maintain law and order even in the highlands. Cromwell was unable to work out a satisfactory constitutional arrangement for England, despite a number of careful attempts. He rooted out radicalism in the army and always assumed that men of property should rule. But the propertied classes came to hate the Republic. They resented the firm military government at the centre and interference in the running of local affairs, which landowning Justices of the Peace saw as their exclusive province. There was high taxation to pay for the army and as many religious restrictions as under the Stuarts.

When Cromwell died in September 1658 the Republic died with him. His son, Richard, resigned the title of Protector which he had inherited from his father. General Monck, the leader of the army in Scotland, took control of the country. The surviving members of the Long Parliament convened and asked Charles II to return as king. Ironically, Britain's only

Oliver Cromwell led the resistance to the king and, with the title Lord Protector, became the leader of the only republic in British history. This painting of him hangs in Sidney Sussex College, Cambridge, where he had been a student.

republic ensured the continuance of the monarchy in some form; it also established the principle of maintaining large armies in wartime only.

The Republic saw the triumph of Puritanism. Bishops were abolished, and Church services made simple (though very long). Frivolous amusements like dancing were scorned, and the theatres were closed. Puritanism was not simply censorious, however. The Puritans believed in the merits of education; all men, they declared, should be able to read the Bible. In 1616 and 1635 Acts of Parliament in Scotland had imposed on landlords the duty of creating and maintaining a school in every parish. Puritan theology – in particular, the belief that all men were equal in the sight of God – had an enormous impact on the political field.

John Milton, who held the office of Latin Secretary to the Council of State during the Republic, produced the greatest religious epic in the English language, 'Paradise Lost', which was completed in 1665 when he had already gone blind. (Milton received £5 for its publication in 1667.) The work tells of the expulsion of Adam from the Garden of Eden and Lucifer's fall from Heaven. So beguiling is the description of Satan, however, that many readers of Milton have considered Lucifer to be the real hero of the epic.

Restoration, 1660–1685

The old order was restored in 1660 – but, significantly, by Parliament. It was clear that future government would be conducted by a partnership of king and Parliament, whether the king liked it or not. The House of Lords and bishoprics which had been abolished by the Republic were restored. The army disbanded, having secured back pay and promises of pensions. Puritans were driven out of public life by a series of laws passed between 1661 and 1665, and central and local government was put firmly in the hands of Royalist landowners and merchants. Puritans who would not agree to the Anglican order of the Church were called Dissenters or Nonconformists, names which have endured to the present day in some areas of England. Many Puritans went to prison. The great religious work *Pilgrim's Progress* was written by the Puritan John Bunyan, while he was in prison. However, only eleven men were executed (those who had signed Charles I's death warrant), and Cromwell's body was disinterred and displayed publicly in London.

Landownership was by far the most difficult and important problem to solve. Many Royalists had sold off property between 1642 and 1660 and they now wanted it back. Understandably, the new owners were reluctant to surrender it. The formula that was worked out was that Royalist land which had been confiscated by the Parliamentarians had to be returned to former owners, but land sold voluntarily by Royalists would remain with the new owners. Many Royalist families were impoverished and embittered; there was little they could do but complain to the king, which they did for many years.

Charles II's declared aim was to remain king, and in this he succeeded. In fact, Charles wanted much more than that, and he gained some of what he wanted. He was a Catholic, though he wisely kept this a secret until his death. He admired the absolutist monarchy of Louis XIV of France, and he disliked dependence on Parliament. In 1670 Charles began secret negotiations with Louis, which culminated in the secret Treaty of Dover. By the terms of the treaty Charles undertook to declare publicly his adherence to Catholicism, whilst Louis promised to help Charles reconvert England with money and soldiers. The two kings also agreed to attack Holland, and war was declared on the Dutch in March 1673. Two days before Charles had issued a Declaration of Indulgence for Roman Catholics and Dissenters, by which he granted permission for these two groups of religious outlaws to hold public office.

Parliament was outraged, first because Catholics and Dissenters were loathed, and secondly because the king had set aside parliamentary statutes in favour of a simple royal declaration. In answer to Charles II's action Parliament passed the Test Act, which obliged all office holders, military and civil, to take the Sacrament according to the rites of the Church of England. The Act reaffirmed Anglican supremacy and drove from public life a number of men close to the king. The king's brother, James (the future king), who had openly declared his Catholicism, had to resign as Lord High Admiral. The Lord Treasurer, Clifford, also resigned. Clearly, if Charles had not agreed to the Test Act, he too would have gone.

The Dutch War was brought to a close in 1674, but Charles continued to receive large financial subsidies from King Louis of France. This allowed Charles the independence necessary to defeat a large party which had grown up, committed to preventing the succession of Charles's Catholic brother, James, and to ensuring that of Charles's natural son, the Protestant duke of Monmouth. Charles was determined that the hereditary principle should prevail and not the wishes of a party of politicians. In the bitter fights over the issue two groups emerged. One was called the Petitioners because it petitioned the king not to prorogue or dissolve Parliament, the king's way of dispensing with a hostile Parliament. The other group was called the Abhorrers because it expressed abhorrence of the Petitioners. These parties were later known as the Whigs and the Tories. Charles called one last Parliament in 1681; thereafter, until his death in 1685, he ruled without Parliament, defying the Triennial Act of 1660, which obliged the king to call regular Parliaments. Charles then instituted a rule of terror against the Whigs and Dissenters. Leading Whigs went to prison. The charters defining the government of towns were remodelled to ensure that Royalists and Tories were in charge locally and that the Members of Parliament returned by these areas in the future would be of the same persuasion. This triumph for Charles and the Tory landowners ensured the smooth succession of James II in 1685. Charles left the monarchy strong and financially secure, a testament to his shrewdness and cool hand in politics. But Charles's reign exhibited the extent of royal power. In 1673 Charles had to give way, but in 1681, with the support of the Tories, increased revenues from customs and French money, he could defy Parliament. The growing revenue from customs resulted from the employment of professional customs officers for the first time and from a greatly increased volume of taxable commerce.

From 1660 until 1700 England experienced a commercial revolution. The Navigation Act of 1660 had the effect of putting nearly all England's trade, and that of her colonies, into the hands of English merchants. Trade increased dramatically, and shipbuilding was in turn stimulated. As more English goods travelled to Europe in English ships, England took control of her own trade with the Baltic. But the most important developments were in colonial trade. England had growing possessions in North America. She had also taken Jamaica in 1655. There were extensive English trading activities and acquisitions in India as well: for example, Charles's queen, Catherine of Braganza, brought Bombay as part of her dowry. By the 1660s the English had established stations on the West African coast and thereby gained access to the lucrative slave trade. Goods flooded into England from the colonies and were either consumed at home or exported to Europe. Some products (like tobacco, which had been a great luxury) became available to society at large. The effect of the expansion of trade on English exports was profound: by the end of the century cloth, which had traditionally been England's sole export, formed only 50 per cent of exports, though cloth production had, in fact, risen.

The new colonies gave English industries an exclusive

market, and this encouraged their development. Colonial trade was thus the stimulus for English industry, which prepared it for the Industrial Revolution of the next century. The government was also bent on using its power to capture trade and colonies. England, which had the largest navy by the end of the seventeenth century, was able to retain and extend this monopoly trade and the protection of her colonial possessions. In a series of wars in the 1660s the English defeated the Dutch, who were until that time the leading maritime power with a growing control of the carrying trade (the carriage of goods between countries). The Dutch had to give up trade which English merchants considered theirs. They also surrendered New Amsterdam in 1664, which later became New York, named after James, duke of York, the future James II. The Dutch Wars were fought against the interests of Scottish merchants and illustrated how little Scotland mattered in the considerations of the king and government after the Restoration.

The Great Fire of London in 1666 swept away not only the plague that had preceded it but many of the buildings. To replace them the architect, Sir Christopher Wren, built a forest of churches, prime among them being St Paul's Cathedral. The skyline of the City of London was to remain much as it looks in this eighteenth-century print until the extensive rebuilding that followed the Second World War.

The year 1665 saw the last visitation to London of plague on a large scale. In the following year the Great Fire destroyed much of the old city, taking with it remnants of the plague bacillus. After the Fire a great rebuilding programme was undertaken, which saw the construction of a new St Paul's Cathedral and fifty-one city churches. The architect was Christopher Wren, a man dominated by Classical ideas from Italy. He planned to create a new city of London, with wide streets and piazzas – a vision which was never realized. Restoration London was no longer confined by the historic limits of the city. It was spreading rapidly westwards. The first of London's parks were established, and theatres and coffee houses catered for the pleasures of the rich. Restoration theatre reflected aristocratic tastes, devoted as it was to heroic tragedy and comedies of manners. (Charles II himself was an ardent theatre-goer. The most famous of his mistresses was Nell Gwyn, who has been thought variously to have been an actress or an orange-seller in the theatre.)

Settlement and Union, 1685–1714

It is amazing that James II could lose such a safe inheritance as that left him by his brother, Charles II. He was rich, and political opposition had been strangled by Charles's tactics at the end of his reign. A rebellion led by the duke of Monmouth in 1685, which was easily suppressed by the royal armies, only served to strengthen James's position, as men of property took fright at the prospect of more fighting and disorder. James was a Catholic. This would not have been a problem had he not tried to come to the aid of his co-religionists, but in two royal declarations, in 1686 and 1687, James ordered the suspension of penal laws against Catholics and Dissenters. The 1687 declaration was particularly insulting to majority Anglican opinion, as the clergy were ordered to read out the text of the Indulgence in their churches. The hostility of the Anglicans was not balanced by gratitude from Dissenters, as they realised that James's measures were really intended to benefit Catholics. This had been made clear by James's promotion of Catholics in the army and navy and his confrontation with the universities in an attempt to force them to admit Catholics. The timing of James's Indulgences could not have been worse, as Louis XIV's revocation of the Edict of Nantes in 1685 began a persecution of Protestants in France and confirmed Protestant fears in England of the menace presented by Catholic France in particular and Catholicism in general.

The archibishop of Canterbury, together with six bishops of the Church of England (usually the most reliable supporters of monarchy), defied James's order to read out the Indulgence. They were sent to the Tower on a charge of seditious libel. But in June 1687 they were acquitted by a jury, and their release was met by great rejoicing in London. This was an ominous sign for James, as London had a reputation for dissent and was usually no friend of bishops. When James's second wife, the Catholic Mary of Modena, gave birth to a son in 1688 there was general despair at the prospect of an unending succession of Catholic monarchs. The only solution was to replace James by Mary, who was his daughter by his marriage to Anne Hyde. Mary was herself Protestant and married to William of Orange, Stadtholder of Holland and champion of Protestantism in Europe. On 1 November 1688 Prince William landed in England with a small army. James panicked and fled abroad. He and his heirs would make attempts to take back the throne, but the Jacobite cause was lost.

'The Glorious Revolution', as the events of 1688 and 1689 have been called, saw the removal of James II, a monarch who had ignored the sentiments of the ruling class and the people at large. William and Mary ruled jointly at the insistence of William, who would not let his wife come to England unless he was acknowledged as king. They were monarchs by invitation, and though the Tories would not admit it, the hereditary principle had been laid aside for the sake of political expediency. A Declaration of Rights was drawn up by Parliament and agreed to by William and Mary. Old ills such as taxation without parliamentary consent and the maintenance of a standing army in peacetime (which James II had reintroduced) were declared illegal. New measures were enacted. There was, for example, a declaration against 'cruel and unusual punishments'. The first measure of religious toleration was granted: Dissenters were allowed to worship freely, though they were still barred from office by the Test Act of 1673. This toleration was most significant in Scotland, where the great majority of the population were Dissenters.

The Presbyterian Church became the Established Church of Scotland in 1690, and the issue in Scotland became the question of whether non-Presbyterians should be tolerated. The Episcopalian Church (like Anglicanism in England) survived, but the authority of the bishops in society had virtually collapsed.

In 1694 a Triennial Act provided that Parliament should meet every three years and also that no Parliament should last longer than three years. The monarchy still retained great authority – it chose ministers and controlled foreign policy – but royal power was now restricted, in practice if not in principle. William used the royal veto on parliamentary bills five times before 1696, but they all subsequently became law. After that William did not use the veto again, and Anne's one veto of legislation in 1708 was the very last in English history.

Control was exercised over the king mainly through finance. Parliament granted customs revenues to the king only for a period of time, and other income did not amount to much. The king was given a sum for life and other sums as needed. There could be no possibility of the king making himself independent of Parliament. The Treasury grew into a professional body of civil servants who remained at their posts when ministers changed. By the end of Anne's reign the Treasury was drawing up annual budgets for the deliberation of Parliament, in the same way that finance in the modern state is administered. Committees of civil servants managed different aspects of government. Towards the end of Anne's reign the Cabinet included all the leading ministers and was responsible for co-ordinating government policy. The Privy Council, the instrument of government favoured by the Tudors, was too large and diverse to be effective and was used less and less, though it continues to exist with little power (in practice) until the present day.

The battle of Blenheim (1704) against the French was commemorated in the splendour of Blenheim Palace, Oxfordshire, built in the baroque style by the famous architect, John Vanbrugh, for the victorious general, John Churchill, first duke of Marlborough. The palace remained the home of the Churchill family and was the birthplace of Winston Churchill in 1874.

The Restoration settlement also took away the king's power to remove judges and instead vested this power in Parliament. Judges held office *quamdiu se bene gesserint* ('as long as they gave satisfactory service') and were removable only by an address from both Houses. The procedure has never been used. The law was freed from the overt political interference of the early Stuart kings.

William used England's financial resources and naval power in his struggle against Louis XIV of France. By the Peace of Ryswick in 1697 the war with France came to an end, and Louis was obliged to surrender virtually all his conquests. The English felt that they had gained little from the war, which had cost them a great deal. A product of the war was the setting up, in 1694, of the Bank of England, which raised £1,200,000 from the public in twelve days.

War with France came again in 1700, during the reign of William III, when Louis XIV accepted the crown of Spain on behalf of his grandson. Louis XIV further aroused English suspicions by recognising King James II's son, James Edward, as the rightful king of England. England's great general was John Churchill, later duke of Marlborough, who was commander-in-chief of the Grand Alliance against the French. He won a series of spectacular victories over the French: Blenheim in 1704, Ramillies in 1706, Oudenarde in 1708 and Malplaquet in 1709. At the end of the war, by the Treaty of Utrecht in 1713, Britain gained Nova Scotia, the Hudson Bay Territory, Gibraltar and Minorca, only the last of which was later to leave the British Empire.

The situation in Ireland was not happy. English governments from Elizabeth I to Oliver Cromwell had adopted the policy of establishing 'plantations' in Ireland. This meant settling English and Scottish Protestants as conquerors on land seized from native Irish landlords. The English Government wanted the Protestant settlers to set an example to the whole of the Irish population by being loyal and hard-working. But much of the land was taken over by absentee English landlords, who remained in England and took no personal interest in their property. The plantation policy resulted in landowners being English and Protestant and the peasantry being Irish and Catholic. Economic, cultural and religious divisions kept the two classes apart. Where there was a large resident population of settlers, most noticeably in Ulster in the north, they were fiercely Protestant, being Scottish Presbyterians, who viewed the Irish around them as improvident and godless.

There was a major rebellion in Elizabeth's reign and another in 1641. Had there been unity among the Irish, the English, who were divided by the Civil War, could have been beaten, but this was not the case. Cromwell completely defeated the Irish in 1649 and carried out a mass confiscation of land belonging to both Irish and English Catholics.

James II sought refuge in Ireland and collected together a large Catholic Irish army. He was decisively defeated at the

Battle of the Boyne by William III. James II escaped, showing that he had no interest in Ireland except as a means of gaining the English throne. William III's government took land and power away from the English aristocracy which had supported James, and from those Irish property owners who had supported the rebellion. Savage laws were passed which forbade Catholics to practise their religion, vote, sit in Parliament or own land (or even a horse over £5 in value). These laws were not relaxed until 1793.

The most important issue of Queen Anne's reign (1702–14) concerned the relationship between her two kingdoms, England and Scotland. They shared the same monarch but little else. Schemes for a union had been forwarded for some time but had come to nothing. The need to guarantee the Protestant succession after Anne's death urged her English government to press for union. None of Anne's seventeen children lived, and the succession was vested in a remote relative, the great-grandson of James I. In Scotland the Jacobite cause had a strong following in the highlands, and there was fear that the House of Stuart, an ancient Scottish house, might be more popular in Scotland than Anne's named heir, George of Hanover.

A Treaty of Union was worked out by English and Scottish commissioners which embodied two main ideas: that the Hanoverian succession should be accepted and that both Parliaments should join together at Westminster. Though there had been some Scots who wanted some form of federation, they had no clear idea of what shape it should take, and the simple plan for complete union won the day. The Act of Union of 1707 came in for almost immediate criticism in Scotland, which has lasted until the present day. There were charges that the Scottish Parliament had only agreed to union because of heavy English bribes. But there is every indication that the Scottish landowners and merchants, whom Parliament represented, saw union as offering them greater opportunities. The smallness of Scottish representation at Westminster also caused annoyance; however, in the eighteenth century interest groups and not individuals were represented in Parliament, and Scotland was in general too poor to exercise much influence in the Parliament of Great Britain. Essentially, the idea that the two nations which lived on the same island should share the same government was a good one. Federation of some sort might, however, have been better. Scottish affairs became only one of many items of business at Westminster, and discussion of Scotland and necessary legislation for the running of the country accumulated and was neglected.

The seventeenth century saw the transformation of English society. James I wrote a book for his son asserting that monarchs were ordained by God to rule, and Charles believed this. By William and Mary's reign it was clear that sovereigns ruled by the consent of Parliament. The philosopher John Locke could speak at the end of the century about government deriving from, and being responsible to, 'the people', though clearly the people in question were the substantial property owners. He outlined a political system in which legislature and executive were separate and a judiciary balanced the two. It was a conservative ideal, but its principles were far from those of Stuart autocracy.

James I was seriously worried about witchcraft; the last trial for witchcraft in England took place in 1712. During the seventeenth century great progress was made in science, and this was marked in 1662, when the Royal Society received its charter; among its early members was Isaac Newton, who discovered gravitation. Religion was an obsessive subject at the beginning of the century; by the end there was limited toleration for Puritans and the tacit admission that there could not be one national Church for everyone.

The seventeenth century saw an upsurge in the quest after scientific knowledge. Sir Isaac Newton, who, among other achievements, established the laws of gravity, is shown here in a portrait by Sir Godfrey Kneller.

England acquired a large empire in the seventeenth century. This brought her wealth and the need for a foreign policy geared to protecting and expanding colonial interests. England's great commercial rival, Holland, was decisively beaten. In the next century England would defeat her great colonial rival, France. English industry had bigger markets abroad. Coal production increased dramatically in the seventeenth century. There were improvements in a whole range of industries; ideas vital to industry came from the Dutch and from French Huguenots. By the end of the century the city of London had overtaken all other cities as a financial centre. In the country landlords were improving their lands and suffering little government interference when small property owners objected to enclosure. The Agricultural and Industrial Revolutions of the eighteenth century have to be viewed in the light of the intensified activity in trade, industry and agriculture of the seventeenth century; political and religious questions had been solved at least to the satisfaction of the political nation: the men of property.

6

The Eighteenth Century

Politics to Mid Century

In 1716 the Septennial Act extended the life of Parliament from three to seven years. There were good reasons for this, as three years was too short a period in which to deal with disputes arising from the general election or to get any business done. It was also a partisan measure favouring the Whig Government at that particular moment. In order to govern, the crown was obliged to secure the confidence of the House of Commons. This was a body of 558 Members – 489 English, twenty-four Welsh and forty-five Scottish. They were all wealthy landowners or rich merchants. Family groupings in the Commons were very important. Great lords probably controlled a number of parliamentary seats. The noblemen themselves would have sat in the House of Lords, but their sons or relatives, or men whom they favoured with their patronage, would have sat in the Commons. Thus if the king included a great lord in his government or in some other way gained his favour, he may have thereby secured the votes of a block of members.

The parliamentary constituencies which the great aristocrats controlled probably formed part of their land or towns near their property, but they may have used their influence and money outside their own territory to gain the election of their candidates. The most famous example of an aristocratic following is that of the duke of Newcastle, who could rely on dozens of members voting as he wished. The king had more money and patronage than anyone else. He could thus command the largest following in the House – about 200 men, known as placemen. Reforms were launched in the 1780s to lessen royal influence in the Commons by excluding men who received salaries from the crown – officers and civil servants, for example.

But the largest group in the Commons was not dependent on great lords or the king. These were the independent Members, country gentlemen who represented the area where they lived and had their own property. They prided themselves on their independence, and voted for or against measures as they saw fit. They had a deep loyalty to the crown and would give the king's government their support unless they believed it was in serious error.

Many of these Members were Tories. Toryism embodied a respect for monarchy and reverence for the Church of England (and sometimes a nostalgia for the Stuarts). Tories wanted sound, economic government by the king. They deeply resented the power of the great nobility and the money they used to secure political advantage. Whigism was inclined to favour government by monarchy and the aristocracy, and toleration of groups outside the Church of England. In the nineteenth century the Tories became the Conservatives and the Whigs became the Liberals.

The monarchy was an enduring institution in the eighteenth century, built as it was on an acceptance of Protestantism and partnership with the Commons. Jacobite revolts in 1715 and 1745 showed that outside Scotland the Stuarts had little real support. The throne was occupied by a variety of monarchs, only one of whom, Anne, was truly English. William was Dutch; he was stiffly reserved and generally disliked. Anne was liked, but she was not clever. She was excessively dependent on favourites and frequently retreated into a fantasy world of her own creation. She stoutly supported the Church of England, liked the Tories and loathed the idea of being succeeded by George of Hanover, whom she kept out of the country during her reign. George was remarkably unprepared to ascend the throne of England. He had very limited English, and did not like the country. Despite these obvious drawbacks, he did establish his dynasty, and his son, George II, who ruled from 1727 until 1760, was quietly capable (though his talents have only been recognised comparatively recently).

Clearly, the Tories who had associations with Jacobitism, were out of favour with the new dynasty, and for half a century governments were almost exclusively drawn from the ranks of the Whigs. From 1722 until 1742 politics were dominated by Sir Robert Walpole. His abilities and success commended him first to George I and then to George II and his powerful queen, Caroline. He pursued peace abroad and the quiet encouragement of trade. Such a policy met a favourable response from county members, often Tories, who paid a relatively low land tax as a result of peace. But Walpole was solidly opposed in the Commons. He was charged with inactivity and with making himself rich at the expense of the public purse. In reality, the opposition was made up of men who disliked Walpole for personal reasons, perhaps because they had not received the honours or advancement they thought they deserved. In fact, this was typical opposition to an eighteenth-century ministry.

In 1739 a war with Spain was forced on Walpole. The ostensible reason for fighting was trivial; the war was basically fought to force Spain to allow British merchants access to the Spanish Caribbean. Walpole could be accused both of not pursuing British interests actively and of fighting the war unsuccessfully, and his opponents in the House of Commons continually pressed these charges until Walpole's supporters began to leave him. In spite of winning a general election in 1741, therefore, Walpole resigned in 1742. He died in 1745.

Walpole has been called the first Prime Minister. In a modern sense this is not true: the crown joined in policy making, and Walpole did not head a government with collective responsibility. But the direction of government affairs by one man, and his ensuring their approval by the Commons, more closely approximates to the modern concept of the premier than anything that there had been before.

Walpole's policies were pursued by his successors, but change came in 1756, with the start of the Seven Years' War between Britain and France. With extreme reluctance George II made William Pitt one of the government's principal ministers. Pitt had vociferously criticised the use of British resources to defend Hanover, which the king obviously did not like. George was also wary of Pitt, an arrogant, abrasive man. Pitt's grandfather ('Diamond Pitt') had made a fortune in the colonies, and Pitt believed wholeheartedly in using Britain's power to pursue an active imperialist policy. It was his conviction, vigour and energy that made it inevitable that Pitt should acquire complete control of directing the war effort in 1757. The duke of Newcastle, who was in charge domestically, had the unenviable task of raising the colossal sum of £11,000,000 to fight the war.

France had a great empire in North America: she had Quebec and claims to lands stretching from the Gulf of Mexico to the valley of the St Lawrence and Hudson Bay. But the empire was weak. Quebec had only 60,000 inhabitants, and the British had control of the seas, which meant that at any time the French colonies could be cut off from France. A great British naval victory at Quiberon Bay in November 1759 ensured that France was unable to help her colonists. In 1759, under General Wolfe, the British captured Quebec City (both Wolfe and the French commander, Montcalm, died in the action), and in 1760 Montreal was captured. The whole of Canada now came under British control. Quebec presented Britain with a problem, as its population was culturally French and Catholic in religion. Wisely, the Quebec Act of 1774 recognised the Catholic religion and French law in civil matters, and the inhabitants were sufficiently satisfied with British rule not to join the American colonists in the revolt against Britain in 1776.

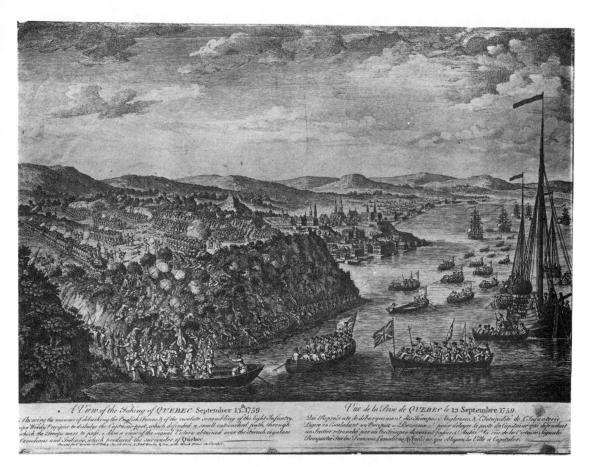

A View of the Taking of QUEBEC September 13.ᵗʰ 1759.

Vüe de la Prise de QUEBEC le 13 Septembre 1759.

Since the seventeenth century Britain and France had possessed important trading stations in India, Britain having Calcutta, Madras and Bombay. Both countries allowed Indian business and affairs to be conducted by private trading companies. In Britain's case it was the powerful and influential East India Company that handled the country's trade with India. As with the conflict in North America, Britain's sea power proved a decisive factor in the confrontation with France. But though the French forces were cut off from help, the French had to be defeated on the subcontinent of India. The British commander, Robert Clive, won a series of spectacular victories over the French, and at the end of the war Britain was left in control of most of India. This did not mean that Britain ruled India. The subcontinent presented a complex picture of states ruled by Indian princes. Apart from a number of trading stations, the East India Company did not have effective control outside Bengal. In 1784 an Act of Parliament laid down that political questions had to be referred by the Company to the British government. This was

The struggle between Britain and France in the New World culminated in General Wolfe's capture of Quebec in 1759 and a year later the whole of Canada passed under British control. This contemporary engraving shows the decisive role played by the navy in the capture of Quebec.

a decisive step in establishing the authority of the British government in the rule of India.

At the conclusion of peace in 1763 Britain agreed to give back to France some territories that had been taken in the war. Pitt violently criticised this moderation, but he could do nothing about it, as he was no longer in the government of the new king, George III. Britain had gained Canada. She had the potential in India to establish a vast and rich empire in the east, which she did in the nineteenth century. Britain could afford to be magnanimous in victory.

Grievances accumulated in Scotland after the Union. There were affronts to national pride when, for example, the Privy Council and the Scottish Royal Mint were abolished. Too many liberties seemed to be granted to episcopalians, which annoyed the Scottish Presbyterian Kirk, the Established Church of Scotland after 1690. Perhaps most important, the upper classes did not think they were getting their share of political rewards and favours, and the populace at large was vexed by the raising of the malt tax. Against this background the Hanoverians succeeded to the British throne in 1714.

But Jacobitism did not sweep Scotland. The Stuarts were Catholics, whom Presbyterians detested. It was apparent that the Stuarts were really intent on gaining England with Scottish support. It was an absurd aim, which did not appeal to most Scots. However, a large army was collected by the earl of Mar exclusively from the highlands and the north-east. James Edward, the Stuart claimant since the death of his father (James II of England and James VII of Scotland), was not an impressive figure; he arrived in Scotland only after the fighting was finished. The Jacobite army was dispersed at Sheriffmuir in 1715 by a smaller government force. The government showed leniency to the Jacobite rebels but began a programme of road and bridge building in the highlands, under General Wade, which would enable it to administer these areas more easily.

In 1745 there was a second Jacobite rising in support of the Young Pretender, Charles Edward, the son of James Edward and grandson of the last Stuart king. Charles was dashing and handsome but not intelligent or particularly loyal to his supporters. Again, support came exclusively from the highlands, from people who had always been poor but who had received nothing from the government since the Union and had little to lose by casting their lot with the Stuarts, who were still regarded as an ancient Scottish family. The government army, led by the duke of Cumberland, annihilated the Jacobites at Culloden Moor in 1746. After defeat, the government dealt with the highlands harshly. There were executions and transportations, and the bearing of arms and highland dress (the tartan) were prohibited. For a generation the clans were put under the direction of loyalist lowlanders. The Stuarts did not come back to Scotland, and the line died out in poverty on the Continent.

The Jacobite rising of 1745 was an attempt to replace the Hanoverians on the throne with Charles Edward Stuart, the Young Pretender. Despite the fact that he was neither astute nor loyal to his followers, 'Bonnie Prince Charlie' has remained a revered legend in the Scottish Highlands. This picture by John Pettie, a Victorian painter, has doubtless helped to perpetuate the romantic image.

The Reign of George III

George III was George II's grandson. He suffered from a blood disease, porphyria, the mistreatment of which may have helped to cause his periods of insanity in the latter part of his reign (in the eighteenth century insanity was, as it is now, a very loosely applied term). He earned the nickname of 'Farmer George' for the interest that he took in new methods of farming; indeed, his interests extended to most branches of science, and he collected both books and pictures. Together with this promising combination of interests went jealousy of his own power, a feeling that royal authority had been eroded in the previous half-century and the conviction that the process should be checked. Such a recovery in royal fortunes was not possible. Groups within Parliament were demanding reforms which would weaken the power of the monarchy, and outside Parliament there were townsmen and countrymen who were beginning to resent the unrepresentative nature of Parliament. The extent to which passions could be aroused in defence of 'liberty' was quickly shown in George III's reign with the drama of the Wilkes Affair between 1763 and 1774.

Arrested on a general warrant (which did not specify the accused) for writing a seditious libel against the king, John Wilkes was later released by the courts as he was a Member of Parliament and thus immune from arrest on such a charge. The Commons intervened to declare Wilkes's action a crime. He was now an outlaw and went abroad. When he returned to England Wilkes went to prison, but he was repeatedly elected to Parliament. The Commons would not acknowledge Wilkes's election until the fourth time in 1774, instead declaring Wilkes's opponent the winner, though he had fewer votes.

George had been insulted by Wilkes's behaviour, and the Commons was not impressed by him. But Wilkes became a symbol of protest against tyranny. 'Wilkes and Liberty' was a popular theme among classes of people who were excluded from politics – artisans in the towns and the owners of small properties in the country. In their thousands they petitioned George on Wilkes's behalf. There were riots and demonstrations in Wilkes's favour in London. The protest movement launched by Wilkes (he did not seek the destruction of property or order) was the beginning of mass radical movements which continued into the nineteenth century and demanded reform on behalf of the people.

Constitutionally, Wilkes's achievement was considerable. General warrants were declared illegal, which removed a wide-sweeping power exercised by ministers. This was particularly helpful to printers, who had been liable to sudden arrest by general warrant. In 1771 the printing of parliamentary debates, hitherto forbidden except by Parliament's authorisation, became free. Most important, the Commons was denied the right to reject a Member elected by a constituency. The electors chose their Members and the Commons had to accept this choice.

The defeat of the French meant that the colonists were no

longer dependent on the British navy and army for protection. The colonists were grieved that they were expected to pay taxes while they received no representation in the London Parliament. They also resented Parliament's restrictions on trade in the colonies, which tied their trade to the mother country, and they were angered by the closure of the frontier, which limited westward expansion. Many colonists had also run up large debts in London, and Virginia planters in particular felt that they were being manipulated by the City.

A group of radical colonists organised protests against Parliament's special taxes so effectively that by 1773 all the taxes had been withdrawn except that on tea. But the radicals could not be expected to be pleased by anything that the government did, and the government was then accused of removing taxes in order to flood the American market with cheap goods. In 1773 a band of activists pitched tea from East India Company ships into Boston Harbour. This move was both a protest at the government's tax and an act of revenge against the East India Company, which had so reduced the price of its tea that smuggling by Bostonians had ceased to be profitable.

Lord North's government was incensed, and the port of Boston was closed. In 1774 a Congress of the colonies met at Philadelphia, and the Americans prepared for confrontation with Britain. War broke out in 1775, when there were skirmishes between troops and colonists. On 4 July 1776 the Americans declared their independence, and their army, commanded by George Washington, waged war in earnest. In 1778 France, which was pleased to do something to repay Britain for her humiliation in the Seven Years' War, allied with the United States and gave the Americans valuable naval help throughout the war. The British army was finally defeated in 1781, when General Cornwallis surrendered at Yorktown. In 1783 the Treaty of Versailles was signed by the Americans and the British; the Treaty acknowledged the independence of the United States.

The loss of the American colonies was devastating. The colonies had a population exceeding 1,000,000, a highly developed economy and great towns. But this very development meant that some change in the political structure of America would have to take place. It is impossible to imagine the United States, with its wealth and complexities, remaining within the British Empire. The British were still left with great possessions. There was Canada and India, the West Indies (which produced Britain's sugar) and the trading posts on the west coast of Africa, which supplied the slaves for the West Indies and the American plantations. By 1779 Captain Cook had circumnavigated New Zealand, explored the east coast of Australia and charted most of the principal groups of islands in the Pacific. In 1788 the first contingent of Britons – convicts and soldiers – landed at Sydney, Australia; the country was used as a dumping ground for prisoners into the nineteenth century.

In 1775 the American War of Independence broke out. George Washington led the colonists in their struggle against the continuance of British rule, and became the first President of the United States.

The British defeat in the American War of Independence caused the resignation of the Prime Minister, Lord North, in 1782 and a severe decline in royal prestige. There was a renewed call for reform. It was, some alleged, a tyrannous king and an unrepresentative Parliament that had let the American situation drift out of control. In 1782 certain classes of government officials were disenfranchised as a consequence of Burke's Economic Reform Act. This was the beginning of a movement to eradicate royal influence in parliamentary elections and the control of Members by royal patronage. But attempts to redistribute parliamentary seats and to bring greater fairness to election procedures failed completely; reform had to wait until the nineteenth century.

Stability returned to the political scene when, in December 1783, George III asked William Pitt, the son of the Elder Pitt, to form a ministry. The Elder Pitt, who had been created earl of Chatham, had remained active in politics until his death in 1778. He had championed John Wilkes and had spoken out passionately against the coercion of America. The Younger Pitt was only twenty-four when he formed his government, and because it was not expected to last beyond Christmas, his government was known as the 'Mincepie Administration'. But in the elections in 1784 Pitt defeated the Opposition, led by Charles Fox, who was a brilliant orator and an avowed enemy of George III.

Though Pitt was prevented by circumstances from enacting any constitutional innovations, he made a number of financial reforms. In 1784 and 1785 he rearranged the tariff system, which had the immediate effect of reducing the volume of smuggling. In 1786 he set up a Sinking Fund to provide annual sums to pay off the National Debt. Pitt's modest reform programme was, however, interrupted by increasing concern in Britain for the fate of France and Europe, following the overthrow of the Bourbons in 1789.

By January 1793 the French had occupied the Austrian Netherlands, thus giving them control of the Flemish coast opposite eastern England. It was traditional British policy to have this coastline in friendly hands, and the French occupation caused serious anxiety. It was France that declared war on Britain, however, confident that an internal revolution would sweep away the old order in Britain as it had done in France. The British fleet defeated the Spanish navy (Spain was France's ally) in an engagement in 1794, but on land all went Napoleon's way. By 1797 (present-day) Belgium and northern Italy had both been annexed to the French state.

In 1798 Napoleon went to Egypt, intending to create a French empire in the Near East. But British control of the seas caused Napoleon to abandon this policy. Under Horatio Nelson the British fleet destroyed the French fleet on the Nile and gained control of the Mediterranean. But with the conclusion of peace in 1802, Napoleon had still not been defeated on the mainland of Europe.

War began again in 1803, and there was a serious scare that

Napoleon would invade Britain. Coast defences were rebuilt, and the militia assembled in towns throughout the country. Again, it was British naval strength that counted, and Nelson's fleet beat the French decisively at Trafalgar, off the southern Spanish coast. Nelson died in his flagship, the *Victory* (preserved to this day as part of the nation's heritage). Napoleon dropped his invasion plans. But France was at the height of her power. An alliance between Napoleon and Tsar Alexander of Russia in 1807 arranged Europe to the liking of the two monarchs. French policy towards Britain was one of economic strangulation. With the Continental system, Napoleon closed the ports of the Continent to British ships. This policy was only partially successful, however, and did not take account of Britain's great colonial trade.

Between 1809 and 1812 the British won a series of engagements against the French in Spain. The Peninsular campaign brought Wellesley, later the duke of Wellington, to the public's attention. Napoleon was broken by his former ally, Russia. Napoleon's invasion of Russia was a disaster; in the retreat from Moscow alone the French lost 50,000 men. In April 1814, with Europe united against him, Napoleon abdicated as emperor.

Between 1812 and 1814 Britain and the United States were at war with each other. The Americans objected to having their ships searched by the Royal Navy for contraband and deserters. The British fleet blockaded the American coast, much to the annoyance of the New England merchants. The Americans tried to take Canada, which had remained loyal to the crown after the War of Independence. But Canada enjoyed a liberal colonial government and had no desire to break with Britain. During the course of the war the British advanced as far as Chicago and Detroit and even burnt the President's residence, later known as the White House. Peace was signed between the United States and Britain at Ghent on Christmas Eve, 1814. News of this did not reach the American and British forces, who fought one of the major engagements of the war at New Orleans on 8 January 1815. Since then there have been no wars between Britain and America.

In February 1815 Napoleon escaped from captivity on the island of Elba and returned to France. At Waterloo, near Brussels, in June 1815 the French army met Wellington, who was commander of the allied armies. Napoleon was defeated and permanently exiled to St Helena. The Congress of Vienna, at which the British representative was Lord Castlereagh, drew up a map of Europe which was to remain largely unchanged until the last quarter of the century. France was encircled by states, which would prevent her from expanding again, as she had tried to do under Louis XIV and Napoleon. Britain wished to play no part in European politics, as long as a peaceful balance existed between the major states.

Britain had emerged as a very strong power in 1815. She had been sustained by her naval power and by the great industrial and agricultural achievements of the eighteenth century, which had supplied the sinews of war. Internally, the war had moved opinion to the right. The magistrates repressed any activities which seemed to favour the ideas of the French Revolution. The constitution remained unchanged, though change was badly needed. The war (like all wars) created employment, but the inevitable recession following peace aggravated the tensions that lay beneath the surface of British life.

There were tensions, too, in Ireland, although the rebuilding of central Dublin in the late eighteenth century in the classical style of the period reflected an economic prosperity and a comparative enlightenment that Ireland had not enjoyed before. From 1782 the Irish Parliament in Dublin was permitted to pass laws on its own initiative. In 1793 the Penal Laws against Catholics were relaxed, and Catholic landlords were allowed to vote (though they could not become Members of Parliament). The wars with France created economic and social tensions; this increased the mistrust between Catholics and Protestants which was always prevalent, and in 1795 the first aggressively Protestant Orange Society was founded to protect the interests of Protestant settlers against the encroachments of Catholic neighbours. An idealistic Protestant lawyer from Dublin, Wolfe Tone, believed that there was enough unity among Ireland's diverse social and religious groups to

The rebuilding of Dublin in the eighteenth century made it one of Europe's most elegant cities. This contemporary print shows Parliament House.

form a united front against Britain and to establish a republican government along current French lines. The rebellion of 1798 failed, however.

The government in Britain believed that the Irish Parliament should be joined with the British Parliament (creating, in 1800, the United Kingdom) as it felt that union would bring firmer government to Ireland. In effect the Act of Union was trying to make the Irish into British as a way of solving the Irish question. But the ending of devolved power pleased no one; even the ascendancy Anglo-Irish landlords and the professional classes resented the closure of the national Parliament. Westminster was remote and could not devote the necessary time to Irish problems. Conversely, in the nineteenth century Irish affairs often dominated the proceedings of the Commons, and the presence of Irish Members complicated political alliances.

Economic Change

In the hundred years from the middle of the eighteenth century the British economy became predominantly industrial; most people lived and worked in towns. Britain's industrialisation made her the workshop of the world and brought her vast wealth and power. Her empire, which became the largest in history, sustained this growth. Politics was obliged to respond to urban growth, changing patterns of population and the appearance of a large middle class and an even larger working class. Britain's industrial supremacy lasted until other countries, with larger populations and resources, themselves became industrialised.

Britain had a good base for industry. She had natural resources: wool, water, coal and some iron ore. Wool was used to make cloth. Water was a source of power in the first phase of the Industrial Revolution and was always necessary to industry for cleaning, cooling and so forth. Coal was a rapidly increasing source of energy after the eighteenth century, and iron ore was vital to iron and steel production. In addition, England had the clays essential to the production of pottery. Other materials needed by industry, particularly cotton, could be imported. (Britain began to import cotton in the seventeenth century.)

As well as natural resources, Britain had other advantages. Britain's climate meant that there could be industrial production throughout the year. There were no insuperable geographical barriers to transport. There was unity and political stability. But these factors had existed for some time. The stimuli to industrialisation were the greater commercial activity of the seventeenth century and a rapid rise in the population, which could be fed by increased food production.

The growth of commerce in the latter part of the seventeenth century gave Britain larger markets for her goods and some raw materials. Imperial acquisitions in the eighteenth century consolidated this position, and America continued to trade with Britain after independence. The wealth from trade increased investment and spending power in Britain. London was the greatest business and banking centre in the world by the end of the seventeenth century, and those with money were willing to invest it in improving land, sinking mines and building factories because the profits were so high. However, industrialisation was not expensive in the eighteenth century, as machinery was simple, so the significance of investment should not be over-emphasised. Wealth with which to buy goods within Britain and markets overseas to which they could be exported were of greater importance.

The population grew dramatically in the eighteenth century. In 1700 there were about 5,900,000 people in Britain and in 1801 about 9,250,000. There were more people to work in the economy and to buy goods. It is not possible to give a precise explanation for the population growth, but certain conditions may have contributed to the rise. There were no large-scale wars and fewer mass epidemics. Hygiene was still elementary, but it was better; soap was a commodity and not a luxury. Cotton clothes, in vogue from the seventeenth century, were easier to wash and were therefore more likely to be laundered. Buildings were better constructed and probably warmer. Yet by the end of the eighteenth century medicine had not improved much, and hospitals still tended to do as much harm as good. The population rose more because people lived longer than because childbirth had become safer or infancy more secure.

The enlarged population was fed, until the mid nineteenth century, mostly with home-produced food. Farming steadily improved throughout the eighteenth century and the first half of the nineteenth century, continuing the progress made in the seventeenth century. This remarkable advance was achieved in spite of farming's declining share of the labour force in the country. Additionally, vast improvements in transport in the eighteenth century resulted in better food distribution as well as the carriage of raw materials for industry.

Industrialisation certainly could not have occurred without technical innovation. New ideas, often borrowed from abroad, were certainly being implemented in the seventeenth century. The trend of innovation and invention intensified in the eighteenth century. The universities and learned societies did not contribute greatly; it was practical men, often owners of industries themselves, who produced the new ideas. How far Protestantism aided industrial and commercial growth by emphasising the dignity and value of work and the competitive spirit is open to question. Dissenters believed in thrift, hard work and, often, abstention from alcohol. This seems good for business. But though there were numbers of Dissenters (particularly Quakers) who became factory owners and bankers, the mass of Dissenters in England and Scotland worked at jobs like everyone else. The Church of England did not have a particular view on industry. Indeed, religion in general failed to meet the response of the Industrial Revolution, and in the course of the nineteenth century the majority of people in towns stopped going to Church. One can also point to the northern Italian towns of the late Middle Ages, which were Catholic and had advanced industry and sophisticated banking and commerce. In the nineteenth century Catholic France and Belgium industrialised.

Having looked generally at the causes of industrialisation, specific attention now needs to be paid to advances in transport, agriculture and industry. They are themes to be viewed not in isolation but as strands in the tangled skein of economic development.

It should be remembered that river and sea transport were always important in England, and where possible these methods of moving goods were used. Coal, for example, was transported from Newcastle to London by ship. But England's roads were deplorable. Parishes responsible for their upkeep were reluctant to spend money on an amenity which might be of more use to people from outside their locality. In the eighteenth century, when government was involved in the provision of services as little as it could help, the initiative in road improvement was taken by individuals who set up turnpike trusts (whereby they built and maintained roads and charged travellers a toll, or fee). Between 1706 and 1790 Parliament authorised nearly 2000 turnpikes. Two distinguished turnpike engineers were John Metcalfe and Thomas Telford, but their road-building techniques were expensive. It was John McAdam (1756–1836) who popularised a cheap road-building technique, known as 'macadamisation': small pieces of stone on a tar base were pressed tightly into place by the wheels of passing vehicles. Essentially the same technique is used to the present day.

The eighteenth century saw the rapid expansion of the canal system. The most famous canal built was that commissioned by the duke of Bridgewater to connect his coal mines at Worsley with Manchester. James Brindley (1716–72), the most distinguished canal engineer, completed 'the Duke's Canal' between 1759 and 1761. As soon as the canal was used to transport coal, the price of coal was halved in Manchester. It was Brindley's plan to link the rivers Severn, Mersey and Trent by means of the Grand Trunk Canal. He began this in 1766, and it was completed after his death in 1772. The result of building the Grand Trunk was that the main industrial areas were now linked with each other and also with the seaports. The canals were useful as a means of transporting not only heavy materials like coal, iron ore, clay and timber but also delicate and fragile items like china ware and machinery. Josiah Wedgwood's famous pottery works at Etruria in Staffordshire stood on a branch of the Grand Trunk.

Agriculture improved steadily in the eighteenth century. Enclosure was most intense in the second half of the century and was especially prevalent in the Midlands, an area with heavy clay soils. By the middle of the nineteenth century enclosure was responsible for bringing under cultivation one-third more land than in 1700. It provided a golden opportunity to consolidate and reorganise land holdings and to construct as many new farm buildings, roads to market and drainage systems as money permitted. Enclosure accentuated the division in the countryside between farmers, who were generally large-scale capitalists, and the rural work force, which was desperately poor both before and after enclosure. The share of people working in the countryside dropped steadily: over 40 per cent of the labour force worked on the land at the end of the eighteenth century; by 1851 it was 21 per cent.

Great proprietors in the eighteenth century, when offering tenants new leases, did so on the understanding that they would use progressive farming methods. These included the growing of root crops (winter food for animals), the rotation of crops and the fertilisation of soils. The seed-drill was invented by Jethro Tull in 1701. It enabled farmers to plant seeds at an even depth at regular intervals. Tull also advocated the continuous weeding of fields, not necessarily an efficient use of labour. Advocates of reform were not always heeded, and frequently the spread of ideas like those of Lord Townshend (called 'Turnip Townshend') amounted merely to the publicising of old ideas. Farming literature seems to have been the reading matter of aristocrats only. But change came about because it was clear that more money could be made out of adopting the ideas, both new and not so new, that best suited one's property. Even when account is taken of new land under cultivation, the rise in grain output by 120 per cent and of livestock (sheep and cattle) by 150 per cent between 1700 and 1850 is impressive.

Textile manufacture was revolutionised by a series of inventions. The flying shuttle of 1733 speeded up weaving, and the jenny of 1767 made faster spinning possible. In 1779 Samuel Crompton produced a spinning mule which spun strong thread even faster. In 1787 Edmund Cartwright produced a power-operated loom which accelerated weaving. By the end of the eighteenth century both sides of the textile industry, spinning and weaving, used water power to operate their machinery, and production outside mills was increasingly rare. The industry changed location when coal was used to produce steam power, but though James Watt patented a steam engine in 1782, its application to the textile industry remained experimental until the nineteenth century.

Technical innovation was taken up much more readily by the cotton industry than by wool manufacturers, whose industry was less adaptable to the new methods. The natural centre of the cotton industry was Lancashire, which could exploit the fast-flowing streams of the Pennine Hills. Woollen manufacture's main (but not exclusive) centre was in Yorkshire,

The Industrial Revolution was built upon technical innovation and improvements in transport. Both are embodied here in the world's first iron bridge at Coalbrookdale, Shropshire, constructed by the great ironmasters Abraham Darby III and John Wilkinson. It was opened in 1779.

on the eastern side of the Pennines. Yorkshire had a large supply of wool as well as the water power of the Pennines. In the nineteenth century, when there was a change to steam power, the abundance of coal in Lancashire further emphasised those areas as centres of textile manufacture. For a time there was cotton-textile manufacture in the Scottish lowlands, and the well established linen industry of Ulster, in the north of Ireland, adopted technical advances in line with the rest of the textile industry.

Iron production was revolutionised. The Darby family discovered how to smelt iron by using coke, and in the 1780s Henry Cort devised a method of making purer iron. The most famous ironmaster of the day was John Wilkinson (1728–1805), who built great ironworks in Shropshire and applied iron to the manufacture of almost everything. He produced the first iron boat which floated, water pipes for Paris and New York and a more accurate cannon. With Abraham Darby III (1750–91) he built the world's first iron bridge.

Eighteenth-Century Society

Industry in the eighteenth century used water power to drive the machinery improved by the great inventors. Steam power produced by burning coal did not take over until the nineteenth century. Dependence on water for energy meant that in the eighteenth century cotton mills, and to a lesser extent woollen mills, were frequently sited in beautiful hilly country. Many of the buildings were of great architectural merit, and the eighteenth-century owners were so proud of their achievement that they often built their homes near their factories. Industrialisation did not supplant domestic industry (people working at home), but it did establish the trend that would see its destruction, as people lived increasingly in large towns rather than in villages. But though many industrial towns grew dramatically during the course of the eighteenth century – especially the cotton towns of Lancashire – the majority of the population continued to live in the countryside. Industrial towns were still small enough to allow people to walk into the country with ease, to fish in the local rivers and generally to mix country with town.

But it is significant that the word 'slum' derives from the eighteenth century. In the growing industrial towns housing was being put up hurriedly and without regard to sanitation. It would have been surprising, given the ramshackle government of the eighteenth century and the capitalist nature of industry, if more care had been taken over housing and town planning. The textile mills, iron foundries and mines introduced workers to industrial discipline: long, joyless hours of work, with no restrictions on the employment of women and children. But no rosy, rural pre-industrial society coexisted with industrialisation. Conditions were hard labouring on the land, and industrial workers were better off than those working in the countryside.

Though water power was available throughout Britain, coal was not, and with the application of steam to industry, the industrialisation of the north, the Midlands, the lowlands of Scotland and the coastal plain of south Wales accelerated. The south of England lost its economic hegemony – but it was spared the grimier aspects of industrialisation as well. The historic split between the north and south of England persisted: the north was industrialised; industry in the south was much less widespread, but there were some important commercial centres, most notably London. In Scotland the division between lowlands and highlands was further accentuated. Industry in south Wales made it distinct economically from rural central and north Wales. In Ireland the area of most intense industrial activity was Protestant Ulster, and industrialisation served to add to religious division in the country.

The writings of the major economist of the eighteenth century, a Scottish academic, Adam Smith, reflected the industrial change that was taking place in the country. He argued persuasively for the division of labour, whereby each worker did a single job and did not 'see through' a task from start to finish. Specialisation of labour in industry advanced rapidly in the nineteenth century. Adam Smith believed that freedom generated enterprise; therefore government should not interfere in industry or put restrictions in the way of trade between countries. This theory, known as *laissez-faire*, was widely supported in the nineteenth century, particularly by the business community. The sector of the economy that advocated protection was farming, but with the transformation of Britain into an industrial society, farming correspondingly lost influence. The amelioration of conditions in industry became a question first of conscience and later of political necessity for parliamentarians, industrialists and philanthropists alike.

It was the writer Dr Samuel Johnson who, in 1763, coined the most celebrated panegyric of London: 'When a man is tired of London he is tired of life; for there is in London all that life can afford.' By the middle of the eighteenth century London probably had a population of 700,000. The city was the political, financial and social capital and handled 80 per cent of the nation's trade. It was not industrialised in the way that the northern cities were, but it supported a range of trades, from printing to silk manufacture and wig making. London probably could meet Dr Johnson's boast. A massive building programme in the eighteenth century resulted in the development of miles of Neo-Classical squares and terraces for the middle classes and the aristocracy; London had theatres, parks, churches and shops.

In contrast, the poor in London lived in warrens of narrow streets. Crime was rife. But entertainment was plentiful. There were boxing matches (without gloves), displays of fireworks and pageantry on state occasions – and even public hangings (until 1783), which were considered social occasions. Crowds would fête the condemned on their way down Oxford Street to the gallows at Tyburn, where Marble Arch now stands. A more tranquil feature of life in the eighteenth-century capital was that it was still possible to buy milk produced by the cows grazing in St James's Park.

Many of the most elegant districts in towns today are those built by eighteenth-century architects. The Clifton area of Bristol was built for the merchants who controlled the slave trade. (It was a Member of Parliament for Bristol, Edmund Burke, who wrote the most eloquent condemnation of the French Revolution.) The city of Bath, near Bristol, was almost entirely remodelled in the eighteenth century to make it a fashionable spa town. People of fashion stayed there, bringing in their wake pickpockets, cardsharps and adventurers. Richard Brinsley Sheridan, one of the greatest eighteenth-century playwrights gives a lucid and amusing portrait of Bath in his play *The Rivals* He treats duelling in a lighthearted way, but to gentlemen the satisfaction of honour was a serious matter and not against the law. An extraordinary individual, Richard Nash ('Beau Nash') became the 'social dictator' of Bath, drawing up precise rules about manners and conduct. The fact that he devised eloquent regulations about the transmission of lies and scandals is clear proof that taking the sulphurous waters there was only the ostensible reason for a visit.

Edinburgh, like London, underwent a building programme on Classical lines, but its title, 'Athens of the North', rested as much on its intellectual achievement as on its fine architecture. Edinburgh was always the centre of law in Scotland, and this did not change after Union, as the two countries continued to have different legal systems; Scotland's was based on Roman law, while England had common law. In the eighteenth century the Royal College of Physicians was founded in Edinburgh which established the city's reputation as the leading centre of anatomical medicine (a reputation which lasted into

107

The fine houses of the east side of St Andrew's Square, Edinburgh, c. 1829, show the style in which the rich lived, at that time.

the twentieth century). Glasgow also built up a formidable medical reputation, but associated with chemistry and physics. Edinburgh (unlike London) had a university; students came from a broad social and educational spectrum. Over the whole of Edinburgh, both new and old, hung a cloud of smoke from the coal fires which kept the houses warm. The cloud was visible from a great distance and earned Edinburgh her other nickname of 'Auld Reekie'. Scotland's national poet, Robert Burns, did not like Edinburgh. It had too many of the pretensions he disliked in society – the privilege of rank, the follies of fashion and the pedantry of the educated. He did not like Calvinism's intolerance, nor the way it dismissed the feminine mind out of hand. His radicalism stirs his poetry, which is not easy for a purely English reader to follow, as it is written in the lowland Scottish vernacular, but which warms the Scottish nation on Burns Night (25 January).

Society in the towns may have been sophisticated and attractive to the wealthy, but the aristocracy and the gentry derived their social position from the land they owned. The abundance of massive houses in the English and Scottish countryside is a testimony to the wealth of the men who built them and to their desire to make their mark in their county. Some of the houses built in the eighteenth century, like Blenheim Palace and Castle Howard, are princely in scale and decoration. But there is not a county without a crop of country houses, built for traditional landed families, for the Anglican clergy (who were invariably upper-class) and for men with money made in trade at home or in the colonies. The desire to maintain a country house (or seat) has been prevalent throughout English history. A sure sign of upward social mobility was the purchase of a stately property in the countryside. Acceptance by the English upper classes has not, on the whole, been difficult – the standard joke is that it takes three generations to make a gentleman. The complexities of rural society (that is, the society of the rich) are beautifully described by the author Jane Austen (1775–1817). Shrewd and ironic, she never questioned the foundations on which her society was based. Her works, by virtue of their skill and insight, mark a turning point in the history of the English novel.

Among the educated there was a growing love for the Classical world. It was in the eighteenth century that the 'grand tour' became popular, when a young aristocrat, accompanied by a tutor, would visit the Classical sites of Italy and perhaps Greece. The taste for the Classical was reflected in the theme of the greatest history written in the eighteenth century, Edward Gibbon's *The Decline and Fall of the Roman Empire*. Gibbon linked Rome's decline with moral weakness as a result of its conversion to Christianity. Gibbon's scepticism of religion was widely shared by eighteenth-century intellectuals. But Christianity had its supporters. The most impressive contribution came from John Wesley, who founded Methodism. This was a movement within the Church of England which emphasised method in one's life. Everyone, Wesley taught, should lead a good, ordered life. Wesley's message was received warmly among the working class, particularly in industrial towns. Wesley lived at a time when the religious needs of the working class were thoroughly neglected, and his achievement was to keep Christianity alive in industrial areas. His Church later split from the Church of England to join the large number of Dissenting, Nonconformist or free Churches, among them the Congregational Church, the Baptist Church and Wesley's own Methodist Church.

The works of Jane Austen (1775–1817) mark a turning point in the history of the English novel. With wit and precision she described the complex society in which she lived. The only picture of her is the one by her sister, Cassandra, in the National Portrait Gallery.

7

The Victorian Age

Protest and Reform, 1800–1850

Britain continued to industrialise rapidly in the nineteenth century. By mid-century the population had risen to 18,000,000 (it had doubled since 1801), and less than a quarter of that population worked on the land. Large numbers of people continued to work in trades that saw little technical change, but the areas of the economy that expanded most rapidly were those in which technological improvement took place and in which the labour force was gathered together in large workplaces. The industry that reflected these changes most clearly was the cotton industry. By 1850 there were 250,000 power looms, and cotton textiles accounted for 40 per cent of the value of British exports. In that year Manchester, described as the 'cottonopolis', had a population of 300,000, a tenfold increase in fifty years. Equally impressive were advances in the coal and iron industries. Coal provided the energy throughout industry, and iron was used in the construction of machinery and the production of consumer goods and rails for the railways.

The great boom in railroad construction came in the 1840s; by mid-century Britain had 8000 kilometres of track. British industry built the railways in many other countries, and this continued to create demands on the iron industry into the twentieth century. The railways bound Britain together, providing cheap transport for people and the fast transportation of goods.

The Industrial Revolution created great wealth. It gave work to the massively increased population. The middle class certainly grew in wealth as well as in size. It is estimated that its spending power doubled between 1815 and 1830, and doubled again between 1830 and 1850. The emergence of a large industrial and urban working class and a rich and confident middle class was bound to cause tensions and change in nineteenth-century society. Economic distress among the working class produced sporadic violence. There was destruction of machinery by workers who felt their jobs were threatened (they were called Luddites). There was destruction of farm property by hungry farm workers in the countryside. There was also the rise of mass working-class movements. Unions were organised, but they collapsed after a short period of time. In the 1840s there was the rise of Chartism, a movement which demanded political rights for workers. Unions and Chartism failed through lack of funds and organisation and the steadfast opposition of authority. The middle class achieved both its political and its economic aims: Parliament was reformed, and free trade and the ending of protection for agriculture were achieved by mid-century.

The shocking condition of life of so many people provoked a response. Reformers, whether moved by religious or political motives, demanded change. The scientific method of investigating abuses was evolved in the early nineteenth century. Royal Commissions gave groups of experts full authority to investigate and report on social evils (as today). It was rare for the reports, rich in statistics, to be rejected by the Commons. The middle class constituted a large reading public to which reformers could appeal. Charles Dickens appealed to his readers' sentiments in his novels and served the cause of reform.

The nineteenth century saw the gradual reform of factories and mines and the reordering of town life, and with this the acceptance by the government of new responsibilities.

Both during the wars with France (which ended in 1815) and afterwards there was acute social tension, a consequence of economic distress. The authorities were nervous, fearful that if radicalism got out of hand, a revolutionary order would be established, as in France. The tense state of affairs was highlighted by an incident in 1819. A great assembly of people, over 50,000, assembled at St Peter's Field, outside Manchester, to hear the radical politician Henry Hunt speak in favour of parliamentary reform. The local magistrates panicked at the thought of the mob under the leadership of a persuasive revolutionary. In fact, the crowd was peaceful and Hunt was moderate in approach. The army moved in, and in the ensuing fight ten of the crowd were killed and hundreds injured. The authorities felt their action had been right: the government congratulated the Lancashire magistrates. The incident, known as Peterloo, became a milestone in working-class history. What is interesting is that Peterloo and other incidents did not lead to revolution. Everyone with property was united against radicalism and willing to back the government's tough approach. Working-class protest was widespread but disorganised.

There was a considerable relaxation of tension in the 1820s mainly because the economic situation had improved. Some repressive legislation was repealed. In the Tory (Conservative) government which was in power from the end of war in 1815 until 1830 there was a change in Cabinet ministers; some men who were associated with reaction in the public mind were replaced by younger men. The Home Secretary, a gifted young man, Robert Peel, pursued major reforms in the criminal law and established the first police force in 1829. This was important. Hitherto in times of trouble only the army could be called on, and its appearance was provocative. Unarmed policemen did not have the same effect.

The most important legislation came at the end of the government's life, when with reluctance, the Prime Minister, the hero of the war, the duke of Wellington, allowed the repeal of the Test and Corporation Acts in 1828 and 1829. This repeal enabled Protestant Nonconformists and Roman Catholics to hold office – they could become Members of Parliament and town councillors, for example – which hitherto they had not been allowed to do. If the government had not repealed these laws, there would have been bitterness and dissent. The provision of basic freedoms, irrespective of religion, is fundamental to any modern state, and that Britain was becoming. In Ireland Catholic emancipation meant that Members of Parliament from that country would continuously and overwhelmingly be Roman Catholic.

The issue of parliamentary reform was not new. It was clear to many in the eighteenth century that the parliamentary electorate was too narrow and that the distribution of parliamentary seats was wildly uneven. Industrial change had sharpened this criticism of Parliament, as industrial cities in the north and Midlands, which were large and rich, were unrepresented. Parliamentary reform was the main aspiration of the middle and working classes. When the government changed in 1830 and the Whigs (Liberals) were returned, some reform seemed certain. But the first Reform Bill was rejected by the House of Lords (to succeed in the British Parliament, a Bill must be approved by both Houses of Parliament, Commons and Lords, and must receive the assent of the monarch). There was a fierce reaction in the country. Bourgeois and working man united against the recalcitrance of the House of Lords and the king, William IV. The Prime Minister, Lord Grey, threatened to resign, which would have left the king in the embarrassing position of having to form a government without majority support in the Commons. William relented, as did the House of Lords after it had been threatened with the creation of new peers to ensure the passing of the Bill. The Reform Bill was passed in 1832. In effect, it gave the middle classes the vote and included the Midlands and the north in the political nation. The passing of the Reform Act helped Britain to acquire political maturity peacefully and spared the middle class the need to use force to gain constitutional change, as happened on the continent of Europe in 1848. 1832 was in fact the first step on the road to democracy, though the number of new voters was relatively small.

A Factory Act passed in 1833 imposed limits on the hours worked by children. The importance of the Act was not its modest achievement but the fact that it established the principle of government intervention in industry to promote health, safety and humanity. In 1842 a Mines Act forbade the employment underground of women and of boys under ten. Most important, an inspectorate was created to supervise the implementation of the Act. In future, industry would not be able to ignore those government regulations which it did not like. By 1850 there had been further reforms in the working conditions of women and children in factories, and by mid-century many factories had, for the first time, introduced a Saturday half-day for their work force. The government's Poor Law Act of 1834, which provided bare subsistence in parish workhouses for those out of work, was not popular. Going to the workhouse became a mark of shame. Men and women had to go to separate houses, and families inevitably split up.

Town government in England, Wales and Scotland was overhauled in 1835, with the creation of new boroughs governed by municipal councils which were elected by local taxpayers. In 1846 a General Board of Health was set up, following the production in 1842 of a momentous report by Edwin Chadwick: 'The Sanitary Conditions of the Labouring Classes'. Local councils were left to set up their own local boards. This was a major step forward in the promotion of healthy living standards nationally but particularly in the cities. In 1833 money was given to two religious societies (Anglican and Nonconformist) to promote education. What is surprising is that England was so slow to take a serious interest in providing state education (compulsory education did not arrive until 1870). England compares badly with Scotland and some Continental countries.

An important reform of the century was the abolition of slavery in 1833. It took some time to put the measure into effect, and the British navy tried, during the nineteenth century, to impose Parliament's ruling throughout the world. The abolition movement was essentially evangelical (extreme Protestant), and testified to Christianity's repugnance of slavery. The campaign illustrated the lesson of success through publicity. Models of slave ships were shown to Parliament, and anti-slavery literature was widely circulated. The slave

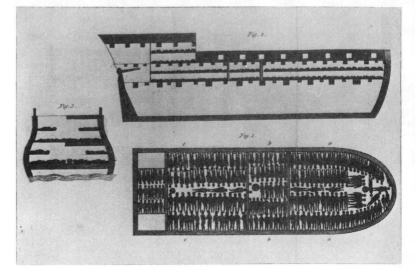

In the late eighteenth century, the Anti-Slavery Movement led by William Wilberforce, mounted a campaign to end the slave trade. Graphic documents, like this drawing of the cramped conditions that slaves had to endure, finally secured the abolition of the trade in 1807 and the abolition of slavery itself in all British dominions in 1833.

interest, which stood to lose a lot of money, mounted a counter-campaign, but with little success.

The 1840s, a decade of uncertain harvests and sporadic economic recession, was dominated by the activities of two great movements. The working class backed the Chartist Movement. The middle class, already enfranchised, wanted major economic reform. It sought the repeal of the Corn Laws, the measures which protected home agriculture from the import of cheap corn. The Repeal of the Corn Laws would, it was believed, bring cheap food. Landowners, on the other hand, were convinced that it would bring their ruin.

The working class had not met with much success in forwarding its own interests. The Grand National Consolidated Trades Union (GNCTU), a union with mass membership, was disbanded in 1834 after only one year of life. Six founder members of the union, who lived in a village in Dorset, Tolpuddle, were transported for their activities (transportation meant being sent to Australia as a convict). Though these men were released and became known as the 'Tolpuddle Martyrs', it was demonstrated that harsh prison sentences could frighten people enough to prevent them from joining unions. The idea of the GNCTU was much too advanced for the early nineteenth century.

The Charter from which Chartism derived its name contained six points which the movement wished to secure: universal manhood suffrage, annual Parliaments, voting by ballot, equal constituencies, no property qualifications for Members of Parliament and the payment of Members, so that working-class men could go to Westminster. The Chartists held mass meetings and collected petitions to present to

Parliament. But the mass meetings did not intimidate the authorities, and Parliament would only accept the last of the petitions (there were three in all). It refused to grant the Chartists' demands. However, the demands were met gradually, on the initiative of parliamentarians themselves and not as a consequence of pressure from without.

A wholly successful movement, by contrast, was the Anti-Corn Law League, founded in 1838. It was led by two able propagandists, John Bright and Richard Cobden. They raised vast sums of money to finance an elaborate campaign to secure public support for the repeal of the Corn Laws. The repealers built the Free Trade Hall in Manchester within six weeks as a meeting place for their movement. The hall could hold 8000 people. The League used the postal service, started by Roland Hill in 1839, to spread their literature through the country. It ran its own newspaper and founded its own magazine, the celebrated *Economist*, in 1843.

How far this organisation influenced the Prime Minister of the day, the Tory Sir Robert Peel (the former Home Secretary) it is difficult to tell. Peel was a man of great compassion, and by 1846 he had come to the conclusion that repeal of the Corn Laws was right. He was in a difficult position. His party, the Conservatives, believed that repeal of the Corn Laws would cause the collapse of the grain market in England, and they therefore strongly supported the measures. There was famine in Ireland, as the potato crop had failed in two successive years and Peel used the argument that the free entry of cheap corn was the only means of saving Ireland. The Irish in fact could not have afforded the cheaper corn. Peel achieved repeal by splitting his party; 112 Tory Peelites and the Opposition voted together, and repeal was carried with a majority of 98.

The economic results of repeal were slight. The price of grain remained steady. Agriculture did not suffer from loss of protection for another thirty years. The repeal caused great political bitterness. The Conservative Party was divided, and in the twenty-eight years between 1846 and 1874 the Conservatives held office for less than five years. Repeal signified the triumph of industrial and middle-class interests over those of agriculture and the landowner.

Also of great importance to the middle class in particular was a measure of Robert Peel's which was passed in 1844. This was the Companies Act, which introduced the concept of limited liability: if a company went bankrupt, shareholders were responsible not for the whole of the company's losses (as previously) but only for the money they had invested in the company. The middle class, with its great wealth to invest, could now more confidently plough money into industry and stimulate industrial growth, the underlying theme of the nineteenth century.

Domestic and Foreign Policy, 1850–1900

The Great Exhibition, held in London's Hyde Park in 1851, was a sumptuous display of British and imperial products. It was a clear indication of Britain's economic hegemony, which was to last for at least another two decades. Britain lost her dominance as the economy of the United States expanded (how, asked one historian, could Britain compete with an entire continent?) and the strength of Germany grew after her unification. This competition became noticeable from the middle of the 1870s. As Britain did not have protection, British agriculture suffered from the import of cheap grain and meat in the last quarter of the nineteenth century. But though British industry experienced periodic slumps, its output increased dramatically in the second half of the century. Exports which were worth £77,400,000 in 1850 totalled £525,200,000 in 1913. All sections of industry grew, and new sources of energy – electricity and oil – were developed. Britain's economic performance was certainly helped by her growing Empire, although large parts of the Empire were undeveloped and in no position to buy British goods. But the fact that the Empire did help the economy and provide employment is not in question. It also gave a new home to millions of settlers.

Britain invested heavily abroad. In 1913 Britons had invested £4000 million overseas (400 times more than in 1815). In the light of Britain's economic difficulties in the twentieth century, it has been suggested that Britain should have invested more money in home industry. There is some truth in this argument, but it must not be exaggerated. Evidence suggests that companies raised the capital they sought. A more justified criticism is that Britain was not only tardy in establishing state education but also developed technical education slowly and late.

By the middle of the century there was a growing electorate. This prompted the two main parties to create nationwide political organisations and to give themselves modern names. The Whigs became Liberals, and the Tories called themselves Conservatives. The Liberals believed in a *laissez-faire* economy and light taxation (if possible, none at all). This suited the middle class well, and the Liberals became the dominant party in the mid nineteenth century, supported by the votes of the urban middle class and the Nonconformists. The

Conservatives had the problem of appearing to be the party of landowners in an increasingly industrial age (by 1913 80 per cent of the population lived in towns – the largest percentage in the world). But under the skilled leadership of Benjamin Disraeli the Conservatives were transformed, in the decades after the repeal of the Corn Laws in 1846, into a party which attracted support from both the middle class and the working class.

The Conservatives backed social reform and, from the 1870s, the cause of Empire – which had a patriotic appeal. Extensive (and necessary) reform was undertaken by both parties. The appearance of socialism at the end of the nineteenth century posed a threat to the two established parties, but particularly to the Liberals, the party more to the left. In the twentieth century Liberalism has succumbed to socialism, but in the nineteenth century the Liberal tenets of peace, retrenchment (saving money) and reform matched the social and political climate.

Though foreign policy changed as governments changed and divided public opinion, certain broad generalisations can be made. Britain was protected from attack by the Channel and her fleet, and was therefore not inclined to become involved in European politics. Her only concern was that no one power should dominate Europe and pose a threat to Britain. At the peace conference in 1815 Britain helped in the creation of barriers to French aggression. There was a genuine concern among many Britons to see the victory of nationalism and Liberalism in Europe. At times during the nineteenth century, therefore, Britain offered help to patriotic movements, although the most she would do was to send naval help, as during the Greek and Italian wars of independence. A dominating fear among many Britons was that of Russian expansion. It seemed possible that the Turkish Empire could collapse and that Russia would take over large parts of the Ottoman lands. This would give Russia control of the eastern Mediterranean and the land route to India. Russia also seemed capable of attacking India directly from the north. Fear of Russia was intensified with the opening of the Suez Canal in 1869, as there was a possibility that Russia might block the newer and quicker sea route to India if she took control of that part of the Mediterranean. Russo phobia caused Britain to give consistent support to Turkey in the nineteenth century – which Britain was reluctant to do, as Turkey oppressed many parts of her Empire, including areas which were Christian.

Britain's only war with a great power in the nineteenth century was with Russia. The ostensible reason for war in 1854 (control of the Holy Places in Jerusalem) was trivial. The war reflected Britain's deep fear of Russian intentions after she had sunk a Turkish squadron and it seemed the Russian navy might take control of access to the Black Sea. Britain and France fought Russia in a war which dragged on until March 1856. The war did not achieve much – certainly not a solution to the Eastern Question, which was the term used to describe the problem of Turkey and her Balkan territories. The war revealed that the British army was very inefficient. The only gain was the foundation of modern nursing by Florence Nightingale, who went out to organise nursing services for the wounded Britons in the Crimea (the area of southern Russia where the fighting took place).

Florence Nightingale's pioneering work in the Crimean war in southern Russia (1854–56) established nursing as a respectable profession. She became known as the 'Lady of the Lamp' and the 'Mother of Nursing' and brought about a transformation in the care of the sick.

The almost continuous Liberal government of the mid nineteenth century was interrupted in 1866 when a minority Conservative government took office. Electoral reform had long been a talking point, and the granting of the vote to working men seemed a possible undertaking for the Liberals after the death, in 1865, of their leader, Lord Palmerston, who was not sympathetic to reform. But the Conservatives in office took the initiative and introduced a Reform Bill which they hoped would gain them support from the new urban working-class voters and would break the Liberal monopoly of government. The Second Reform Act, which emerged in 1867, was far more radical than the Conservatives (and most Liberals) had planned. Its most important feature was the granting of the vote to the artisans and more prosperous workers in the towns. In the election which followed in 1868 the Conservatives were not returned (gratitude cannot be expected from voters). Instead there was a Liberal government, headed by W. E. Gladstone, a leader of massive stature and intellect. This government undertook sweeping reforms. Limited schooling, which was to be the responsibility of local school boards, was made compulsory in 1870. In the same year competitive entry to the Civil Service was established. In fact, the examinations were difficult and produced a high standard among civil servants, which was particularly important when Britain had a large empire to administer. There were significant reforms in the army; commissions could no longer be bought, and punishments for soldiers were made less severe. In 1872 the Secret Ballot Act made voting a private business and not, as it had been, a carnival-like process characterised by bribery and intimidation.

In 1874 a Conservative government was returned. The Prime Minister, Disraeli, was of Jewish ancestry, and he had had to fight hard for his obvious talents – he was a brilliant debater – to be allowed to outweigh his unconventional background. Disraeli was most interested in foreign affairs, in which he had marked success. In 1875 he bought a half-share in the Suez Canal. At the peace conference in Berlin in 1878, following war between Turkey and Russia, Disraeli obtained Cyprus for Britain, which secured Britain's interests of keeping Russia out of the Mediterranean. It was his government which gave Queen Victoria the title Empress of India in 1877. The title pleased Victoria, and it acknowledged the overwhelming importance of India within the British Empire. Disraeli and the queen basked in mutual admiration (she disliked, and was probably a little afraid of, the severe Gladstone), and the imperial title was the greatest compliment Disraeli could pay to the queen.

Gladstone's second government completed electoral reform in 1884 by giving the vote to working men in both town and country. But it was affairs overseas that dogged his government. Britain had become involved in Egypt and the Sudan, as a result of her part-acquisition of the Suez Canal. A British expedition, led by General Gordon, was sent to Khartoum to evacuate the Egyptian army. But Gordon stayed on against Gladstone's wishes, and consequently the Prime Minister would not send him relief forces when he was under fierce attack from Sudanese tribesmen, under their leader, the Mahdi. When Gladstone finally agreed to send relief in 1885 it arrived too late to save Gordon and his forces. There was widespread indignation in Britain; Gladstone was branded the 'Murderer of Gordon' (this was based on a reversal of Gladstone's affectionate nickname, the 'Grand Old Man').

A problem which confronted Gladstone, as it did all nineteenth-century statesmen, was Ireland. The country was poor and had suffered famine and mass emigration. The members of Parliament returned from Ireland demanded Home Rule (which gave the Irish a Dublin parliament to run Irish internal affairs). This was resisted by most parliamentarians, as they thought that home government for Ireland would endanger the future of the British Empire. Ireland had been linked with England for centuries, and it was assumed that the tie should continue. Westminster was not oblivious to Irish problems. In 1881 the Land Act passed by Gladstone's second government laid down that fair rents were to be decided by a tribunal, and there was to be fixity of tenure for those tenants who paid their rents. This was a far-reaching measure in a predominantly agricultural country. But Ireland was plagued with violence, as when the Chief Secretary of Ireland, Lord Frederick Cavendish, and his Under-Secretary were assassinated while walking in a Dublin park. Such an act enraged public opinion and bolstered determination not to concede Home Rule.

Gladstone became convinced that there should be Home Rule for Ireland (he seems, undoubtedly, to have been right), and he introduced a Bill to that effect in April 1886, at the end of his third government. Ninety-three Liberals voted with the Conservative Opposition and the Bill was lost; but though the Liberal party in the Commons saw the splitting off of a Unionist wing (opposed to Home Rule), the parliamentary party was not damaged in the long term. In the House of Lords, however, the Liberals were left with even fewer supporters. In effect, the Upper House became a Conservative preserve. This was not good for the Liberals and was harmful to the constitution. In his fourth government Gladstone introduced another Home Rule Bill, but it was heavily defeated in the House of Lords in 1893. A settlement of the Irish question did not come until after the First World War.

By the end of the century organised labour was an established third force in British politics. In 1851 the first successful union was established, by engineers who could afford to pay big subscriptions and whom the employers were not in a position to sack. In 1868 the Trades Union Congress (TUC) was formed, with 1,500,000 members. It became the national voice of unionism. Workers in a relatively weak position organised and met with success in demanding higher wages. In 1888, for example, the girls who made matches for the Bryant and May company went on strike and won because they gained general union and public support. In 1892 Keir Hardie, a socialist, was elected to Parliament. (He posed for cameras outside Westminster in miner's gear). In 1900 the Labour Representation Committee was set up to co-ordinate the efforts of the various socialist groups in getting left-wing

The working man gained the right to vote by the Reform Acts of the nineteenth century. Keir Hardie, a Scot, became the first socialist elected to Parliament, in 1892.

candidates elected. This was the beginning of the Labour Party which in the twentieth century was to replace the Liberal Party as the party of the left.

Empire

The British Empire reached its zenith at the end of the century; Britain had possessions all over the globe and authority over a quarter of the world's population. Maps showed British territories in red – a source of pride to millions of ordinary Britons who only in exceptional circumstances ever left the country. The possession of an empire in the twentieth century perhaps made Britain seem stronger than she actually was. In the post-Second World War period, following the rapid dismantling of the Empire, Britain has been left with the psychological problem of adjusting to the status of a middle-weight power – albeit with worthwhile ties with former territories. Throughout the world today there is ample evidence of the influence of British institutions and culture, and English is the main international language, partly as a legacy of the Empire and partly because of America's size and power.

India was the most important territory in the Empire. This was reflected by the care taken to secure the sea routes (and routes overland) from Britain to India and the Far East. A series of British bases was established at strategic points. In 1815, after the war with Napoleon, Britain's possession of Gibraltar and Malta was confirmed. These were important acquisitions and assisted in the control of the Mediterranean. (Cyprus was acquired in 1878.) Britain also took Mauritius from the French and the Cape and Ceylon from the Dutch. Singapore was acquired in 1819 and Hong Kong (which still remains a British colony) in 1842. In 1839 Britain conquered Aden and thereby acquired a vital base from which to control the Red Sea. The bases provided fuelling and repair facilities for British ships.

India exported tea, wood, cotton and jute and later imported a whole variety of British products, especially cotton textiles. The country had a vast population with religions and cultures far more ancient than Britain's; its complexities and divisions enabled Britain to gain a foothold in the first place. After a mutiny of Indian soldiers in 1857 – because of accumulated anxieties over changes made by the British – the East India Company was obliged to hand over the rule of India to the British government. A viceroy and an executive council were appointed and later a legislative council, on which some Indians sat. India presented a patchwork of areas of direct rule by British officials and provinces where the native rulers still had some administrative responsibilities. The Indian Civil Service was highly capable, and corruption was rare.

By their very presence in India the British fostered the spirit of nationalism which was eventually to demand and obtain independence. How the two races regarded each other has been the subject of literary speculation for a hundred years. The image of the British in India which has been presented by many books (as, for example, E. M. Forster's *A Passage to India*) is that of an aloof race, typified by reserved civil servants stiffly doing their duty. Indians, who often received a classical English education, resented their non-acceptance at a social level. But to think that India would have remained British if there had been friendlier social contacts is not realistic. Indians who saw in operation British representative institutions like Parliament asked (as other peoples did) why they should not have them too.

India was the jewel of the British Empire. Although most of the subcontinent was under British control by the mid-eighteenth century, the British government did not rule there directly until after the army mutiny of 1857. Then some states were administered by colonial service officials and others by native rulers with the assistance of a senior British official.

It was a response to a crisis in Canada that produced the constitutional device which ensured the evolution of the British Empire (and saved it from revolution, as in America in 1776). In 1837 there was a rebellion in Canada, which led to a Commission of Inquiry by Lord Durham. In his report, completed in 1839 (one year before his death), he recommended that the Cabinet in Canada be made responsible to the Assembly on matters of colonial concern. This vested internal control of the country in the electorate of the country itself. The Canadian provinces joined in confederation in 1867. This union was in part brought about by the withdrawal of British troops and the need for Canadians to stand together to avoid piecemeal absorption by the United States to the south. (The last province to enter the confederation was Newfoundland, in 1949.)

The system of self-government worked out for Canada was applied to the other two territories with white populations, Australia and New Zealand, in 1855. Australia (New South Wales particularly) was first conceived as a convenient place to send convicts, who at the end of their prison term (usually seven years) were expected to settle in the country. As British courts transported people of both sexes and all ages for the most trivial crimes, Australia got a wider cross-section of settlers than at first might be imagined. But demands came from within Australia for this practice to stop, and by 1840 it had almost come to an end (it finally ended in 1868). The economy of Australia was built on sheep (there were 13,000,000 in 1850). The merino produced a fine wool and could stand up to the Australian climate. Gold strikes hoisted the population. But Australia developed into an essentially urban society around the Australian coasts. In 1901 the Australian states adopted a very loose federal structure and became the Australian Commonwealth.

New Zealand, by contrast, became a tightly knit union in 1876, with a capital at Wellington, sited between the islands (the selection of Ottawa and Canberra as the capitals of Canada and Australia avoided the difficult choice of one of the big cities as the centre of national life). After the invention of refrigeration in 1882 New Zealand sent nearly all her lamb and her dairy products to Britain – a trade pattern guaranteed by Britain's control of the seas before the threats from Common Market competition of recent times. Unlike Australia, New Zealand had a large native population, the Maoris. Missionary activity was keen in New Zealand, and the missionaries invariably took the side of the Maoris against the settlers. New Zealand society was essentially pastoral and democratic, without any very distinct differences of class. Its governments pioneered much radical social legislation and imposed high taxation on the rich, which forced the division of large estates into small farms. Together with the radicalism went a very British way of life.

British interests in Africa developed in a piecemeal fashion. The West Coast of Africa gradually came under British control – the Danish and Dutch sold their stations to the British in 1850 and 1871. The Cape began as a British base, but climate, fertile soils and mineral wealth led to British expansion and conflict with the Boers.

The opening of the Suez Canal in 1869 drew Britain into the

The gothic splendour of the Houses of Parliament in Ottawa recalls the British origins of the majority of Canada's people. The Canadian Confederation of 1867, however, allowed for the differences engendered by sheer size and cultural diversity by ensuring maximum independence for the individual provinces within Canada.

affairs of Egypt and the Sudan. The British government did not have anything approaching a policy towards Africa until the end of the century. British governments did not want extra territories to administer at great cost. Much of the exploration of Africa was left to private individuals: missionaries and businessmen. David Livingstone, the Scottish missionary, explored much of east-central Africa. Cecil Rhodes, explorer, businessman and settler, aimed to establish a great empire for Britain in Africa and to build a railroad from Cairo to the Cape, traversing the continent entirely on British territory.

Rhodes's enterprise secured Rhodesia. British influence was similarly extended to Nigeria, Kenya and Uganda through private companies. The Cape–Cairo railway had to wait until after the First World War, as Germany controlled the territory between Rhodesia, Uganda and Kenya (however, a narrow strip of land granted by Belgium symbolically linked these British lands).

British governments became seriously interested in Africa only when other European powers did, particularly France, Germany and Italy. In the 1890s arrangements were made between the European powers over the partition of Africa. Britain and France came to an amicable understanding over territories (despite a temporary crisis in 1898), as both countries already owned vast tracts of land. The newcomers, Germany and Italy, felt grieved that they, as great European powers, had such comparatively small lands in Africa (and none elsewhere). But it would be erroneous to think that the First World War was fought over colonial issues. Diplomatic alliances enmeshed the great powers, and Germany and Italy in fact fought on opposite sides.

The century ended in war, the outcome of continual friction between the Boer (Dutch) and British peoples living in South Africa. The Boers wanted their two inland states, the Transvaal and Orange Free State, to have complete independence. Certainly, the Boer leader, Kruger, envisaged Dutch control of the whole of South Africa. The British were angry that their citizens in the Transvaal were denied political rights (the gold mines of Johannesburg attracted many Britons). Milner, the British High Commissioner in South Africa, believed that it would be best for South Africa to be within the British Empire. The Boer War lasted from 1899 until 1902. It was fought between Boer farmers, with a superb knowledge of the country, and the regular British army, which was overwhelming in size. The British army should have won a quick victory, but the war dragged on. It was hugely expensive and very embarrassing for Britain. The Boers portrayed the British as aggressors, and this view won international support, particularly from Germany. The British army had a very difficult job fighting an army on its own ground using guerrilla tactics, but its prestige suffered badly. In Britain there was mounting concern about the lack of success, the cost and the British use of concentration camps, the first in history, to detain the civilian population. (An English woman, Emily Hobhouse, had toured these camps and she denounced them in the British press.)

Peace was concluded in 1902. A new Liberal government conferred self-government on the Transvaal in 1906 and on the Orange Free State in 1907. There were two Boer and two British states in South Africa, with their own tariff systems. For economic reasons, and because Boers and Britons constituted racial minorities in South Africa, a union of the states was proposed. It came about in 1910. London did not insist on special safeguards for the freedom of the native Africans, as it did not wish to endanger relations with the Boers. Union staved off, but did not solve, problems. Antagonism between Boers and Britons continued. The Boer War had developed Boer nationalism as perhaps nothing else could have done. Union, in the form in which it was set up, did not allow for the inevitable demands of black South Africans for political rights.

The Empire was a collection of territories at varying stages of development. The white dominions had virtual independence. African countries had been brought into existence with scant regard for historic tribal traditions and did not involve Africans in their administration. India was treated respectfully but ruled nonetheless.

The Empire provided vast opportunities for trade until the 1930s. This helped to sustain Britain's position, particularly with the decline of European markets in the last decades of the nineteenth century. The Empire also gave a home to millions of Britons and employment to thousands more. The British built the infrastructure (roads, railways and so on) in most of the imperial countries; education came usually with missionaries, as did some measure of social welfare; and British law was established everywhere.

Social Life in Victorian Britain

After a period of undistinguished kingship Queen Victoria's achievement was that she redeemed the monarchy and raised it to a new pinnacle of popularity. Victoria was thrifty, hardworking, religious and devoted to her family – she was a paragon of those qualities held dear by Victorians. The queen's imperiousness well fitted an age in which Britain was supremely confident and successful.

Victoria was only eighteen when she came to the throne in 1837, and in her early days as queen she was guided by the Prime Minister, Lord Melbourne, who treated her in a kindly, avuncular fashion. In 1841 Victoria married her cousin, Prince Albert, with whom she was dearly in love and whom she took as her ideal even after his death in 1861. The queen mourned Albert so deeply that she retreated from public life until the 1870s. A small republican movement even sprang up in reaction to the queen's shunning of her public duties. This glimmer of republicanism was rapidly extinguished when Victoria was made Empress of India in 1877, and the monarch emerged as a glorious symbol of the rapidly growing Empire. In the Diamond Jubilee celebrations in 1897 Victoria was virtually deified.

There were never good relations between the queen and Edward, the prince of Wales. Victoria claimed that Edward's wild ways had contributed to the death of Albert. Edward was allowed little part in the affairs of state until the last years of the century, and this lack of practical experience in government was unfortunate for a future king (there were traditionally poor relations between monarch and heir in the Hanoverian family, though Victoria had, in fact, been liked by her uncle, William IV). Victoria held strong views on political questions, but the age had passed in which the monarch could reject as Prime Minister a man with different views from those of the crown. Early in her reign, in 1841, Victoria had to accept Sir Robert Peel as Prime Minister, even though she thoroughly disliked him. Eventually she came to respect and like Peel, but she was never reconciled to Gladstone. He treated her formally, even brusquely, and Victoria responded to a softer, more charming approach, such as that of Disraeli. Despite her dislike of Gladstone, the queen had to have him four times as her Prime Minister.

Victoria had a generally conservative view of society. The queen cared for the dignity of the crown and hierarchy in society. She would agree to only a few additions to the peerage, with the result that the House of Lords emerged in the twentieth century as a body quite remote from the main stream of society. Victoria followed foreign affairs closely, and as she was related to most of the royal houses in Europe, she often had channels of communication and influence superior to that of her government. On the whole, Victoria disliked the emergence of nationalism in Europe in the nineteenth century and did not approve of the unification of Italy. She gave enthusiastic support to the British armies in the Crimean and Boer wars and publicly made known her sympathies for Gordon in the Sudan (public knowledge of the monarch's political opinions would be unthinkable today).

Victorian Britain saw a considerable revival in religion. In 1833 a group of churchmen at Oxford released the first of their 'Tracts for the Times', which emphasised the eternal authority of the Church rather than its foundation on the Reformation settlement of the sixteenth century. A number of Tractarians left the Church of England and joined the Roman Catholic Church. One of the most distinguished converts was John Newman, who eventually became a cardinal. The Tractarians

Queen Victoria (1837–1901), seen here in her old age, ruled for much of the nineteenth century and became Queen and Empress of more than a quarter of the world's population. Despite her retreat into mourning after the death of her husband, Albert, she was greatly revered as the symbol of a confident, expanding empire.

within the Church of England remained a powerful and traditionally-minded minority, who did much to strengthen the fibre of Anglicanism. Conversely, evangelicals within the Church of England emphasised the authority of the Bible and the need to preach to the people. There was often considerable hostility between the Tractarians, or High Church men, and the evangelicals, or Low Church men, in the Established Church. But the enthusiasm both groups generated helped to stem the decline in the Church's strength which had begun with the Industrial Revolution. Nonconformists also gained a new energy, and by 1851 there were 318,000 Protestant Sun-

Public schools became an important institution in the nineteenth century. Thomas Arnold, the headmaster of Rugby School, was particularly influential. The public schools were in fact more private than public, demanding sizeable fees in return for educating their pupils as Christian gentlemen. The photograph shows pupils of Rugby School in the Edwardian period.

day school teachers in Britain. In 1856 the Catholic Church was allowed by Parliament to establish dioceses in Britain for the first time since the Reformation. There was some alarm among Protestants at the number of Catholics who appeared in society. Between 1895 and 1903 the fabric of the great Roman Catholic cathedral at Westminster, in London, was completed.

The publication in 1859 of Charles Darwin's *The Origin of the Species* was the culmination of a series of writings which swept aside the fundamental biblical view of Creation and history, substituting for it evolution and natural selection. T. H. Huxley, Darwin's greatest disciple, claimed for Darwin a place in science comparable with Galileo's and Newton's, but many scientists believed that Darwin had destroyed the moral basis of scientific studies. Another indication of the changing beliefs of the age was that in 1886, after much debate and three re-elections to Parliament, an atheist, Charles Bradlaugh, was allowed to take his seat in the Commons.

The two English universities, Oxford and Cambridge, which had reached a deplorably low state in the eighteenth century, gradually revived in the nineteenth century. In 1825 University College, which was open to members of all religions and non-believers, was founded in London. It was to provide an education for the bright offspring of the middle class. The foundation of new universities in the largest cities of the country continued throughout the nineteenth century. Public schools (private and fee-paying) were similarly transformed. Thomas Arnold, the headmaster of Rugby School in the early part of the nineteenth century, believed that the purpose of education was to produce Christian gentlemen. Moral as well as intellectual training was to become an aim of the public school, whose popularity increased with the growth of a middle class which could afford the fees and an expansion of the railways which could transport boys from home to school. With the growth of the Empire in the late nineteenth century, there was a need for large numbers of well schooled men who could take up posts in the army, the Civil Service and business.

Victorians were certainly class-conscious, but the vast wealth produced by the Industrial Revolution enabled people of all classes to improve their social position. One of the most popular books of the nineteenth century was Samuel Smiles's *Self-help*, published in 1859, which claimed that success was the product of four virtues – thrift, character, self-help and duty. Dickens's novels are filled with characters aspiring to better themselves. The colonies and America were an important outlet for people who wished to break with the constraints of home and chance their luck. Disraeli spoke of a divided society in his novel *Sybil*, and Karl Marx had Britain in mind during the composition of *Das Kapital* in the Reading Room of the British Museum. The British were inclined to think they had avoided upheaval by virtue of their glorious constitution and their acceptance of gradual reform. This argument may have had some merit, but Britain's wealth increased dramatically in the nineteenth century, and though its distribution was highly uneven, the increase in prosperity among the working class was sufficient to give its members a growing feeling of betterment and security.

The prosperity of the nineteenth century is evident from the great number of buildings erected. Advances in engineering enabled structures to be bigger and more daring than ever before. Between 1829 and 1864 the Clifton Suspension Bridge was erected in Bristol by Isambard Brunel and his successors. In 1868 the enormous arch at St Pancras Station was finished. It was designed by W. H. Barlow. St Pancras was the prototype

Victorian prosperity owed much to the increasingly fast and efficient communication brought by the railways. Architects celebrated the marvels of steam engines by the creation of monumental stations such as St Pancras in London. W. H. Barlow designed the great arch of the railway shed shown here and the main building, which incorporated a huge hotel, was the work of Sir Gilbert Scott.

CASSELLS OLD & NEW LONDON. PLATE 7.

THE MIDLAND RAILWAY STATION.—ST PANCRAS.

of the great railway stations that were to appear throughout the country. The station in Bristol was built to look like a medieval fortress. In all towns a need for civic buildings demanded the construction of town halls, schools, hospitals, museums and libraries.

The new interest in religion was paralleled in architecture by the movement known as the Gothic Revival, which regarded the Middle Ages as an age of faith, whose Gothic style of building should be emulated. Two of the greatest exponents of the Gothic Revival were Sir Charles Barry and Augustus Pugin. After the Houses of Parliament burnt down in 1836, Barry won the competition to rebuild the Palace of Westminster. Augustus Pugin was responsible for the rich decoration which embellishes the interior of the great structure. Sir Gilbert Scott, who was considered to have betrayed the Gothic movement by building the new Foreign Office building in Whitehall in a Classical style, built the memorial to Prince Albert in Kensington Gardens in a highly Gothic style. The nineteenth century invariably demanded Gothic for any ecclesiastical structure.

Victorian interiors were rich and crowded; in reaction to this profusion and quantity, the Arts and Crafts movement at the end of the century attempted to reintroduce simple, functional furniture and furnishings. A leading member of the movement was William Morris, who designed over 500 patterns for wallpapers, textiles, carpets and tapestry, many of which are still used today. Morris envisaged a simpler society, in which men might live by the skills of their hands and without the pressures and squalor of industrial society. The rejection, in whole or in part, of the Industrial Revolution – regarded generally as the most significant achievement of late eighteenth-century and nineteenth-century Britain – divided the intelligentsia from the rest of society.

The divorce from urban Britain was most marked in the Romantic poets of the early nineteenth century, who shunned the cities and lived in remote country areas. William Wordsworth and his sister, Dorothy, tramped through the Somerset countryside with their friend, the poet Samuel Taylor Coleridge, engaged in endless discussion. The move of the Wordsworths to the Lake District in the north-west of England inspired William Wordsworth, and the Lake District is as inextricably linked with him as Stratford-upon-Avon is linked with William Shakespeare. The English Romantic poets abroad were uplifted by both the majesty of the past and the wonders of nature. Wordsworth was stunned at the beauty of the Alps. Lord Byron and John Keats were both moved by Switzerland, 'the home of freedom'. The ancient world exerted an even greater attraction, however. Byron went to Greece to aid the Greeks in their struggle against the Turks – and he died at Missolonghi in 1824. John Keats lived and died in Rome, and his greatest friend, the poet Percy Shelley, was drowned at sea off Leghorn and cremated on the beach near Viareggio in Italy.

The novelists Emily and Charlotte Brontë lived a life of seclusion in a rectory in a remote part of Yorkshire. In their isolation they produced two of the finest novels in the English language, *Wuthering Heights* and *Jane Eyre. Wuthering Heights* extols the beauty of the wild, desolate countryside, which is matched by the passions of the characters. *Jane Eyre* is set in an out-of-the-way country house. The story concerns a governess, the role allotted to many Victorian women of gentle birth but no wealth who, by teaching the children of the rich, could stay within the world of gentility.

Seaside resorts like Weston-super-Mare expanded greatly in Victorian times. This picture shows Weston as mid-century host to the elegant and wealthy. By the end of the century it was catering for working-class holiday-makers from the great industrial cities.

When novelists did turn their attention to the cities they were scathing. The very title of Mrs Gaskell's novel *North and South* illustrates the profound split in nineteenth-century England between the rural south and the industrial north. It was a cold, hard world that Mrs Gaskell saw in the north. Charles Dickens in *Hard Times* comes as close as he ever does to condemning Victorian society, when he portrays a small northern industrial town with an oppressed working class and a ruling elite dedicated to making money. It was a long time before writers could see anything worthwhile in the industrial working-class culture that was emerging in the nineteenth century – a culture which embraced brass bands, outings to the seaside, music halls and hymn singing in Nonconformist chapels. It was cheery, lively and vibrant and was the culture of the majority of Britons by the end of the century.

8

The Twentieth Century to 1960

Britain and the Great War, 1900–1922

The Edwardian period, which extends from the accession of Edward VII in 1901 to the outbreak of war in 1914, has been characterised by the rather ostentatious lifestyle of the rich, including that of the king. The sobriety and correctness of Victorian Britain disappeared, but Edward VII turned out to be capable and competent, contrary to his mother's expectations. His extravagant tastes were anyway combined with a generosity and charm which made him popular, and the queen, Alexandra, was very well liked. The popping of champagne corks, the patronage of Continental resorts (a number of which Edward helped to make fashionable), the horse racing and the yachts should not obscure the fact that the Edwardian period was one of tension and occasional friction at home and abroad.

Strikes, which had become increasingly successful and bitter in late Victorian Britain, continued in the new century. Living standards were higher than before, but wages were low when weighed against the profits from industry. There was militancy in other (and perhaps unexpected) quarters. Women, by and large from the middle and upper class, began to voice ever more strident demands for the vote. Ironically, the more violent women became in demanding their rights, the more their opponents could present them as unfitted to have the vote.

The nineteenth century had produced no solution to Ireland. In the twentieth century two sharply divided parties existed in Ireland; the Catholics demanded Home Rule (in effect, independence), and the Protestants (in the north) refused to be part of a Catholic Ireland and wished to remain in the United Kingdom. Irish Home Rulers and Unionists saw violence as a means to an end. An impressive number of arms were in both Catholic and Protestant hands and civil war in Ireland in 1914 seemed imminent. Conflict in Ireland was averted until after the First World War. But a major collision occurred between the Liberal government of the day and the predominantly Conservative House of Lords.

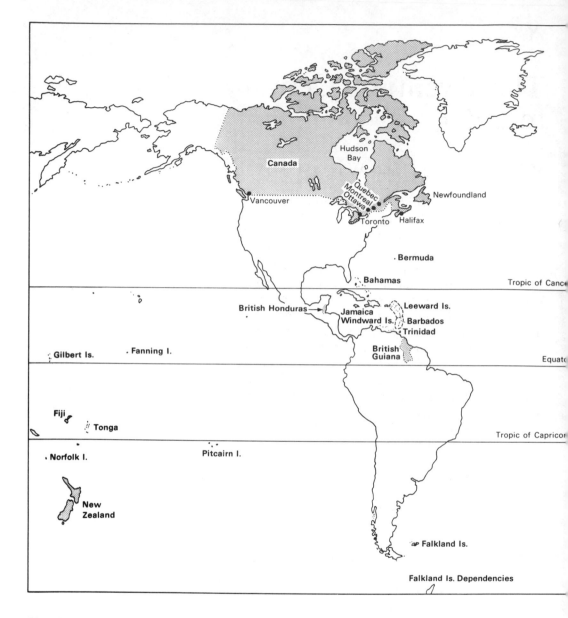

The British Empire in 1914

Finally, the cloud of war hung over the international scene. Admittedly, tensions had eased by 1914, but suspicion was so deeply rooted and the alliance system so binding that war broke out almost automatically, following the assassination of an Austrian prince in the Balkans. The First World War constituted a definite break in European history (three empires ended). In Britain the war brought momentous changes. Two pre-war issues were solved: Southern Ireland gained virtual independence and women won the vote. The war extended the activities of the state. Unions co-operated with the govern-

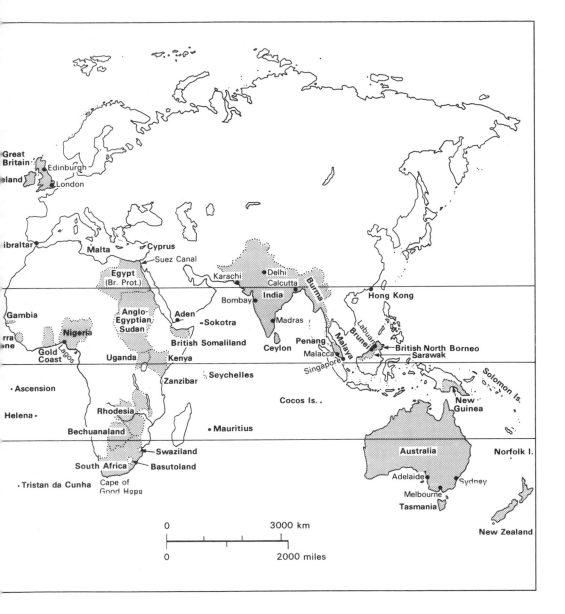

ment in winning the war. For the first time in their lives, millions of men left their homes and travelled, albeit in the gravest of circumstances.

There was a decade of Conservative government, from 1895, when the government was headed by Lord Salisbury, and from 1902 by his equally accomplished nephew, Arthur Balfour. The most important measure of the Balfour administration was the Education Act of 1902, which in effect introduced secondary education on a national scale. The Act was obviously important, but what was of particular interest and concern was the fact that the organisation of secondary education came so late in Britain, and when it was organised there was no specific provision for technical education. Unlike German and American industry, British industry, though very strong, was not being stimulated by a flow of new ideas. New ideas had to come from men with scientific skills (or a flair for organisation), and therefore a broad system of higher education was indispensable. The private sector and the universities produced good men for the professions, business and administration at home and in the Empire but markedly few scientists and engineers.

Though the Liberals formed the new government in December 1905, the interesting feature of the election had been the return of fifty-three Labour members. The Liberals were a party of reform, and therefore their introduction of social legislation was to be expected; but the rise of a party which could take away their left-wing vote guaranteed that they would choose a programme with appeal to the working class. In 1908 the Liberals introduced a Bill to provide small old-age pensions (this meant that old people without money or family no longer needed to go to the workhouse, a highly unpopular institution). The Bill became law after some pressure had been put on the Lords. But in 1909 the Liberals, and in particular their Chancellor of the Exchequer, an eloquent Member from Wales, Lloyd George, suggested further changes, which caused a confrontation with the Lords and a constitutional crisis.

The Liberals proposed certain measures, such as the setting up of labour exchanges, which were not controversial. What caused anger was the financing of the new schemes. In particular, there seemed to be taxes aimed specifically at the rich – a rise in death duties (a tax paid on property and real estate when a person died), the levying of land duties whenever land changed hands and a super-tax to be paid for the first time on incomes over £3000 a year. The budget had a popular appeal, but it provoked a strong Conservative reaction (many Liberals, in fact, did not like the budget either). The Conservative leadership was ill advised enough to let the House of Lords reject the government's budget. The Liberals called an election and were able to present the matter as a constitutional issue (they claimed to be defending the supremacy of the elected Commons over the unelected Lords). The Lords rejected the budget again, together with a parliamentary Bill which proposed to curtail the powers of the Upper House. There was a second election in December 1910, and a large Liberal majority was returned again. This convinced the new king, George V (Edward VII died in May 1910, while the crisis was still on) that he should agree to use his power to create enough Liberal peers to pass the government's legislation, should the House of Lords block the Bill again.

In July 1911 the House of Lords allowed the legislation to pass. Inevitably, constitutional change came as well. By the Parliament Act important money Bills could become law, if need be, without the consent of the Lords. The Speaker of the Commons was left to determine which Bills fell into this category. Other Bills rejected by the Lords, if passed by the Commons in three successive sessions, could after two years become law (this became one year in 1949). Finally, the length of each Parliament was reduced from seven to five years (the present length of a Parliament).

In 1911 Lloyd George's National Insurance Bill was passed, which provided sick pay of ten shillings a week for large groups of workers (falling to five shillings in cases of prolonged illness). This scheme, like the provision of pensions, was an important step in providing state security for citizens in need. In 1911 a measure was also passed to provide for the payment of Members of Parliament. It was intended to make it easier for a working man to be a parliamentarian. Payment had been a radical demand from the time of the Chartists in the early nineteenth century. In fact, the Labour Party was able to finance its members from union funds (still an important source of income for the Labour Party).

The Liberal government, and particularly the Prime Minister, Herbert Asquith, would not give way to demands to give women the vote. A militant movement grew up under the

Although male householders of all ranks had gained the right to vote, women remained excluded. The early years of the twentieth century saw the rise of a militant suffragette movement Yet victory when it came probably owed more to the First World War than to their violent protests.

leadership of a mother and daughter, Emmeline and Christabel Pankhurst. The movement's noisy demonstrations, smashing of shop windows in London's West End and other acts, on the whole tended to shock rather than sway public opinion. The authorities' most controversial action was the force-feeding of suffragettes who went on hunger strike while in prison. The vote was achieved peacefully in 1918, when all women over thirty were enfranchised and all men over twenty-one. In 1928 the voting age for women was lowered to twenty-one as well.

Nothing had been decided about Ulster by 1914. A Home Rule Bill introduced in 1912 caused vigorous protest in Protestant Ulster; a large (and illegal) army of volunteers gathered in readiness to defend Ulster's 'freedom'. The Liberals then agreed to let Ulster vote in a plebiscite on the question of Home Rule, but the situation had reached an impasse by the time war broke out.

In 1914 Germany stood by Austria against Russia and her ally, France. Britain was not (intentionally) tied by any alliance and could have remained neutral. But a treaty of friendship had been concluded with France in 1904, and though Britain had had serious doubts about Russia throughout the nineteenth century, since the latter part of that century Germany had seemed a greater peril to British interests. When Germany invaded Belgium (which she had to do in order to attack France) Britain declared war on Germany. The occupation of Belgium, and possibly of northern France, by an enemy power awakened traditional fears in Britain.

The British entered the war with enthusiasm. It was a popular and patriotic war at the start, and there was no need for the conscription of men for the army until 1916. Ordinary soldiers believed that they were fighting tyranny and that the world after Germany's defeat would be a better and more peaceful place. German things, from dogs to sausages, became instantly unfashionable, and it was the war that obliged the royal family to change its name from Saxe-Coburg-Gotha to Windsor. Conscientious objectors who refused to fight had a hard time. Many were forced into the army; many others went to prison; some worked on farms. This coercion caused bitterness and was not repeated in the Second World War.

The war was one of stalemate and increasing disillusion. Both armies confronted each other from row upon row of trenches, dug from Switzerland to the Channel. There were occasional charges from the trenches, when the armies would try to make modest advances, but they resulted in appalling casualties on both sides.

Though the British navy was superior to Germany's and

The First World War required more manpower than any other in history. Recruiting efforts such as this poster of Lord Kitchener, a popular general, helped Britain to assemble a vast volunteer army in the early years of the war. Later, conscription became necessary for the first time. In all, three million troops from Britain and the Empire died or were seriously wounded.

beat Germany in the only serious naval engagement of the war, the Battle of Jutland in 1916, German submarine warfare was seriously affecting Britain's supply lines in 1916–17. It was the attacks by U-boats on American shipping which finally decided the United States to enter the war on the side of the Allies. The solution to submarine attacks was the convoy system (groups of merchant ships travelling together, protected by naval vessels), an idea which the Admiralty only accepted under pressure from the Prime Minister, Lloyd George. He had succeeded Asquith in 1916 and brought a vigour and determination to the conduct of the war which was lacking under Asquith. Lloyd George took over factories for war production; he redirected labour; and in 1918 he introduced rationing – an unprecedented extension of the powers of the state. Russia dropped out of the war in 1917, but America's involvement brought the Allies fresh troops and great supplies of machinery (tanks were particularly important). Germany was too overstrained to continue fighting, and she surrendered in 1918.

Victory had been bought at a great price. There had been a colossal waste of material resources. In all, 3,000,000 troops from Britain and the Empire had been killed or seriously injured. An influenza epidemic in 1918–19 killed a further 150,000 people; resistance was low at the end of a tiring war.

Among many people there was deep disillusion. Certainly, the literature of the period, a flowering of poetry by such people as Siegfried Sassoon and Wilfred Owen, was a bitter condemnation of war and military leaders. The scars of the First World War were so deep that there was a revulsion in the following decades against any action that might lead Britain into such a terrible conflict again.

At the peace conference of Versailles Lloyd George was one of the moderate voices. Even so, a large number of territories which belonged to Germany and her ally, Turkey, were absorbed into the Empire. Tanganyika went to Britain, South-West Africa to South Africa, New Guinea to Australia and Samoa to New Zealand. In the Middle East Britain acquired mandates over Palestine, Iraq and Transjordan (during the war a British army officer, T. E. Lawrence – Lawrence of Arabia – had inspired the Arabs to unite against the Turks). In 1917 Arthur Balfour, the former Tory premier, had stated that Palestine should be a home for the Jewish peoples, and after the war Jews from all over the world began to make their homes there. Balfour's statement was well meant; he did not envisage the confrontation that would develop between a Jewish nation and the Arab world in the post-Second World War period.

The First World War brought about the collapse of the Ottoman Empire. T. E. Lawrence, 'Lawrence of Arabia' – an Englishman more at home in Arabia than in his own country – helped to organise widescale opposition to the Turks and, indirectly, to foster Arab nationalism.

A casualty of the war was the Liberal Party. It had traditionally been the party of peace, yet it had led Britain into the war. Many of the conscientious objectors had been Welsh Liberal Dissenters. Lloyd George and Herbert Asquith, now personal enemies, became the leaders of rival groups of Liberals. Lloyd George's Liberals joined the Conservatives in a coalition, and this coalition won a great victory in the 1918 general election. Lloyd George remained Prime Minister, but with predominantly Conservative support. The official Liberals, under Asquith, did very badly in the election and won only twenty-eight seats. Lloyd George was able to pass several pieces of legislation – the setting up of a Ministry of Health in 1919 and the extension of the 1911 Insurance Act to cover all workers. But his leadership was under threat. Many Conservatives were deeply suspicious of Lloyd George, the former radical Chancellor, and there was deep concern about his scandalous private life and ostentatious sale of titles to gain money and support. The Conservatives made Bonar Law, a wealthy Canadian Scot, their leader, and in 1922 he replaced Lloyd George as Prime Minister.

Clearly, at the end of the war the Irish question had to be tackled again. In 1916 there had been the Easter Rising in Dublin when a small group of republicans tried to seize the Government. The rising failed and savage repression followed, which only served to increase massively the sympathy for republicanism in the south. After the war the republicans established their own parliament in Dublin. Lloyd George's government would not accept this situation and used the British army against the republicans. Force again failed. In 1920 the Government partitioned Ireland between the Protestant north and the Catholic south. Each part of Ireland was to exercise a degree of home rule. But the south would not accept this solution, and in 1921 the British government was obliged to grant the south dominion status (such as Canada and Australia had), which gave it virtual independence. The north remained part of the United Kingdom as it does to this day.

Northern Ireland (Ulster) included many Catholics (a third of the population) and among this Catholic minority there were many who wanted unification with the south and claimed that they were oppressed by the Protestant majority. Ulster, though part of the United Kingdom, has its own cultural and religious background, which has made it not only different from the south but also from Britain. The south, with a Celtic and Catholic heritage many centuries old, continued to be independent of the United Kingdom. It did not fight on the British side in the Second World War but remained neutral and in 1948 the south became the Republic of Eire and left the Commonwealth.

Britain between the Wars

Throughout most of the 1920s there was economic stagnation in Europe. In America dizzy speculation in the late twenties ended in the collapse of the stock market in 1929, which caused severe recession in the United States itself and in the advanced economies all around the world. Democracy fared badly. Two major states, Italy and Germany, acquired rightist dictatorships, and Russia (never democratic) was undergoing a communist revolution. Britain had economic troubles and political and social tensions, particularly in the thirties; set against the international scene, they do not seem extraordinary, but this is not to minimise the discomfort and exasperation of the millions of Britons who could not find work. Bad memories of the thirties have endured to the present, and the avoidance of mass unemployment has been a high priority in modern politics.

In the twenties the economy was marked by periods of prosperity and periods of recession. But even when there was an easing of economic conditions, unemployment never fell below 1,000,000. With the collapse of international trade between 1929 and 1932, the number of unemployed rose to 3,750,000. It did not drop below 2,000,000 until after 1935. The most significant aspect of unemployment was its concentration in Britain's old-established industries – coal mining, iron and steel production, ship building and textile manufacture. These industries were particularly dependent on world markets, which had never recovered from the dislocation of the First World War. Additionally, developing countries could not get good prices for their raw materials, which meant that they were not in a position to buy many manufactured articles from countries like Britain.

But 'new' industries, which catered essentially for the consumer at home, experienced rapid growth. These industries included car production, the manufacture of electrical goods, the manufacture of synthetic textiles like rayon and aeroplane construction. The building trade also did well, helped enormously by the government's intention to house people better. As industries suffering decline were concentrated in the areas which had industrialised first, and as the new industries grew up elsewhere, unemployment and its attendant social distress became associated with particular regions. South Wales, the north-east of England, central Scotland and parts of Northern

Ireland were especially hard-hit. The new industries grew up in the Midlands and the south (particularly around London, though not, significantly enough, in London's East End, which remained very poor), and they experienced relative prosperity. When therefore in 1936 workers marched in protest to London from Jarrow, a town in the north-east of England in which 80 per cent of the working population was unemployed, they were greeted with some incredulity (but respect) in the south.

Britain was governed for most of the inter-war period by Conservative administrations. The Labour Party formed two short-lived governments, reflecting the fact that it was a mass party and had succeeded in supplanting the Liberals as the alternative government to the Conservatives. Government was bewildered by economic problems and unemployment. Refurbishment and relocation of British industry was a possible answer – but out of the question. Also, the economy needed to be revitalised by spending, and that all governments were reluctant to do. Conservative governments believed in financial orthodoxy. Unnecessary spending was cut. Britain even returned to the Gold Standard in 1925 (until 1931), which had the effect of making British exports less competitive. Stanley Baldwin, the Conservative premier, demonstrated his personal belief in traditional remedies by paying half of his large fortune into the National Debt, in the hope that others would follow his example and that the Debt would be wiped out.

Free trade was finally abandoned in 1931, and British industry was protected from the entry of all but imperial goods. There was also social legislation which consolidated welfare for the sick and unemployed and made the period much less tense than it might have been. Despite its efforts, government in this period was unadventurous and appeared complacent to those suffering from economic change (obviously, though, the electorate as a whole thought the approach was correct, as the Conservative vote was consistently high). Industry reorganised considerably (large companies became larger), but there was a lack of investment in research programmes and a reluctance to finance new industrial techniques.

The election called by the new Conservative premier, Stanley Baldwin, in November 1923 was fought against a background of high unemployment and bitter discussion over tariffs which the Conservatives wished to introduce. The result was that the Conservatives were the largest party, with 258 seats, but they did not have an overall majority, as Labour had 191 Members and the Liberals (now united) had 159 Members. The Liberals made it clear that they would not keep

The Depression of the 1930s brought chronic unemployment. The north-east of England suffered particularly, and in 1936 workers marched in protest from Jarrow to London. The quiet dignity of the marchers won great respect, but their situation remained unchanged.

the Conservatives in office, and so the king, George V, called upon the Labour Party to form a government. Britain's first socialist administration roused great expectation on all sides, but apart from the fact that the government did not have a majority, its leadership was cautious and committed to the philosophy of gradual change. The most memorable act of the government was the restoration of diplomatic relations with the Soviet Union. The government was weak, but two incidents speeded its end. The Conservative Opposition accused the government of withdrawing for political motives a prosecution against the *Worker's Weekly*, which, it was alleged, had incited soldiers to mutiny. There was a debate on the issue in the Commons, which the Government lost. The second incident was a letter (later discovered to have been forged), from The Third International, exhorting the British Communist Party to cause an insurrection in Britain. The letter was published by the popular Press, and the election was fought with passion.

In the 1924 election the Conservatives were returned to office with a decisive majority. The Labour Party claimed that it was the 'Red Letter' that had lost it the election. Neville Chamberlain (a future Prime Minister), as Minister of Health, considerably extended social services: for the first time pensions were provided for widows and orphans, and old-age pensions could be claimed at the age of sixty-five instead of seventy. Chamberlain already had a reputation as a reformer, as in 1923 it was his action that had speeded up house building. The return to the Gold Standard in 1925 was regressive, however, and the prediction that there would be trouble in industry, and particularly in coal-mining, was accurate.

The background to mining was one of unemployment and conflict between mine owners and miners. Huge investment was required in mining, and a Royal Commission after the war had suggested the nationalisation of the mines for this purpose. The idea had been turned down, much to the chagrin of the miners. Trouble was caused in 1926 when a government committee suggested, among other proposals, that miners' wages should be reduced. Life in mining communities was grim. The miners began a strike on 26 April, and the TUC, to show its sympathy, called a stoppage in some industries which was to begin on 3 May. As the industries selected included transport, gas, electricity and printing, the strike was considered 'general'. Neither the TUC nor the government wanted a confrontation, but both sides drifted into a situation in which neither side felt that it could give way; on 3 May Britain's first general strike began.

The government handled the situation well. It maintained essential services with the help of middle-class volunteers, and it was helped incalculably by the radio, which already had about 2,000,000 regular listeners. Optimistic news was broadcast instead of news about the strikers' solidarity. If this tradition of government interference in broadcasting had continued it would have been highly detrimental to broadcasting, but the British Broadcasting Corporation (BBC), set up in 1927, decided that it should never be used as a political vehicle again. The TUC called off the strike on 12 May, though the miners continued to fight in great bitterness for another six months.

Workers did not have good memories of 1926, and the strike was a scar on industrial relations, but there had been a marked moderation on both sides. There was some victimisation after the strike, and the government's Trades Disputes Act (1927), which made sympathetic strikes illegal, was highly unpopular with unions and the Labour Party (it was repealed by the socialist administration after the Second World War).

As if to signify calm after the strike, the most acrimonious debate in the House of Commons in 1928 was over the Church's choice of a new prayer book, which Members rejected as being too Catholic (it would be difficult to imagine such a situation now; though the Church of England is still a state institution, its affairs are very much under the direction of its bishops and councils).

Baldwin called a general election in 1929, but his theme of 'Safety First' was rejected by the voters, who preferred the idea of change represented by the Labour Party. Labour won

144

the largest number of seats in the Commons, though it was still in a minority. The second Labour government was formed under its leader, Ramsay MacDonald; Margaret Bondfield became the Minister of Labour, and thereby the first woman Cabinet Minister in parliamentary history.

Almost immediately the government had to deal with the economic crisis which hit Britain, as it did other parts of the world, after the Wall Street crash of October 1929. Unemployment rocketed. The government tried to create jobs by initiating a public works programme, but the Chancellor of the Exchequer, Philip Snowden, would only allow limited spending, as he feared the effects on Britain's financial position. Despite Snowden's actions, in February 1931 the Conservative Opposition tabled a vote of censure on the government for extravagance, and the committee set up by the government to answer these criticisms produced a black report. In the crisis that this provoked MacDonald resigned. But the king asked him to stay on and form a national government of all three parties, Labour, Conservative and Liberal. When MacDonald agreed the Labour Party and the trade union movement were outraged. Only twelve Labour Members supported the new government, while 242 opposed it. MacDonald, Snowden and their group were reviled as men who had betrayed the movement, surrendering to partisan criticisms instead of holding firm.

The national government presented an emergency budget, took Britain off the Gold Standard and decided on a general election. The government received overwhelming support – 60 per cent of all votes cast and 521 seats. The great majority of the new members were Conservatives, and MacDonald's government was only 'national' in name. Labour lost 1,750,000 votes, but its mass support remained, and in the general election of 1935 Labour recouped its losses and gained almost the same number of votes as in 1929 (and, in fact, a higher percentage of all votes cast).

The new government decided on the general protection of British industry, and in 1932 a 10 per cent customs duty was levied on most imports. Free trade had been dying for some time. It was good for Britain when her industry was supreme, but clearly in the twentieth century British industry was suffering from stiff competition. Some industries, like car manufacture, had always enjoyed protection, and the 1932 measure should therefore be seen as the extension of a principle rather than its first application. In the same year an imperial economic conference was held in Ottawa, and a partial system of free trade in the Commonwealth area was agreed upon. The term 'Commonwealth' was now coming into use. It indicated the idea of a group of states of equal status governing their own affairs, rather than the principle of empire, which implied dependence of colonies on the mother country. The dominions – Canada, Australia, New Zealand and South Africa – had manifested their independence by representing themselves at the peace conference in 1919. The Liberals, unprepared to sanction further attacks on free trade which the tariff agreements with the Commonwealth had brought, left the national government, but this made no difference to the government's majority.

In July 1935 MacDonald was replaced by Baldwin as leader of the government, and in November he won a large victory in the general election. Economic improvement continued steadily, though unemployment remained endemic in the old industrial areas.

Shortly after the new government came to power, in January 1936, the death occurred of the king, George V. He was a traditionalist, earnestly trying to do his best for the country, and he had been deeply respected. His son's accession brought problems. Edward VIII, as prince of Wales, had commented publicly on the unemployment situation. This had brought him popularity but had embarrassed the government. Edward, with his definite views on domestic and foreign policy, was not likely to meet the approval of the cautious Prime Minister, Stanley Baldwin. How far Edward's personality and outlook contributed to the establishment's willingness to let him abdicate is difficult to say. The issue which arose was simple. Edward wished to marry Mrs Simpson, an American who had

In 1936 Edward VIII, after less than a year as king, decided to abdicate in order to marry Mrs Simpson, a divorcée. They became the Duke and Duchess of Windsor and the throne passed to Edward's brother, George VI.

146

divorced two husbands. The government, the Churches, the leaders of the Commonwealth and probably majority opinion in the country opposed a royal marriage that would make Mrs Simpson queen. Edward had the clear choice of remaining king or abdicating and marrying Mrs Simpson. He chose to abdicate on 11 December 1936 and went abroad to live in order to cause the royal family the minimum of embarrassment. Both he and his wife remained popular figures, and their romance has often been fondly recalled in books and newspapers and, later, on television. Edward's brother, who became George VI (father of Queen Elizabeth II) quickly established his popularity. He had to overcome both shyness and a stutter, and the efforts he made (particularly when making radio broadcasts) were greatly admired.

Just as the economy of the inter-war period presented the contrast of industrial decay and industrial growth, so there was a marked contrast in society. There were dole queues (the dole was unemployment pay) and soup kitchens in areas of high unemployment. There were protest marches by workers, and there was the bitterness of the General Strike. But there were also growing signs of prosperity and more varied lifestyles. By 1938 there were 2,400,000 motor cars, and the lorry had taken over from the horse and cart. Every town of any size had a cinema. Around many towns, particularly in the Midlands and the south, suburbs proliferated, often made up of identical semi-detached houses with generous gardens. Consumer goods had made their appearance. Many homes had a radio, electrical fittings and sets of books given away by newspapers to boost their sales. Women's clothes, now made out of synthetic fabrics, became easier to look after. Skirts no longer touched the ground, and cosmetics were widely used.

The freedom from repressive Victorian conventions was particularly pronounced in literature. D. H. Lawrence wrote explicitly about sex. One of his novels, *The Rainbow*, was prosecuted as obscene in 1915, and *Lady Chatterley's Lover* (1928) was not published in unexpurgated form for thirty years. He approved of the irrational and stormy side of life; sober marriage and compatibility with society was not for his characters – nor, in fact, for him. James Joyce's *Ulysses* (1922) treated sexual themes in a way that was considered shocking, and the book could not be bought readily for many years because of the disapproval of the courts.

Both Lawrence and Joyce wrote autobiographical novels which describe their home background with care and, on the whole, affection. In *Sons and Lovers* Lawrence portrays the north Midland mining area from which he came; London, to which one of the main characters moves, seems utterly remote

The solid, semi-detached suburban house typical of the thirties still remains a popular choice for middle-class home owners.

147

One of the features of literary and intellectual life of the early twentieth century was the dominance of the Bloomsbury Group. It centred upon the novelist Virginia Woolf whose troubled life ended in suicide in 1941.

from the pit villages of Nottinghamshire. Joyce's *Portrait of the Artist as a Young Man* reveals the joys and tensions of life in Ireland, which was strongly influenced by family and the Catholic Church. The weight of Ireland burdened Joyce, and his adult life was spent away from his country, though his novels are always dominated by his homeland. If sexual liberation was championed in literature, so too was social justice. George Orwell condemned the conditions of life of people in mining towns, industrial centres and the corners of the big cities. Like other English and American writers, of whom the most famous was Ernest Hemingway, he went to Spain to fight Fascism. Developments in Europe appeared to him to show exactly where right and wrong lay.

Virginia Woolf was at the centre of a group of writers called the Bloomsbury Group. Their aims were diverse. What brought them together was the association of intellect and generally stylish surroundings. They were unashamedly highbrow. Virginia Woolf's was probably the last of London's literary salons. Their elitism marked the growing separation of writers (particularly poets) from society.

The Second World War and Reconstruction

The 1930s witnessed a considerable deterioration in the international scene, as Japan, Italy and Germany extended their territories by force. The League of Nations, the agency set up to promote harmony between countries at the end of the Great War, had little success in dealing with aggressors; the democracies, France and Britain, took modest action late; while the United States retreated into isolation and did not wish to become involved in world affairs at all.

The developments which caused mounting alarm in Britain and which pushed Britain into increased activity was the expansion of Hitler's Germany in 1938. Britain's Prime Minister, Neville Chamberlain, reluctantly accepted the *Anschluss* (union between Germany and Austria) in March 1938, when German troops marched into Austria and opposition to Nazism there was suppressed. Hitler called on the powerful argument that he was only uniting two Germanic peoples. He used the same argument to justify his demand for Germany to occupy Czech Sudetenland. It was true that this area had a predominantly German population, but it also contained Czechoslovakia's main industrial centres and lines of defence, and its loss would jeopardise Czech security and independence.

Chamberlain had three meetings with Hitler over Czechoslovakia. At the first, held in Germany on 15 September 1938, Chamberlain conceded to Hitler's demand to take the Sudetenland. But at the second meeting, on 22 and 23 September, Chamberlain rejected Hitler's proposal. There was a general feeling that there would be war; Chamberlain met Hitler in Munich again on 30 September. Critics of Chamberlain see 'Munich' as a betrayal, because Chamberlain conceded to Hitler's demands on Czechoslovakia and thereby ended the life of the Czech nation. Chamberlain's critics believe that if he had remained firm, Hitler would have had to give way, as at that time he did not have enough support from the German military to undertake war against Britain and France. A strong line from Britain, it has been argued, would have preserved Czech and Polish independence and enabled their armies and resources (Czechoslovakia had a fine army and large munitions works) to be used against Germany – which, under Hitler's leadership, was bound to go to war sooner or later.

This argument seems sound, but Chamberlain was not a natural belligerent. Chamberlain detested Hitler, but he believed at that time that he could be placated. The British Prime Minister had a distinguished domestic record, but in foreign affairs he was unskilled. If Britain had had a different premier – Churchill or perhaps Baldwin – the course of events might have been different. However, when Hitler occupied the whole of Czechoslovakia, in defiance of the Munich agreement, Britain was put on a war footing. In March 1939 guarantees were given by Britain to Poland that Britain would

When the Prime Minister, Neville Chamberlain, returned from talks with Hitler in Munich in 1938 he believed that he had secured 'peace with honour'. Later his appeasement of Hitler's ever increasing demands was seen as wishful thinking doomed to failure.

come to her aid if attacked. Guarantees were extended in April to Romania and Greece. On 23 August Hitler scored a great diplomatic coup with the signing of a non-aggression pact between Germany and the Soviet Union. Hitler felt confident that Britain and France would not take action when he invaded Poland on 1 September. In this he was wrong. Britain and France declared war on Germany, and the British dominions (with the exception of Ireland) followed Britain with their declarations of war.

The Battle of Britain in 1940 was one of the most heroic actions of the Second World War. RAF spitfires like these confronted and defeated German fighters over the Channel.

Germany occupied large parts of Europe with lightning speed and came to an arrangement with the Soviet Union over the partition of Poland. Britain expected an invasion at any moment and massive air strikes, but this did not happen; these first few months of the war have been called Britain's 'Phoney War'. Disillusion with Chamberlain, who was identified with appeasement, was widespread, and in May 1940 he resigned as Prime Minister and was replaced by Winston Churchill. Churchill had had a long career in politics, but he had been regarded with some suspicion by established politicians. He was not willing to compromise on imperial issues (particularly the granting of self-government to India), and he had a marked anti-Labour image. But Churchill's lack of compromise was ideal for a war leader. He believed implicitly that Hitler was evil and had to be defeated. (Churchill's avowed intention to preserve the power of the British Empire was outdated, but he was not to play a part in shaping policy after the war had been won.)

The Phoney War was decisively over by May 1940, when Norway was taken; the fall of Belgium and Holland followed, and finally there was the defeat of France in June. A British army stationed in northern France had to be evacuated quickly. This gave rise to one of the most heroic exercises of the war: a flotilla of small ships, ranging from fishing boats to pleasure steamers, took the troops from Dunkirk to England (the navy could not spare the ships but provided defence). The

Winston Churchill, the leader of the war-time Coalition government, with his familiar cigar and walking stick, joins the people to inspect the devastation following an air raid. Churchill's determination never to surrender inspired and fortified the British at a perilous time in their history.

massive bombardment of Britain, so long feared, began, in preparation for a German invasion, called 'Operation Sea-Lion' by Hitler. But the invasion was not mounted. The German airforce could not gain air superiority. The British airforce's confrontation with German fighters over the Channel, called the Battle of Britain, was another heroic victory. The occasion prompted one of Churchill's most ringing speeches, when he said in praise of the Fighter Command: 'Never in the field of human conflict was so much owed by so many to so few.'

When Germany attacked the Soviet Union in 1941, and Germany's ally Japan attacked the United States, the two greatest military powers were ranged against Germany on Britain's side. It then became fairly certain that the human and material resources of the United States and the Soviet Union would ultimately overwhelm Germany and her Axis partners.

The German invasion of Russia was a complete disaster.

The German armies lost 250,000 men and had to retreat westward, with the Russian armies in pursuit. By 1943 North Africa was in the hands of the Allies (the British general was Montgomery), and in July 1943 the Allies – American, British and Commonwealth troops – landed in Sicily. Italy, having surrendered to the Allies, was slowly occupied, and in June 1944 there was the Allied invasion of northern France. The war ended on 8 May 1945, and Japan surrendered on 14 August after America had dropped atomic bombs on Hiroshima and Nagasaki. By 1945 about 303,000 British men and women in the armed services and about 60,000 civilians had been killed (many fewer than in the First World War), but the country was drained financially, and many cities had been devastated by German airforce bombardment, known as the Blitz.

Britain experienced a remarkable unity in the Second World War. There was barely any opposition to the war, and conscientious objectors were treated humanely. Even the leader of British Fascism, Sir Oswald Mosley, was released from prison in 1943. The war caused the mobilisation of most of the working population for military service or work in industry. There was severe rationing of food and clothes for everyone, and even the royal family insisted on the presentation of ration books at royal receptions. Indeed, the monarchy shared the spirit of resistance and common suffering. The royal family stayed in the capital, despite the bombing, wore uniform and did what it could to boost morale. Many women and children were evacuated from the cities; the arrival in country towns and villages of city children in particular, who were often thin and poorly dressed, did much to highlight the harsh conditions prevailing in Britain's cities (just as in the First World War mass medical examination of recruits showed how many among Britain's industrial work force were underfed or suffering from disease). There was a general desire that a better society should emerge after the war. The unions insisted on action even during the course of the war, and the government recognised the effect that social legislation would have on the morale of the people. In December 1942 Sir William Beveridge, a Liberal, produced a report which argued for a comprehensive system of social benefits and state medicine for everyone – proposals which were to form the basis of the welfare state. In 1944 the Minister of Education, a Conservative, R. A. Butler, saw the passage of the Act which bears his name, which provided for the reorganisation of secondary education and the raising of the school leaving age at the end of the war.

Churchill was partly responsible for his own electoral defeat after the war. He portrayed Labour as a party with totalitarian leanings and claimed that socialism would lead to a totalitarian state. Labour, on the other hand, mounted an impressive campaign, paying tribute to Churchill's war leadership but detailing the changes Labour would make in their reconstruction programme. Whereas after the First World War there had been a desire to return to the normality of pre-war days, there was no such desire to return to the thirties in 1945. The British people were ready to experiment. In the election in July (many thousands of soldiers voted abroad) Labour won a convincing victory, taking 47.6 per cent of the poll and 393 seats. It was the first socialist government with a majority in Britain's history. The new Prime Minister was Clement Attlee, a quietly competent figure and a member of the professional classes, who had been educated at a leading public school, Haileybury.

The legislation his government passed in the economic field appears radical because it saw the nationalisation of about 20 per cent of the British economy. But in fact most of the enterprises that were nationalised had never been in private hands or were in such a state of collapse (like the railways) that nationalisation was the only way of redeeming them. A fierce struggle did ensue, however, over the nationalisation of iron and steel and road haulage. The Conservatives pledged themselves to denationalise this part of the economy when they were returned to power, and these industries duly returned to private enterprise in 1955. The debate over the steel industry continued until 1967, when it was nationalised by the second government of Harold Wilson (by this time it was in need of massive investment and restructuring).

Wartime austerity continued into peacetime, partly because recovery after the war would take time and partly because the government deliberately retained controls on finance and imports to repress consumer appetites at home. The government wanted to boost exports at the expense of home consumption. Britain was considerably helped in this, as many of Britain's industrial rivals had been devastated by the war; American industries were busy supplying home demand, and her exports of cars, for example, actually declined. The government pumped enormous sums into old industries like the coal industry, textiles and railways. Wartime help for agriculture also continued. But the growth sector of the British economy was still the 'new' industries, which continued to cause problems of regional poverty, as it had before 1939.

The lead which British industries had gained could only be maintained in the post-war period by reorganisation and the introduction of innovation. There is an argument that the total destruction of industry is a blessing because it enables the building of a new industrial structure. This happens if capital is available, and Marshall Aid from America gave vast sums to Europe and Japan. Britain received £2,400 million from America; other finance from the United States was in the form of loans, which were paid back. American money, on the other hand, provided a new industrial base for Germany, on which German ingenuity built and produced the economy which, by the fifties, was taking the lead in Europe.

Britain's position as a banking and finance centre was unchanged in the post-war period. This was lucrative for Britain and gave employment, but the need to maintain a high pound was constantly put forward by financiers (and the Treasury), while exporters frequently sought a lower pound.

Structures in the union movement remained unaltered. There were several big unions and many smaller ones, and there was a tendency for their activities to overlap. Ironically, British trade unionists helped to establish the rational system of trade unions in Germany, while at home plans for restructuring the unions and preparing a new and permanent method of working out wage increases and so forth were shelved. Class structures also remained unchanged, despite the brief comradeship of the war. The Butler Education Act (1944) provided universal secondary education to the age of fifteen, but its provision for technical schools was not implemented. The private sector of education also remained weak in technical and scientific education.

Thus the problems of the British economy were deep-seated after the Second World War. For a second time national resources had been prodigiously depleted by war. The old industries were in decline; the reconstruction programme had limited finance; and there were deficiencies in the school and union system.

Despite austerity, the government followed the lines of the Beveridge Report and set up the Health Service. The National Health Act of 1946 set out to provide free medical treatment and medicine. This was popular, humane and necessary. The National Insurance Act of 1946 provided everyone with sickness and unemployment benefits and retirement pensions. The Conservative Party accepted the principle of the welfare state and argued only over the details of its application. A theme of post-war politics was the question of which of the two big parties could run the Health Service best.

The post-war period saw significant developments in Britain's relations abroad. The independence of India and Pakistan in 1947 (they became republics within the Commonwealth in 1950 and 1956) marked the end of the British Empire. India had been Britain's largest and richest possession, and many British territories around the world were maintained to guard the routes to India. In Europe the Council of Europe was founded in 1949, and the European Coal and Steel Community was established in 1951; these institutions were to develop into the European Economic Community (EEC). Neither the Conservatives nor the socialists showed any interest in this manifestation of European unity, and so Britain did not become part of European movement at the beginning. Britain was still the third power in the world and looked upon Europe as only one area of interest. But clearly Britain was the junior partner in the Western Alliance. It was the United States that took the initiative and stood against Soviet threats to Berlin, organising the Berlin airlift in 1948 and 1949. It was the United States that was the prime mover in the setting up of the North Atlantic Treaty Organisation (NATO), the alliance of non-communist Western states. America and the Soviet Union both emerged from their isolation after the war and took the lead in foreign affairs which their size, wealth and military strength demanded.

The Fifties

The government was obliged by law to hold an election by July 1950, but it chose to go to the country in February. Labour lost seats but still remained the government, with a slim majority (seventeen). Whereas during the war the British people had accepted controls as a necessity, in the post-war period government restrictions on business and finance were considered increasingly irksome. The economic situation was worsened in 1950 by the Labour government's agreement to give aid to the American war effort in Korea, where the United States had intervened to defeat communism. This increased defence spending (which was already high) put a further strain on the economy. In addition to the economic problems the government faced, there was friction within the government over its proposal to make some modest charges for items provided by the National Health Service (spectacles and false teeth) which had previously been free. It seemed to some left-wing Cabinet Ministers that the principle of a free health service was under threat.

In the election fought in the autumn of 1951 the Conservatives appeared vigorous and capable. They offered more freedom and opportunity, while at the same time they were careful to underline allegiance to the welfare state. The Conservatives won 321 seats against Labour's 295. At the age of seventy-six Winston Churchill returned as Prime

Minister. Sir Anthony Eden was marked out as his heir apparent, and R. A. Butler was Chancellor and prominent in the shaping of Conservative policy.

The management of the economy in the fifties was characterised by a lifting of controls wherever possible, though the government imposed restrictions on finance at periodic intervals (when there were exchange crises). Exports did well in the fifties; there was growing prosperity. But there was a weakness in export industries which domestic prosperity camouflaged. The unions' role was to demand more money for their members. Though union members were appointed to government committees and the like, they did not share in the pains and pleasures of directing industry. The foundation for a new relationship between government, unions and employers was not laid. In prosperous times there seemed to be no need; in the late sixties and seventies it would be regretted that industrial relations were not better in Britain. The fifties did not see any narrowing of the gap between the prosperous Midlands and the south, and the poorer north and west, with their old industries. This was reflected in politics; old industrial areas piled up huge majorities for Labour, but industrial areas in the south often had no fixed political allegiance.

When the Korean War ended in 1953 the level of defence expenditure was frozen, as was spending on the social services. Income tax was steadily reduced and, with the appearance of so many new consumer goods, a long boom in consumer spending began. This was helped by the general acceptance of buying on credit (usually by weekly instalments).

The government decided that too much money had been spent on social programmes (schools, etc.) and not enough on housing. It therefore encouraged local councils and private builders to aim for a target of 300,000 new houses a year. In 1953 the Minister of Housing, Harold Macmillan (a future Prime Minister) was able to announce that the target had been met. The house-building boom gave a colossal boost to the economy; it also pushed up property and land prices and saw the start of speculation in office building, which was particularly noticeable in London.

Churchill resigned in April 1955. Almost at once there was a general election, in which the new Conservative leader, Anthony Eden, increased the Conservative vote substantially and took 344 seats compared with Labour's 277. It was said that Eden's elegance and good looks had won him support from women electors. Certainly, the electorate saw no reason to change from the Conservatives when the economy was going well and Labour appeared to be divided on basic issues. Labour, too, changed leadership in November 1955. Hugh

Gaitskell, the new leader, had to contend with Labour's internal divisions over defence (the question of whether or not Britain should have nuclear weapons) and the Party's approach to the economy. He also had to deal with a question central to the Labour movement: whether the unions or the parliamentary Party should have ultimate control of the Labour movement. Gaitskell, who was considered right-wing by his socialist opponents, ultimately won the battle over Party control and policy, but divisions among the socialists helped the Conservatives to maintain their political supremacy until 1964.

In 1956 Anthony Eden's government was faced with the gravest crisis in foreign affairs since the end of the war. It began on 26 July, when the President of Egypt, the energetic and reform-minded Colonel Nasser, announced the nationalisation of the Suez Canal, which had been run by the Anglo-French Suez Canal Company since 1888 – an arrangement endorsed by the Egyptian government as recently as 1954. Nationalisation came in response to the West's refusal to provide loans for the building of the Aswan High Dam, a project Nasser considered vital for his country's future.

Opinion throughout the world and on both sides of the House of Commons was hostile to Nasser's move. In August 1956 a conference of twenty-two countries with an interest in the Suez Canal was held in London, but the conciliatory scheme offered to Egypt was rejected when Colonel Nasser was assured of Soviet backing. In response, Britain and France ordered the withdrawal of the Suez Canal Company's pilots, thereby hoping that the Canal would be unable to operate and that Nasser would have to come to terms. The United States did not endorse Britain and France's action, preferring instead the idea of putting pressure on Egypt through a Canal Users' association. Britain and France considered such an association ineffectual from the start. In October, after the Suez question had been referred to the United Nations, France's and Britain's new proposals (which were, in fact, similar to those of August) were vetoed by the Soviet Union, and in a mood of anger and determination France and Britain decided upon direct action.

In collusion with Britain and France, Israel attacked Egypt on 29 October. The next day Britain and France called on both sides to withdraw, and when Egypt rejected this ultimatum Britain bombed Egyptian airfields. On 5 November paratroops were dropped near Port Said, and the city was taken. Israel had meanwhile taken the Sinai Peninsula. Opposition to the action of Britain, France and Israel was swift and fierce.

At home the Labour Opposition condemned Anthony Eden and the government, and vast protest meetings were held in London. Even one or two Conservative Members expressed their opposition to the government's action. President Eisenhower conveyed his wrath to Eden on the phone, and the United States made it plain that she would not support Britain and France. On 2 November the General Assembly of the United Nations (UN) passed, by sixty-four votes to five, a resolution calling for an immediate cease-fire. Israel agreed at once, as she had achieved her military objectives. Reluctantly, Britain agreed to the resolution on 6 November, though France wanted to continue the operation. British and French troops eventually withdrew, and the Canal Zone was policed by UN forces.

Suez has been seen as a turning point in history, an occasion when it became clear that Britain could not act alone on the international stage (though it had been apparent since the war that Britain's status had changed). America called the tune in the West and the Soviet Union in the East. There was considerable bitterness in right-wing circles in Britain, about the American stance but this did not alter Britain's relations with the United States. In France, however, the idea grew up that Suez had failed because of the collapse of British and United States backing. This feeling fed the fires of Gaullism, and though Britain's relations were ostensibly excellent with France, in reality a current of annoyance was evident beneath the surface.

Whether from ill health alone or not, Eden resigned as Prime Minister in January 1957 and was succeeded by Harold Macmillan, who had Edwardian manners, charm and immense determination to succeed. His appearances on television (now an important factor in a politician's life) were convincing and often entertaining. Macmillan seemed to bring with him the optimism of his successful housing campaign. The financial pressures caused by Suez – a run on the pound and withdrawal of reserves from Britain – quickly eased. The economy was performing well; Macmillan decided to stimulate it further. In 1958 the new Chancellor of the Exchequer, Heathcote Amory, reduced the bank rate sharply and relaxed credit restrictions. In 1959 the standard rate of income tax was reduced. The effect on the economy was instantaneous. A great boom in consumer spending began, aided by hire purchase and encouraged by mass advertising. Many people bought household goods or cars which they had never owned before. A sentence (taken out of context) in one of Macmillan's speeches seemed to sum up the sentiment of the time: 'You have never had it so good.'

In October 1959 there was a general election. The Conservatives took over 49 per cent of the vote and increased their number of seats to 365; Labour dropped to 258 seats. It was not an easy election for Gaitskell to fight. It did Labour no good to revive charges against Eden and the Conservatives over Suez, as the issue had faded and the greatest fear of the West (that oil and other supplies might be cut off) had proved to be unfounded. New, larger tankers now went via the Cape.

Labour attacked the Rent Act passed by the Conservatives in 1957. This had removed all rent and tenure controls on privately rented flats and houses. It had put more property on the market, but it had also bred an unscrupulous type of property exploitation called Rachmanism (after Rachman, a notorious property dealer). The Rent Act caused some bitterness (Labour repealed it in 1964), but it cannot have lost the Conservatives much support. In fact, it had been widely welcomed by millions of small landlords with savings invested in property, who thought that the measure was designed to protect their interests. The Labour Party also raised the question of education in its election campaign more prominently than ever before. It attacked the system of secondary education set up by the Butler Act, whereby the results of an examination taken at the age of eleven (known as the Eleven Plus) determined which type of secondary school a child should attend. Those children who passed the examination went to grammar schools (the pass rate varied from county to county – the range was between 10 and 30 per cent); the rest went to secondary modern schools, in which the emphasis was on technical rather than intellectual accomplishment. Labour believed that such selection was harmful educationally and socially, and it advocated a single type of school for all children after the age of eleven – the comprehensive school. As each county has a large measure of control over educational matters, an Act designed to change the educational system cannot bring about immediate change (as Labour found out later). The battle over comprehensive education was a long and contentious one.

There was trouble throughout the fifties in Cyprus, as a Greek Cypriot force, EOKA, used terrorist tactics in pursuit of independence. Eventually, in 1959, independence was granted to the island (though a British military base remained) under the leadership of Archbishop Makarios. Colonial conflicts (like that in Cyprus) were disturbing to the public at home. A large body of opinion did not like the idea of retaining colonial possessions anyway. Those who believed that Britain's role demanded a presence abroad were not happy with the use of the army and the loss of life. Conscription for the army – generally called National Service – was not popular (there was a long tradition in Britain of reluctance to maintain large armies in peacetime). There was also a feeling among army leaders that conscription was not an efficient way of running an army. Training was long and costly, and it was not worthwhile to train short-term, and often reluctant, recruits. The army was also becoming more dependent on highly advanced technology, and careerist soldiers with specialist training were required. With all these considerations in mind, conscription was ended in 1957. It has not been brought back, though occasionally its restoration is demanded as a way of giving young men a sense of discipline, among other things. Its reinstatement would probably be unpopular with the electorate at large.

Britain's Empire was already well on the way to dissolution before the fifties. Imperialism was unpopular, and all the European countries with territories overseas were having to give way to independence movements. France, for example, had retreated from South-East Asia. In Africa Britain withdrew from the Sudan and granted independence to Ghana in 1957 and to Nigeria in 1960. Where there were few white settlers, as in West Africa, the problems of decolonisation were limited, but in East Africa, where there were large and established British communities, there was friction. In 1952 the Mau Mau revolt broke out in Kenya, and the British army had to be called in to restore order. Jomo Kenyatta, the future President of the country and a great figure in African nationalism, was put in detention. Peace was restored in Kenya for the time being, and in 1954 a scheme was worked out for the rest of East Africa which, it was hoped, would be permanent. A

The austerity of the war and immediate post-war years were effectively banished in the Festival of Britain in 1951. The Royal Festival Hall was the centrepiece in the festival and later formed the nucleus of the great arts complex on the South Bank of the river Thames.

federation of the Rhodesias and Nyasaland was set up, which was intended to combine the manpower of Nyasaland, the mineral resources of Northern Rhodesia and Southern Rhodesia's agricultural wealth. The Federation was put under the chairmanship of an energetic ex-railroad man, Sir Roy Welensky.

The emergence from austerity was marked by the Festival of Britain, which was held in London in 1951 (just one hundred years after the Great Exhibition). It gave some joy at the end of a depressing period. The Festival Hall, built for the occasion, is at the centre of the arts complex on the south bank of the Thames. This concert hall, dedicated to classical music, symbolised one element in the nation. The fifties was also the era of rock music, of Elvis Presley, greased hair and powerful motor cycles. There was a current of restlessness which reflected the feeling that things were changing but in an uncertain manner. Suez ended imperial adventure; Kenya and Cyprus were nasty experiences. In John Osborne's stage play *Look Back in Anger* the angry young man rejects the values of middle-class Britain. He does not suggest anything in their place. The most impressive public meetings were those held by the Campaign for Nuclear Disarmament, which were addressed by the philosopher Bertrand Russell. The atomic bomb was seen as a very real threat to life; Britain, it was felt, should show the world that the bomb was a danger and should ban it.

But without doubt the most popular occasion of the fifties was the crowning of the young Queen Elizabeth II in 1953. People admired her youth and her courage. They liked the idea of a new Elizabethan era, combining tradition and adventure. But it was more of an adventure in uncharted waters than anyone had imagined.

The fifties began with the memory of wartime austerity fresh in everyone's mind; the decade ended enveloped in a cosiness produced by mass consumerism and a booming economy. Of the many comforts and gadgets that entered British homes, by far the most important and the most eagerly awaited was the television. Queen Elizabeth's coronation was televised from start to finish and caused a rush to shops to buy sets. Upholders of standards were alarmed at the influence that television viewing (the Coronation excepted) might have on the population. America did not seem a healthy example. But the BBC Television Service, initiated in 1946, was under stoutly old-fashioned management. Announcers wore evening dress and melodious classical music accompanied the (many) intervals. Independent television companies started broadcasting in 1955; with their bigger funds from advertising (the

The teddy boys of the fifties had an immense influence on the fashions and mores of the young just as their successors – mods, rockers, skinheads and punks have had in later years.

161

government had a tax bonanza from this source) their output was much brasher, though they had to comply with rules about programming which ensured quotas of serious viewing.

9

Contemporary Britain: from 1960

Conservatives in the Early 1960s

Conservatism in the late fifties had been rather ebullient. It was not in the sixties. There was a continuing problem with the balance of payments, as the growing demands of consumers increased imports, which were not met by a sufficient rise in exports. In 1960 the bank rate was raised; restrictions were put on credit; and government spending was reduced. The government announced that it would not give increases to the people it employed and hoped, rather optimistically, that the private sector would follow suit. The economy did not respond to government efforts, and in 1961 Selwyn Lloyd, the Chancellor of the Exchequer, called for wages and salaries to remain static from July 1961 to March 1962. The government was only able to enforce its will in the public sector. It turned down pay claims from nurses and postman, low-paid groups with a record of public service, who won widespread sympathy and brought the pay policy into disrepute. Selwyn Lloyd's budget in 1962 put a tax on short-term gains which was aimed particularly at land speculators. This was a serious step away from Macmillan's *laissez-faire* approach to money-making in the late fifties.

Believing that a more carefully planned approach to the economy was required, the government set up both the National Economic Development Corporation (NEDC), which was to produce indicative plans for the economy after consulting various industries, and the National Incomes Commission, which was to investigate pay claims submitted to it. The TUC (representing the unions) did not like the government's plans at all and would not co-operate. Macmillan believed that his Cabinet needed a new (perhaps more youthful) image, and he sacked the Chancellor and six other members. This was drastic action – the newspapers referred to 'Mac the Knife' – but it did not seem to reassure the public. The government lost a safe seat (Orpington, in the London commuter belt of Kent) to the Liberals in a by-election, which was sensational and seemed to show that many disillusioned middle-class voters might switch to the Liberals.

The new Chancellor, Reginald Maudling, believed that the economy had to be reflated if higher growth rates were to be achieved (as NEDC wanted). Even if there were balance-of-payments deficits, it would be possible, it was argued, to pay off the debts when the economy was booming again. Economic experts anxiously pointed to the more rapid growth of other European economies, which their marked prosperity made apparent to the most casual observer. But by April 1964 reflation had accelerated too much, and the Chancellor brought in a series of taxes on consumer goods in order to reduce the public's spending power. The Conservative government's alternating economic restraint and relaxation prompted their critics to accuse them of running a 'stop–go' economy. Economic difficulties seriously undermined the government's standing with the electorate, which had had a decade of rising living standards and which naturally wanted affluence to continue.

Macmillan was a world figure and believed that he had a role to play in bringing together East and West in an attempt to reach agreement on the limiting of nuclear tests and the build-up of nuclear weapons. Macmillan's diplomacy had been excellent, but the resulting conference in London in May 1960 was a failure, Khrushchev and Eisenhower parted on bad terms. In 1960 Macmillan spoke well at the United Nations, but Britain's apparent leadership of the Western Allies vanished when John Kennedy was elected President of the United States in 1960 and assumed complete control of Western diplomacy. Macmillan and Kennedy were great friends, but that did not stop the President from settling the Cuban crisis in 1962 without any reference to Britain.

The fact of Britain's decline in world importance was illustrated by Suez and again by Cuba. Britain did not have the resources to keep up with the nuclear race in which the United States and the Soviet Union were the contenders. Atlee's government had decided to build the atom bomb, but this comparatively cheap weapon was superseded in the late 1950s by the development of inter-continental ballistic missiles. Britain tried to develop her own rocket, *Blue Streak*, but it had to be abandoned in 1960. At first Britain tried to buy the *Skybolt* rocket from America, but in 1962 the United States ceased production. Britain then purchased American *Polaris* submarines, from which nuclear rockets could be fired (Britain currently has four nuclear submarines, each equipped with sixteen *Polaris* missiles). Clearly the vague idea Britain had of maintaining an independent nuclear armoury as a deterrent had been abandoned by Macmillan's day. Her nuclear weapons could only be used in conjunction with those of the United States.

A change in Britain's world position, and a belief that it was necessary to be associated with large economic units in a competitive world, prompted Macmillan's government to announce in July 1961 that Britain was applying to join the European Economic Community, or Common Market. Edward Heath (a future Prime Minister), who had shown toughness and ability as Chief Whip (organiser of the Conservative Party in Parliament) at the time of Suez, was picked out to lead the British team of negotiators. Britain had a special case to put to the EEC. Arrangements had to be made for Britain's traditional trading patterns within the Commonwealth to be phased out gently. Additionally, Britain's farmers had to be integrated with European producers. British farmers received subsidies, and peasant farmers in Europe were afraid of competition from Britain's technologically advanced farming methods. But although provisional agreement had been reached over British entry by June 1962, General de Gaulle, the French President, made clear his opposition to the British application at a Press conference, with the result that negotiations were broken off on 29 January 1963. France did not like the special provisions associated with Britain's proposed entry, and West Germany, the strongest country in the EEC and well disposed to Britain's entry, was not prepared to risk endangering her 'understanding' with France by insisting on British admittance (this pattern was to be repeated).

The Commonwealth was changing fast. Those countries in

A post-war British invention of considerable potential was the hovercraft. The first was the SRN–1 built by Sir Christopher Cockerell in 1959.

165

Africa which did not have independence wanted it rapidly. Macmillan recognised this mood, and while on a visit to South Africa in 1960 he said in a speech, 'The wind of change is blowing through the Continent,' which was interpreted to mean that Britain would not resist a move towards independence by African territories. The speech disappointed right-wing Conservatives, who had hoped that Macmillan would revitalise and not abandon the Empire. Uganda, Kenya and Tanganyika (Tanzania of today) achieved independence in 1962, 1963 and 1964 respectively. The federation of the Rhodesias and Nyasaland, which had never really worked, broke up in 1964. Nyasaland became the new state of Malawi, and Northern Rhodesia became Zambia. Southern Rhodesia, with its large white population, remained a colony, though with a considerable measure of self government. The new constitution in 1961 gave black people representation in the Rhodesian Parliament for the first time, and the British government agreed that the constitution could not be altered without the consent of the Rhodesian government and legislature. Botswana and Lesotho became independent in 1966 and Swaziland in 1968. In 1960 South Africa decided in a plebiscite (of white voters, a majority of whom were Boers) to become a republic, and in 1961 South Africa left the Commonwealth. Britain's relations with South Africa were going to be a subject of great debate. All political parties in Britain were distressed by *apartheid* (the policy of segregating blacks and whites), but there was a wide range of opinion among politicians about what Britain's relations with South Africa should be. Some advocated a complete break with South Africa; some proposed that normal relations with the country should be maintained because South Africa was a big importer of British goods, and she was also strategically important to the West.

Between 1955 and 1960 233,200 Commonwealth immigrants came to Britain. They were predominantly West Indian and Pakistani, and they came in response to job opportunities created by the growing economy. Against a background of economic recession and growing concern that so many people of different races and cultures could not be integrated satisfactorily at such speed, a law was enacted in 1961 which severely restricted the entry of immigrants. A further 218,000 immigrants came into Britain before the Act came into force in June 1962. The Commonwealth resented the Immigration Act, and the Labour Party opposed it fiercely. (Labour, however, tightened this legislation in 1968.)

In the early sixties Britain was shaken by a series of trials which illustrated the alarming degree to which the Russians had been able to penetrate British defence and security. In the summer of 1963 the newspapers suggested that the Minister of War, John Profumo, had been keeping the company of Christine Keeler, a well-known figure in Soho, one of London's less respectable districts. When questioned in the Commons about this relationship, Profumo denied that there had been any impropriety. It was later proved that this was not true, and Profumo resigned from office. The government was considerably embarrassed, as Profumo's association with the underworld raised the question of whether national security had been put at risk. A Royal Commission under Lord Denning was appointed to investigate the Profumo scandal, but it found that Profumo had not leaked any official information. Nevertheless, the image of the Conservative government had been damaged, and the fact that the Prime Minister knew nothing about the affair suggested that he did not know his Cabinet very well.

Plagued by problems and criticism, Harold Macmillan became ill in the autumn of 1963 and had to resign the premiership. He refused to back the deputy leader, R. A. Butler, as leader, and after a complicated contest Lord Home, an elder statesman of the Conservative Party, became leader and Prime Minister. Lord Home, with his highly aristocratic Scottish pedigree and his seat in the House of Lords, did not seem the best choice at a time when the Opposition was accusing the Conservatives of being out of touch with the British people. But Home had steely determination and the respect of his colleagues. Taking advantage of a change in the law in 1960, Lord Home renounced his title and became Sir Alec Douglas-Home. He then fought a by-election and became a Member of the House of Commons. Almost from the beginning of Home's premiership there was speculation about the date of the next general election. It eventually came in the autumn of 1964, after a summer in which opinion polls showed that the Conservatives were rallying under Home's leadership and were reducing the popularity which the Labour Party had enjoyed. The Labour Party emerged after the election with a small majority. It polled 44.1 per cent of all votes cast and had 317 seats. The Liberals increased their share of the poll to 11.2 per cent but won only nine seats. A Liberal revival did not materialise; those voters who had voted Liberal returned in the main to their traditional party allegiances. The Liberal Party complained – and they have continued to do so – of an electoral system which gives seats to the candidate who receives most votes *in each constituency* and fails to take account of the *national* vote of the party. The Liberals advocate proportional representation (a system which would allocate seats in Parliament according to the total number of votes cast for each party), but as long as one or other of the two main parties is, under the present system, bound to form the government, there seems no likelihood that the system will change. Proportional representation would, in all probability, see no one party with a clear majority in the Commons. This would necessitate government by coalition, which could be successful but might lead to political instability.

Harold Macmillan was obviously not at ease in the sixties. The gravity of the economic situation forced on him a change in style. His fine wit was kept on a tight rein, and he adopted an impassive seriousness when dealing with questioners and critics. He often seemed lugubrious rather than inspiring. Macmillan's style, his appearance and especially the delivery of his words became the subject of a growing satire industry. A Saturday night television programme *That was the Week that Was* lampooned the Conservative administration and helped to foster the belief, true or not, that Conservatism was remote from the society that was changing around it. Macmillan had enjoyed the prosperity associated with his premiership, not merely for the obvious reason, but because he believed in prosperity. He had represented a depressed working-class constituency in the 1930s, and he wanted a stimulated economy and vital people in contrast to those grey days. His concept of Britain was of a property-owning democracy in which everyone owned his own home and benefited from the security that was a consequence of that.

Macmillan himself was many things at once. He was a classical scholar, a country gentleman, a shrewd businessman (Macmillan's is a very businesslike publishing house) and a diplomat. But in the next general election, held in 1964, Britain voted for a new style of leadership.

The Wilson Government, 1964–1970

Harold Wilson, who had become leader of the Labour Party after Gaitskell's death in 1963, was a strong and decisive leader. He produced almost instant unity in the Labour Party. Despite the government's small majority of five (which fell to three after a by-election defeat in January 1965), Wilson determined to govern with confidence. Labour was faced with a balance-of-payments deficit of £800 million; British industry was visibly falling behind its foreign competitors; and Britain had a bad strike record. Wilson believed there had to be consistent direction of the economy through planning, that declining industries should be restructured and that technology must be stimulated.

Consequently, the government announced its intention to produce a national plan, which would set out the probable development of the economy until the end of the decade. With its aid, government and employers would be able to detect general trends and plan accordingly. A Ministry of Technology was created, directed by Frank Cousins, a well-known trade-union leader on the left of the Labour movement. Overall command of the government's economic strategy was given to George Brown, who had contested the Labour leadership against Wilson in 1963. He became head of the Department of Economic Affairs.

This machinery of planning would not, it was thought, be any good unless rises in prices and incomes were also successfully regulated. In March 1965 the Prices and Incomes Board (PIB) was set up, headed by Aubrey Jones, a chairman deliberately chosen from outside the ranks of the Labour movement; he had been a Conservative Cabinet Minister and was prominent in the City. The TUC endorsed the Board's view that wages should not rise by more than 3 or $3\frac{1}{2}$ per cent, and the Board met with some success in restraining rises. But by the summer of 1965 it was clear that prices and incomes were running well ahead of productivity. The government decided, therefore, to introduce a Prices and Incomes Bill, which would give the PIB power to delay pay or price increases for up to three months while applications were referred to the Board for investigation and report. The Bill never became law, as the government decided to call a general election in March 1966. The government asked for a mandate to continue the work it had started; it received this and gained forty-seven extra seats in the Commons.

In July 1966 the government reintroduced its Prices and Incomes Bill, but this time asked for power to freeze wages and prices for six months and to subject them to severe restraint for a further six months. Fines of up to £500 could be imposed on employers who paid wage increases without the PIB's permission and on trade unions who took action to force employers to pay increases. The employers did not like the idea of penalties for increases in wages which they were obliged to give because of pressure from workers (not necessarily the trade unions). The TUC reluctantly agreed to the measures, but the left protested vigorously, and Frank Cousins resigned from the Ministry of Technology. Public disenchantment with the freeze (July–December 1966) and severe restraint (December 1966–June 1967) increased, as it seemed that wages were being controlled more effectively than prices.

While restraints were being imposed on prices and incomes, the other part of the government's policy, the direct stimulation of industry, continued. The Department of Economic Affairs came to an end; many socialists alleged that this was because of the hostility of the Treasury, which did not wish to see the formation of a rival body. The Ministry of Technology did co-ordinate plans for the revitalisation of industry and met with some success. The most important agency created by the government to stimulate industry was the Industrial Reorganisation Corporation (IRC), which put money into ailing industries and encouraged the merger of companies to make more effective units. The most famous IRC action was the merging of Leyland Motors with the British Motor Corporation in 1968 to make British Leyland. In June 1967 the government ended its freeze on dividends as an encouragement to would-be investors in industry, but simultaneously (June 1967–December 1967) it imposed further restraint on wages.

The government met with considerable success, though the frustration of the public with measures aimed at curbing its spending was considerable. However, two strikes, by seamen in 1966 and by dockers in 1967, had a crippling effect on the economy. There was a severe balance-of-payments crisis and overseas investors lost confidence in Britain. With reluctance, the Wilson government devalued the pound by 14.75 per cent in 1967, hoping that this would help exports, relieve the balance-of-payments crisis and restore confidence. Devaluation caused widespread public anger, not merely because of the resulting price rises, but also because the government had emphasised at the election in 1966 that it would not devalue the pound. Harold Wilson was bitterly attacked in the Press, and a period of extremely bad relations between Downing Street and Fleet Street began.

At the end of restraint in December 1967 it was impossible to keep wage increases at $3\frac{1}{2}$ per cent, and in the following year they rose by 8 per cent. The TUC made clear its hostility to the prices and incomes policy, and thereafter there was little the PIB could do to regulate the economy. The government considered, and the Press believed most earnestly, that much damage to the economy was caused by unofficial 'wildcat' strikes. The government therefore proposed legislation to invoke tough sanctions against this type of strike. The TUC, believing that legislation would not solve the problem of industrial action (which they thought was exaggerated by observers anyway), refused to endorse the measure to control strikes. The government dropped the idea (which was to be taken up by the Conservatives again in 1970).

There was economic recovery under the Wilson government, and the balance of payments showed a surplus. But progress seemed slow to people who were burdened by restraint on incomes and rising prices (the inflation rate was 7 per cent). In the general election which Wilson called in June 1970 the economy – and particularly the high price of goods in the shops – was the central issue (it was, in fact, called the 'Shopping Basket' election).

The Wilson government was faced with other questions of great importance. The settlement of Rhodesia in 1961 was not permanent. The white Rhodesians, fearful that the British government would grant independence and majority rule, issued their Unilateral Declaration of Independence (UDI) on 11 November 1965. Even if the Wilson government had wished to recognise the new arrangement in Rhodesia, the hostility in Africa to British endorsement of permanent white minority rule would have been intense. The three major parties condemned UDI (though the Southern Rhodesians were supported by a number of Conservative Members of Parliament and Tory lords, in particular Lord Salisbury). The government imposed economic sanctions on Rhodesia, including an oil blockade.

While the 'wind of change' had brought independence under black rule throughout most of Africa, the whites entrenched their position in the south. Ian Smith attempted to perpetuate white rule in Rhodesia by making a unilateral declaration of independence (UDI) in 1965 and for some years maintained his position despite international sanctions and British efforts at diplomatic solutions.

The Rhodesians were led by Ian Smith, a tough (some would say obstinate) man – he had been a fighter pilot in the Royal Air Force in the Second World War – who would not give way to British and world pressures. In November 1966 Smith met the British Prime Minister on board HMS *Tiger*, off Gibraltar. Though the two leaders agreed on a new draft constitution, they could not agree on how the Rhodesian government could 'return to legality'. The United Nations then imposed sanctions on Rhodesia. In June 1967 Lord Alport went to Rhodesia to try to arrange fresh talks – which, when they eventually took place in October 1968, ended in deadlock. In June 1969 the white voters of Rhodesia overwhelmingly endorsed a new constitution proposed by Ian Smith, whereby Rhodesia became a republic.

In Britain the general question of the integration of coloured immigrants was causing concern by the late sixties. To stop discrimination on grounds of race and religion in questions of housing, employment and the use of public places, the first and second Race Relations Acts were passed in 1965 and 1968. A Race Relations Board was set up to supervise the working of the Acts. Important as this legislation was, social acceptance of the 'new Britons' would only come with time.

There were powerful spokesmen who warned Britain of the imminent dangers it faced with a racially 'divided' society. The most prominent figure to speak along these lines was

Tensions between white and black have from time to time caused problems in Britain's inner cities since the post-war influx of Commonwealth citizens settling in Britain. However, this scene at the annual Notting Hill Carnival shows the friendly relations that can prevail between the police and citizens of whatever colour.

Enoch Powell, a former Conservative Minister of Health and a member of Edward Heath's Shadow Cabinet. In 1968 he made a powerful speech, laced with emotive imagery, which put forward the argument that by the end of the century Britain would face the same problems over race as the United States. Heath disassociated himself from the speech and sacked Powell from the Shadow Cabinet. But Powell throughout the country received widespread support, which cut across party lines. The strength of Powell's support can be judged from the general election in February 1974, when he advised people to vote against the Heath government, and the Conservatives lost a number of west Midland seats. Mr Powell is an eloquent and factual debater, not a street orator (he was once a professor of Classics), and his critics have found him formidable in argument. Inevitably, there was a resurgence of support for extremist parties with a racial platform. Fascism, anti-Jewish in the thirties, became anti-coloured in the sixties. However, the National Front Party has never had electoral success.

Since the division of Ireland in 1920 many Catholics in the north (a part of the United Kingdom) had been dissatisfied with their status and economic condition. In the late 1960s some Catholics began civil rights protests and marches. On 5 October 1968 there was a bloody confrontation between protesters and police in Londonderry (Catholics called the city 'Derry'). Disturbances spread throughout the province, and the Northern Ireland Cabinet (Northern Ireland administered its own internal affairs) was obliged to ask the Westminster government to send troops to restore order. The Wilson government was disquieted by the injustices of Ulster society; it dispatched the army, and it also imposed a wide-ranging reform programme. This included the ending of discrimination against Catholics, changes in the electoral system, the restructuring of the police force and the establishment of machinery for the investigation of citizen's complaints.

But this programme did not avert the rapid spread of violence. British troops, which had at first been welcomed by both Protestants and Catholics, were soon regarded by many as enemies. The Irish Republican Army (IRA), which for many years had lain dormant, sprang to life. The official IRA was rapidly overtaken by the newly established Provisional IRA, which was prepared to use extreme and violent means to attain its ends. These were never specific but included the withdrawal of British troops and the unification of Northern Ireland with Eire in the south. The Labour government clearly could not hope to find solutions to such deep-seated problems, though there was fortunately agreement between the main political parties at Westminster on the question of Ireland and a growing understanding between the British and Eire governments.

The question of the EEC arose again at this time. Harold Wilson was convinced that membership would be good for Britain on the right terms. Wilson described his conversion to Europe (he had not been in favour of the Macmillan initiative) as his 'historic decision'. But Britain's application to join the EEC in May 1965 was finally rejected in 1968 by General de Gaulle, who thought that, without radical transformation,

173

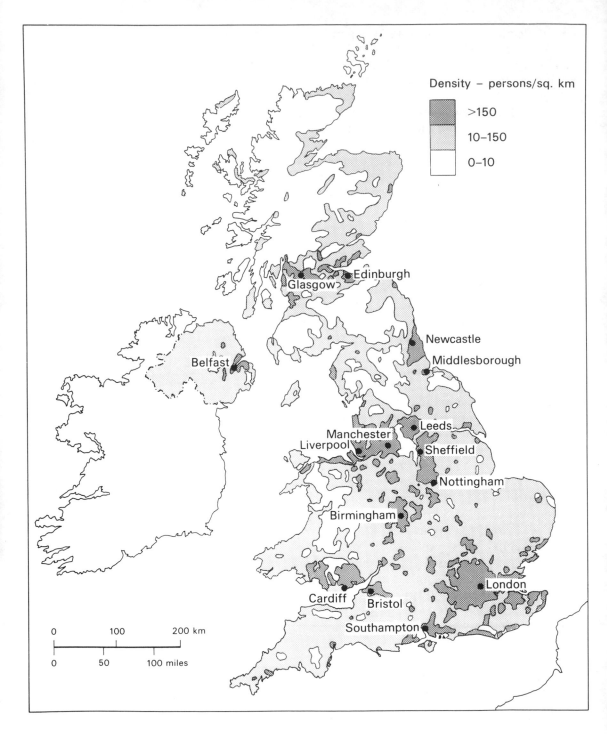

The population density in 1971

Britain was not ready to join. This rejection pleased certain members of Mr Wilson's own party but few others. The left opposed membership of what it considered to be an ostentatiously capitalist club. Ironically, the extreme left was joined in its opposition to EEC membership by the right of the Conservative Party, which disliked the prospect of any threat to Britain's sovereignty.

It was confidently predicted by the opinion polls that the Wilson government would win the general election called for June 1970. However, there is doubtless some truth in the view that Harold Wilson had built up a reputation for smugness, even arrogance, which did him no good on polling day. Certainly, there was strong hostility to him in the Press. The electorate proved the opinion polls wrong: the new leader of the Conservative Party, Edward Heath, who succeeded Sir Alec Douglas-Home in 1965 (Home was generally considered an interim leader), led the Conservatives to victory. He believed the economy needed rapid stimulation, but the Conservative campaign was remembered particularly for the Party's claim that under a new government 'prices would be cut at a stroke'.

The Heath Government, 1970–1974

Edward Heath appeared to his colleagues to be a man of action, a man who would tackle the problems of government vigorously and would not shirk difficult tasks. As Heath saw it, the economy had to be stimulated quickly to achieve a higher growth rate. A booming economy would create jobs for the 500,000 people who were out of work. Together with this reflationary policy, the Heath government believed that a legal framework had to be introduced into industrial relations. Though at first the government's desire to expand the economy was uncontroversial, the idea of attempting to legislate for harmonious industrial relations was bitterly criticised from the start.

Labour's Prices and Incomes Board was abolished, and taxes were reduced in successive budgets. In 1972 measures were passed to allow expenditure on plant and machinery in industry to be written off against profits for tax purposes. There were government grants to assist regional development, and the government gave selective aids to industry and took a stake in assisted companies. The economy took off. In 1971 there was a record surplus of earnings over expenditure abroad. The stock market soared and property prices climbed dramatically. At the same time there was a rapid increase in inflation,

Four British Prime Ministers off duty.

(far left, top) Harold Macmillan, Conservative Prime Minister 1957–63, had a deceptively old-world image. His nickname, 'Supermac' was a caustic reference to his talents and shrewdness.

(far left, bottom) Edward Heath, Conservative Premier 1970–74, has always been a passionate European. He has written books about his two pastimes, music and sailing. Heath is seen here as orchestral conductor.

(centre left) Harold Wilson headed four Labour Governments between 1964–70 and 1974–76. He is a keen golfer and enjoys sailing. He has spent much time writing since resigning office.

(left) Sir Alec Douglas-Home was Conservative Prime Minister 1963–64. A member of the Scottish aristocracy, he pursues the country sports of Scotland. Outside his country he was a respected international statesman.

which was not nearly matched by a growth in productivity. The government decided, at the end of 1972, to abandon its policy of bargaining freedom and changed to a policy of strict supervision of prices and incomes, which lasted until the end of the Heath administration in 1974. The unions argued that wage increases were not responsible for inflation; the culprit was government policy. They strenuously opposed pay restraint, together with the government's legislation on industrial relations.

The government's Industrial Relations Act of 1972 made written collective agreements enforceable at law. It required the registration of unions with an Industrial Relations Board; failure to register meant that financial penalties would be imposed on the union concerned. The Act set up the Industrial Relations Court, which had the power to impose a sixty-day cooling-off period in respect of any proposed strike or lock-out if the Court were satisfied that such action would cause grave injury to the national economy. This was intended to prevent sudden strikes and to allow time for reasoned discussion. If there were any doubt about whether workers wanted a strike, a secret ballot of union members was to take place.

The trade union movement bitterly resented the entire Act. They believed that their freedoms were being curtailed without precedent or consultation, while the owners of capital remained free to do what they wanted. There was, nonetheless, strong public backing for what seemed to be an attempt to impose order on a disordered field. Other countries, it was argued, had similar legislation, so British unions should not become emotional about the subject. The unions' united opposition to the Act, and consequently the resistance of half the work force of the country, was remarkable. A number of unions refused to register and paid fines throughout the period of the Heath government. Strike ballots, when held, confirmed union members' desire to follow their leaders' advice to strike. The whole atmosphere of labour relations was further inflamed by the imprisonment of two building workers for picketing violently.

Against this background of industrial tension, it does not seem surprising that the government did not obtain from the unions voluntary agreement to restrictions on wage claims. Therefore, in November 1972, the government brought in a compulsory ninety-day standstill on prices, pay and dividends. At the end of this period, called Phase One, the government announced the continuation of its counter-inflationary policy. Wage increases were limited to £1 a week plus 4 per cent of the current pay bill or £250 per annum per head – whichever was the lower figure. A board was set up to supervise wage increases, while a Price Commission had the task of controlling price increases. In October 1973 the government relaxed its guidelines in what was called Phase Three, when higher wages were allowed. It also proposed a £10 bonus for old-age pensioners at Christmas and a lowering of mortgage rates from 11 to 8.5 per cent for first-time home buyers.

The government's counter-inflationary policy did not work. The period of economic *laissez-faire* had produced massive inflation (30 per cent at its highest) and highly priced capital which forced many middle suppliers out of business. Mr Heath spoke of 'the unacceptable face of capitalism' when referring to the sharp practice of some financiers who had taken advantage of the boom and had behaved unscrupulously. The economy could not alter direction so quickly after such heady activity.

Such hope as the government had of making its policies work was dashed by a sudden increase in the world price of many commodities, in particular oil. The government brought in measures to reduce oil consumption – for example, a speed limit of eighty kilometres per hour. Energy supplies were also threatened by a ban on overtime by coal miners, who believed they should receive bigger wage increases than Phase Three allowed. Coal supplies were severely reduced. The government was faced with a grave crisis, and on 12 November 1973 it announced a state of emergency: lighting in shops, offices, restaurants and most other public places was to be reduced by 50 per cent. On 17 December stringent measures were announced which limited weekly consumption of electricity to 65 per cent of normal use. A three-day week was introduced in industry. Television closed at 10.30 p.m. Christmas 1973 was undoubtedly the drabbest since the war.

In December a rail dispute began which heightened the tension in the country. There was a polarisation of opinion. Edward Heath was seen either as the instigator of unprecedented economic and industrial troubles or as the defender of the national interest against subversive elements. On 30 January 1974 Mr Eldon Griffiths, a government Minister, in an open letter to Mr Wilson, asked what he intended to do about communist 'leverage' in the unions and the resulting 'influence' in the Labour Party. To resolve what was considered by the government to be an economic, social and constitutional crisis (the Conservative theme was: who rules Britain, the government or the unions?) a general election was called in February 1974.

In fact, the period of crisis had thrown into focus a number of interesting points about British industry. As much was turned out by the factories in three days of production as in five. It was clear, therefore, that much could be achieved by the better deployment of labour and use of existing machinery; some observers even saw at this time a brief revival of 'national spirit'. Strikes were another matter. They dislocated industry and prevented delivery dates from being met, which irritated foreign (and British) buyers. The period from 1970 to 1974 saw the highest numbers of working days lost through strike action since the war.

Edward Heath had long been committed to the ideal of a united Europe, and it is not surprising that he made British entry to the EEC a matter of priority for his government. By May 1971 Britain had reached agreement with the Community over the position of British agriculture and the import of sugar from the Caribbean. On 28 October 1971 both Houses of Parliament voted in favour of entry. The vote revealed splits in the two major parties on the issue (the Liberals had always been consistently in favour of Britain's membership of the EEC). While the Labour Party opposed British entry on Conservative terms, eighty-nine Labour members voted for entry and thirty-nine Conservatives voted against. Three prominent Labour pro-Marketeers – Roy Jenkins, George Thompson and Harold Lever – resigned from the Shadow Cabinet in April 1972 because they thought Labour's attitude was hardening against the EEC. Harold Wilson's position was that though he agreed with entry for Britain in principle, he did not consider that the Conservative terms were right. He said that a future Labour government would ask for negotiations to be reopened (this in fact happened). Britain, together with Denmark and the Irish Republic (countries with strong trading links with Britain, whose entry to the EEC was very much dependent on Britain's decision), joined the European Community on 1 January 1973. Roy Jenkins, the eloquent and intellectual spokesman of moderate social democracy in Britain, was later to become President of the EEC.

The reform programme initiated by the Labour government in 1968 was not sufficient to bring peace to the province of Northern Ireland. There was sporadic IRA violence in 1970, and in 1971 the IRA campaign increased in intensity. By 1973 IRA activities had extended to the mainland of Britain. In Britain the IRA selected army camps and pubs used by soldiers as their targets. When this failed to bring results the campaign was broadened to include 'civilian targets'. These were public places, like pubs, shops, restaurants, Underground stations and exhibition halls. The IRA hoped that public indignation would take the form of massive pressure on the government of the day to withdraw totally from Northern Ireland. Parliament remained steadfast in its commitment to keep British troops in Ireland as long as they were needed and to maintain British sovereignty over Northern Ireland until a majority of its people democratically expressed their desire to break the connection.

In Northern Ireland Protestant extremist organisations such as the Ulster Defence Association, the Ulster Volunteer Force and the Ulster Freedom Fighters, claiming that they were defending the Protestant community against the IRA, began a campaign of violence against Catholics associated with the Republican cause. They attacked Catholic targets and inevitably ran into conflict with the police and army. British troops found themselves under attack from both Catholic and Protestant extremists.

In March 1972 Mr Heath's government considered that Northern Ireland had reached such a state of political instability and violence that its Parliament should be prorogued and the province should be ruled directly from Westminster. Authority over the province was vested in the hands of a Secretary of State. The government took extraordinary powers to protect Northern Irish, and later mainland British, society. Internment was introduced in August 1971, which allowed the

The conflict between Protestant and Catholic extremists in Northern Ireland and the British forces brought in to keep the peace has been a major factor in British politics since 1969. Yet in the streets of Belfast life goes on.

authorities to hold without trial a person suspected of terrorism.

The Detention of Terrorists Order 1972 upheld this power. This in turn was superseded by the Northern Ireland Emergency Provisions Act of 1973, which provided that crimes of a terrorist nature might be tried by a court without a jury. The Act also provided that an interim custody order issued on the authority of the Secretary of State might hold a suspected terrorist for up to twenty-eight days. A Commissioner for Determination had then to decide whether a person had charges to answer as a terrorist or whether his detention was necessary for the protection of the public. In November 1974 the Prevention of Terrorism Act was passed. This proscribed the IRA and made it an offence in any way to aid or assist the IRA. It gave the Home Secretary power to make exclusion orders against people concerned with terrorism. It gave the police powers to arrest and to hold for up to forty-eight hours anyone reasonably suspected of being involved in terrorism. The Act also provided for the examination of travellers entering or leaving mainland Britain or Northern Ireland. Continuing and growing co-operation between the governments of Britain and Eire led to the passage of legislation which allowed the courts of the two countries to try crimes of a terrorist nature committed in either Britain or Eire.

The earliest discussions on a future administrative structure for Northern Ireland were held in September 1972, at Darlington. Northern Ireland politicians and the Secretary of State agreed that a settlement could be found which was likely to be acceptable to the mass of Northern Ireland's people. On 8 March 1973 a plebiscite on the border was held to determine whether the Northern Irish people wished to remain part of the United Kingdom or be joined to the Irish Republic. More than 600,000 voters out of a total electorate of just over 1,000,000 voters went to the poll, and of these 591,870 voted to remain part of the United Kingdom. The Roman Catholic population decided not to take part in a plebiscite which they could not hope to win. The Northern Ireland Constitution Act, passed on 18 July 1973, restated the government's position, which was that Northern Ireland would be part of the United Kingdom until a majority of the people of Northern Ireland, voting in a plebiscite, made it clear that they wished this arrangement to change.

The Assembly Act of 3 May 1973 laid down that Northern Ireland was to have a single-chamber Assembly of seventy-eight members. The Act also proposed that there should be an executive which reflected the balance of power in the Assembly. The Assembly Act hoped that the different parties in Northern

Ireland would be brought together and would work in co-operation. But many Protestants did not like the idea of an Assembly and wanted the return of the Parliament that had existed before direct rule from Westminster. Neither did they like the voting system that had been proposed, nor the power-sharing executive, which they claimed were novel ideas which politicians in London would not try in other parts of Britain. In the election to the Assembly held in June 1973 Unionists opposed to the government's constitutional proposals gained twenty-six seats; those Unionists who supported the proposals won twenty-four seats; the Social Democratic and Labour Party, which represented most Catholics, won nineteen seats; the middle-of-the-road Alliance Party won eight seats; and the Northern Ireland Labour Party one seat.

The first meeting of the Assembly was in July 1973. On 1 January 1974 the power-sharing executive came into being. In December 1973 there had been a conference at Sunningdale between the leader of the Northern Irish executive designate and ministers of the United Kingdom and of the Irish Republic. An agreement was reached whereby a Council of Ireland was to be set up consisting of seven ministers from the Irish Republic and seven members of the Northern Ireland executive. The agreement also affirmed the permanence of the border. The Council was generally to foster good relations between north and south. But a growing number of Protestants opposed the new constitution and the Sunningdale agreement, and in the general election of February 1974 this hostility was expressed. Protestants opposed to the Heath government's settlement gained 51 per cent of the votes and eleven of the twelve parliamentary seats. The Assembly continued, but its days were numbered.

To some people the troubles in Ireland seemed anachronistic; however, the animosity between Catholics and Protestants was provoked not by doctrine but by questions of nationalism and, to some degree, by economic and social considerations. The Protestants had dominated the economy of the north of Ireland for centuries. Though the situation was changing fast, the traditional economic advantages of the Protestants and the exclusion of Catholics from prosperity could not be erased overnight.

Though politics was dominated by the economy and Ireland, several other questions caused a stir during this period of Mr Heath's government. In particular, there was the government's education policy. The new Minister of Education (and, later, first woman Prime Minister) was Mrs Margaret Thatcher. She was forceful and dynamic; sweeping all objections aside, in July 1970 she withdrew the former government's circular which had urged local authorities to make their secondary schools comprehensive. Mrs Thatcher's action was a reprieve for the selective system and especially for the grammar school. In April 1971 Mrs Thatcher announced a new programme: large sums of money were to be allocated to the clearance of slum primary schools, of which there were an estimated 6000. The Conservative government also announced the ending of free milk for children in secondary schools.

In September 1972 the government decided to airlift the Asian community from Uganda, following President Amin's decision to expel them. The Asians held British passports, and their plight was considered serious enough to relax the Immigration Acts. The Ugandan Asians were mainly professionals or lower middle class. They spoke good English and quickly integrated into British society. Many of the Ugandan Asians became proprietors of small shops, which delighted local neighbourhoods by staying open much longer than was usual. The airlifting of the Ugandan Asians was a compassionate move. But it served, too, to remind Britain that the acquisition of an empire brings with it responsibilities as well as benefits.

In February 1971 a White Paper (an informative report issued by the government) proposed the reorganisation of local government: the country was to be divided into forty-four counties, some of which were entirely new. The reform of local government had begun in 1966, when Greater London came into being, an area which embraced the city and its suburbs. The changes of 1971 followed the same principle, that a city should include the suburbs, and even the smaller towns, which depended on the city economically. Since the war there had been a general movement from city centres to the surrounding countryside. New metropolitan counties therefore included large cities and their surroundings. Other changes in the county structure were the break-up of some old historic counties and the merging of two or more together. In fact, it caused great annoyance to some towns like Bristol, which had been autonomous in local government since the Middle Ages, to become part of a new county. The restructuring did, however, try to take account of tradition; in Wales, for example, the new counties and their names are rooted in the ancient divisions for the country – those that existed before the sixteenth century when an essentially English reorganisation of administration was imposed on the land.

The general election held on 28 February 1974 was bitterly fought. Mr Heath hoped for a mandate to deal authoritatively with the economic and industrial situation. The results dashed his hopes. Though it seemed that Conservatives remained loyal to Conservative policies and the rightness of the

Heath approach, the voters (who were not committed to any one party and tended to decide which way to vote on the day of the poll) turned against the Conservatives, as they thought the Party would provoke a confrontation between the government and the labour force. But Harold Wilson did not acquire an overwhelming mandate either (essentially he advocated careful planning and the complete dismantling of the Industrial Relations Act). The Conservatives gained 296 seats and Labour 301. The Liberals, with fourteen seats, were in a strong position, as for the first time since the First World War they held the balance of power in Parliament. On 4 March the Liberals decided not to join a coalition with the Conservatives. Mr Heath resigned as Prime Minister, and Harold Wilson was invited to form a government.

Edward Heath remains one of the most impressive figures in British politics, but his period in office was marked by confrontation and polarisation. He misjudged the strength of the unions, and he failed to recognise the fact that changes in industrial relations would have to be brought about without the use of the force of government and the law. Edward Heath was not a rightist aggressor (he had previously had good relations with the unions), but he appeared hostile to the TUC, which was naturally suspicious of Conservatives. It is doubtful if he would now adopt the same approach to industrial relations.

If Edward Heath's terms for Britain's entry to the EEC were not the best that could have been devised, he did take Britain into the Community and created a body of opinion which believed that the destinies of Britain and Europe were linked.

Labour Government, 1974–1979

The third Labour government of Harold Wilson, though it did not have a majority in the House of Commons, could be assured of the support of the Liberal Party and the minority parties (particularly the Nationalists) if it proposed legislation of which they did not disapprove. The government was able to abolish the Pay Board and the National Industrial Relations Court set up by the previous administration, but without a majority the government was unable to prevent the passing of Conservative amendments to its own Labour Act, which preserved part of the Industrial Relations Act. In October 1974 Wilson called a general election (there had been a fever of excitement about the possibility of an election throughout the summer, but the Prime Minister appeared very cool and detached). Labour increased its strength in the Commons to

The issue of nationalism has been much debated both in Scotland and in Wales, and feelings run high, sometimes breaking into violence. This Welsh eisteddfod represents a more peaceful determination to preserve Welsh traditional costume, language and culture. Some 590,000 people out of 2,774,000 in Wales are Welsh speakers.

319; the Conservatives dropped to 276. The Liberals had thirteen seats.

An interesting result of the election was the return of eleven Scottish Nationalists and three members of Plaid Cymru, the Welsh Nationalist Party. For some time there had been growing support for nationalist parties in Scotland and Wales. Nationalism could be seen as an expression of many things, among them irritation with the two major parties, a desire for Westminster to delegate power and authority to Scotland and Wales or a wish for complete independence. In both Scotland and Wales there was deep-seated patriotism. Scotland had always been a separate kingdom with marked differences in law and education from England. Wales had been administratively merged with England (for example, most statistics treated the two countries as a single unit, whereas Scotland and Northern Ireland were quoted separately). But Wales had 590,000 Welsh speakers (they usually spoke English as well) out of a population of 2,774,000. This alone was a basis for a

Prince Charles carries on the tradition begun in 1301 that the monarch's eldest son is Prince of Wales. Queen Elizabeth II and her husband, the Duke of Edinburgh, attended the ceremony of his Investiture as Prince of Wales in 1969.

feeling of difference. Both Scottish and Welsh national parties believed that their countries were maladministered from London and that the economic decline they had suffered (in common with the old industrial areas of England) could have been avoided. The appearance of nationalist Members of Parliament on a large scale prompted both Labour and Conservatives to take a new interest in Scotland and Wales and to attempt to devise a means to stem the nationalist tide.

Harold Wilson's fourth government repealed the Conservative amendments to its Labour Act, and thereby the industrial relations legislation of the previous administration was ended. From the very start the basis of the government's economic strategy was the 'Social Contract', by which the TUC undertook to operate a voluntary incomes policy in return for the government's achievement of social aims. The government set up the Arbitration, Conciliation and Advisory Service (ACAS) in the spring of 1975 (it was put on a statutory basis in November 1975) to provide a professional body devoted to the promotion of industrial harmony. Its members were drawn from the unions and the Confederation of British Industry (CBI), a body which represented the employers and there were independent members. The TUC liked the idea, but the CBI said it was one-sided. The government also tightened up the rules on unfair dismissal, and an industrial tribunal was established to decide cases. Again, the CBI claimed that this measure would deliberately favour the unions.

The government instituted the National Enterprise Board (NEB) in February 1975. Its aim was to prevent the transfer abroad of the control of manufacturing undertakings, and to provide assistance to industry, in the hope of promoting industrial efficiency and international competitiveness. The NEB was to work closely with the trade unions and to provide them with information about industry. The government argued that priority had to be given to industrial development rather than consumption and social objectives. In May 1975 the government injected £15 million of new capital into Ferranti, the electrical and electronics group (the government took $62\frac{1}{2}$ per cent of the total equity, including half of the ordinary voting capital), and in July £25 million was allocated to Alfred Herbert, the machine tool group and the government took a majority stake in the firm. In the autumn of 1975, in its biggest financial undertaking of this sort, the government provided money to keep in operation British Leyland, the motor company; in December 1975 it committed £162.5 million to saving the operation of the American Chrysler car company in the United Kingdom. The TUC favoured the extension of funds to companies, but it envisaged a much broader plan for the nationalisation of a large section of the economy – and, indeed, aircraft and shipbuilding were nationalised in March 1977.

On the whole, the government was not in a position to push through controversial legislation like nationalisation, as the Labour Party had a small parliamentary majority, which dwindled steadily. The Liberals and most Northern Ireland members did not like nationalisation, and the Nationalists were prepared to offer their support only on condition that their cause was forwarded.

The exploitation of Britain's offshore oil fields, which were the most optimistic element in the economy, was vested in both private and public control. A petroleum revenue tax of 45 per cent was imposed on the private oil companies. In 1975 the British National Oil Corporation was established with wide exploration and production powers. Self-sufficiency in oil production was anticipated for 1980. The successful development of oil resources did much to boost the economy in the late seventies and the manufacture of pipelines gave a stimulus to the steel industry.

The government counted on pay restraint to assist the success of their economic programme. In June 1974 the TUC agreed to co-operate in limiting wage claims, but with rampant inflation and the decline in the pound (the pound was allowed to float in 1973 and dropped below the $2 mark in 1976), Labour felt it necessary to bring in three phases of compulsory pay restraint. Until 1978 the TUC was generally willing to support government measures, as the economic situation was manifestly grave; in fact, the unions backed measures which had the effect of reducing the living standards of their members. By mid-1978 the inflation rate was down to 7.4 per cent, the lowest figure since September 1972.

In July 1975 the government announced Phase One of its income policy. A £6-a-week limit on wage increases was imposed, and no rises were permitted for those who earned over £8,500. Phase Two, which ran from the summer of 1976 until the summer of 1977, limited increases in wages and salaries to about $4\frac{1}{2}$ per cent on average, with cash minima and maxima of £2.50 and £4.00 per week. After negotiations on Phase Three of the incomes policy the TUC declined to give further guidance on pay to its members, but there was an understanding that pay increases should be kept below 10 per cent. At the same time, in July 1977, the Price Commission (first established in 1973) was given power to impose a two-month freeze on price increases. The government's counter-inflation policy for the twelve months from 1 August 1978 envisaged pay increases of not more than 5 per cent, continued price restraint and an extension of statutory powers to control dividends. The package was rejected by the TUC. There was an increase in the number of strikes in support of pay claims, though these were undertaken without TUC backing. In 1978 the government came under strong criticism from the Opposition for its compilation of a 'black list' of firms said to have exceeded the 10 per cent guideline for pay increases. The government declared that it would penalise these companies by withholding government contracts. In November 1978 Denis Healey, the Chancellor of the Exchequer, announced sanctions against Ford for settling pay claims over the limit.

By the end of 1978 there was considerable frustration over pay. The TUC urged the government to hold an election in the autumn of 1978 at the end of the government's Phase Three. But the Labour government continued in office until May 1979.

In Northern Ireland the Heath government's constitutional arrangements finally collapsed in May 1974, when the Ulster Worker's Council, claiming to represent 300,000 workers, called a general strike, which paralysed the province. On 28 May Mr Faulkner and his Unionist followers resigned from the executive and on 29 May the Assembly was prorogued.

The next scheme the government thought of was the setting up of a Constitutional Convention. Its task was not to govern but to try to find a pattern of government for Northern Ireland. The Northern Ireland Assembly was dissolved at the end of March 1975, and elections to the Convention took place on 1 May. Of the seventy-eight members of the Convention, forty-six represented the Loyalist coalition, consisting of the main Protestant groups: the official Unionists, the Vanguard Unionist Party and the Democratic Unionist Party. No scheme was found which commanded support from the Protestant and Catholic parties in the Convention. The Loyalist coalition did not seek power-sharing of any kind but wanted a return to rule by Stormont, the Northern Ireland Parliament. The Catholics demanded power-sharing of some kind, as otherwise they saw themselves permanently excluded from power. Early in 1976 opinion polls in Northern Ireland indicated that a majority of Protestants were willing to agree to power-sharing. Though there was a widespread demand among the vast majority of the people of Northern Ireland for a return to peace and harmony in their society, a political solution proved impossible to find – despite the fact that international opinion had hardened against the IRA terrorists. Many European Catholics ceased to see the strife as the result of the suppression of religious freedom. Many Americans shed their belief that the IRA was connected with the freedom fighters of 1916. Terrorism became a fact of life in Britain itself. It forced the passing of illiberal measures which were disagreeable to an enlightened Home Secretary like Roy Jenkins.

In November 1975 the government published a White Paper on the devolution of power to Scotland and Wales, based on the Kilbrandon Report of October 1973. The Paper rejected separatism but advocated assemblies for Scotland and Wales with wide powers, though the raising of revenue was kept as a preserve of the central government. The government ran into difficulties with a group of its own Members, represen-

Age		2–5	5–7	7–11	11–16/18	
A	THE STATE SYSTEM	Nursery School (a limited number exist)	Infant School	Junior School	Grammar School or 11–16 Secondary Modern School	16+ Some Technical Colleges and Sixth Form Colleges
			Infant and Junior Schools may be combined in a Primary School			
		2–5	5–7	7–11	11–16/18	
B		Nursery	Infant	Junior	Comprehensive School	
		2–5	5–8/9	8/9–12/13	12/13–16/18	
C		Nursery	First School	Middle School	Comprehensive School	
		2–5	5–8	8–13	13–16/18	
D	PRIVATE	Nursery	Pre-preparatory School	Preparatory (or Prep) School	Public School	

The education system in **England** and **Wales**

tatives of economically depressed northern constituencies, who did not think that Scotland and Wales should receive 'special treatment'. Two Scottish Labour Members opposed to devolution broke away from the Labour Party, which they thought was putting the unity of the United Kingdom in danger. The Nationalists were not delighted with the Government's White Paper, but they believed that, for the time being, it was better than nothing. The Conservatives, by nature opposed to devolution, were hostile to the measure. After much debate it was decided to hold referenda on devolution in Scotland and Wales.

On 1 March 1979 the referenda took place. In Scotland the electorate voted by a narrow majority for the establishment of an assembly (the 'yes' vote in Scotland was 32.85 per cent, the 'no' vote 30.78 per cent). In Wales the idea was decisively rejected (11.92 per cent were in favour of a national assembly and 46.92 per cent against). The decline in nationalist fortunes was reflected in the general election of May 1979, when the Scottish Nationalists were reduced from eleven members to two, and Plaid Cymru lost one seat, to stand at two. Support had swung away from nationalism towards the main parties. The Nationalists talked of apathy, even reaction, among voters. The main parties believed that the reason for this change of attitude was that the Scottish and Welsh peoples were unwilling to surrender their destinies to an unknown system of government.

The government tried to establish comprehensive schooling throughout the state system by its Education Act of 1976 (comprehensive schools already took over 60 per cent of the pupils in secondary education). But those counties which rejected the comprehensive system were able to delay their plans for reorganisation so long that selection in education continued, despite the government's displeasure. In fact, in the seventies the educational debate had changed, and the comprehensive issue was beginning to lose some of its fire. The subject of discussion was 'standards'. A group of educationalists attacked some of the modern methods of teaching (for example, new reading techniques and the absence of 'streaming' – the grouping together of pupils with similar abilities – in schools). They claimed that educational liberalism had produced poor results. There could be no agreement on this subject, but the seventies saw a movement away from experiment. The public school system (fee-paying private schools) still continued to take a tiny percentage of the school population (5 per cent). Its image had changed. Training in leadership and command were hardly mentioned as attributes of a public school education, let alone moral training. Reflecting the seventies' concern with academic standards, the public schools emphasised the thoroughness and hard-working nature of the schooling they offered.

A contentious issue throughout the seventies was private medicine. By an Act of 1976 private beds were to be phased out of the National Health Service. Doctors had, on the whole, wanted private patients to remain within the hospitals, but hospital workers objected furiously and refused to service private rooms and wards. Those in favour of private beds saw their existence as a fundamental freedom and argued that private patients injected money into the Health Service. The main counter-argument was that private patients were able to purchase treatment earlier than thousands of others who were waiting for operations. The phasing out of pay beds meant an increase in the number of private clinics, already a booming industry by virtue of the large number of foreigners who were coming to Britain for private treatment.

Mr Wilson was pledged to renegotiate the terms of entry to the EEC and to subject any new terms to the British people for their approval in a referendum. Britain's partners in the EEC were disgruntled at having to concede anything to Britain in new negotiations, but at the same time they were fearful that Britain might leave the Community. Concessions were therefore made over Britain's contribution to the Community budget, the working of the Common Agricultural Policy (CAP) and imports of New Zealand dairy products after 1977. In March 1975 Wilson said that in the forthcoming referendum on membership of the EEC he would recommend the British people to vote in favour of staying in. The referendum was held on 5 June. In answer to the question: 'Do you think that the United Kingdom should stay in the European Community (the Common Market)?', an overwhelming majority of those voting said 'Yes'; 67.2 per cent of the voters supported continued membership, while 32.8 per cent voted for withdrawal. In only two of the sixty-eight voting regions (the Shetland Islands and the Western Isles of Scotland) was there a majority of 'no' votes. It was the first time that the referendum had been used to decide a major issue in British politics (some constitutionalists considered that the introduction of the referendum as a permanent feature of political life was worthy of consideration).

The British still have deep reservations about the EEC. Its critics in Britain maintain that the referendum was not fought over EEC issues but was engineered into a campaign against the left, who militantly fought against membership. Though the vote may reflect a show of strength against extremism, it should not obscure the fact that the British would be in a real dilemma if they had to choose an alternative economic union to the EEC.

The problem of terrorism continued. In November 1974 a bomb planted in a pub in Birmingham killed twenty-one people, most of them young men and women. In response to this bombing, the government, with the full backing of the

After much public debate and a referendum (a very unusual event in British politics) Britain joined the European Economic Community in 1975.
A pro-Market rally in Trafalgar Square, London, is shown here. The speaker is Reg Prentice.

193

Opposition (there was an all-party approach to Ireland), passed legislation in one day which gave the Home Secretary tougher powers against terrorist organisations. Further legislation followed in March 1976, after more pub bombings in Guildford and Woolwich. The Home Secretary was empowered to proscribe organisations and to exclude and expel from the United Kingdom persons suspected of involvement in terrorist activities. In February 1976 the Home Secretary was faced with the difficult problem of how to treat a terrorist imprisoned in Britain who went on hunger strike. Force-feeding is a nasty business, and the authorities decided to let the prisoner in question, Frank Stagg, take his own life if he wished. The IRA did not intervene to stop Stagg from refusing food.

By the 1970s Britain was a land of owner-occupiers: in 1976 53 per cent of the people owned their own home. There was an acknowledgement by both parties that the British liked to own property. However, the Conservative Party extended this concept further than the Labour Party and empowered local authorities to sell the properties they owned (these were houses and flats, built with money provided by taxes and local rates, which were rented to people who did not own their own homes). The purchasers were generally the people who were already living in them. The Labour Party strenuously opposed the idea, saying that council houses must be reserved for people who were not in a position to buy. The Conservatives believed that each person should be able to buy the house he had lived in (there may also have been a political motive, as home owners tended to Conservatism while council-house occupants tended to have Labour sympathies). The subject was divisive and represented a fundamental difference of approach at the general elections of 1974 and 1979.

A matter of some contention was Labour's Rent Act (1974), which gave security to long-term tenants in furnished and unfurnished accommodation alike. Because they feared that their tenants would now have a permanent claim on their property, many landlords, it was argued, had withdrawn their accommodation from the market. It was claimed that perhaps a third of the privately rented accommodation in London had disappeared because of this, making the housing situation in London even worse. The seventies saw the illegal occupation of premises by squatters. Sometimes the authorities turned a blind eye if the squatters were homeless families (an estimated 100,000 people in London are without their own homes and live with other families or in hostels) or if the buildings were council-owned and would be empty for some time. On other occasions there were bitter confrontations between squatters and the authorities.

Though there were differences between the two main parties over social questions (schools, hospitals and housing), there was a surprising degree of unanimity. The parties were united on Ireland. There were few scuffles over foreign affairs. In fact, the only major excitement in foreign affairs in the seventies was the so-called 'Cod War' between Britain and Iceland, when Iceland extended her territorial waters to 322 kilometres and thereby closed rich fishing grounds to British boats. There was a virtual concession to all Iceland's demands by Britain at the Oslo Conference in 1976 (much to the chagrin of British fishermen). The question of Rhodesia continued without resolution, but the United States participated in the search for a solution to the southern Africa situation. The Common Market did not divide parties, though the issue caused tension within the Labour Party. Even economic issues were not as divisive as they might have seemed throughout much of the seventies. There was a grudging recognition in the country that severe restraint was necessary, and it was clear that Labour's traditional supporters, as well as everyone else, were affected by the curbs on pay.

By the election of 1979 many Labour supporters would not tolerate restraint any longer. It was also evident that the Conservative Party could not continue to hold down the economy. There was a feeling in 1979 that private initiative needed encouragement, and the Conservatives reflected this mood for change. In the words of the Conservative leader: 'The balance in society had been increasingly tilted in favour of the state at the expense of individual freedom.'

The three major parties all had new leaders in the election held on 3 May 1979. In February 1975 Edward Heath stood for re-election as leader of the Conservative Party, but was defeated by Mrs Margaret Thatcher. The result was a surprise to all but the best informed. Edward Heath's handling of the unions had been unsuccessful, and his television image was not good (this factor was increasingly important to Party managers). Mrs Thatcher was cool and decisive and seemed capable of matching Harold Wilson's performances in the House of Commons. Mrs Thatcher's election represented a turn to the right in the Conservative Party – her ideas on economic freedom and individualism were much more clear-cut than Heath's. They both came from similar backgrounds: Mrs Thatcher's father was a grocer and Heath's father had a small building firm. Socially, they did not represent the aristocratic or plutocratic element within Conservatism but its mass support from small business people who worked hard and had modest incomes. Mrs Thatcher, like Heath, had gone to Oxford; she had studied chemistry (a scientific background

Jim Callaghan became Labour Prime Minister from the time of Harold Wilson's unexpected resignation in 1976 until the defeat of Labour at the general election of 1979.

was highly unusual for a parliamentarian), though she later became a barrister. The Soviet Union once in annoyance called Mrs Thatcher the 'iron lady' – but Mrs Thatcher turned it to her advantage and saw it as recognition of the fact that she was a woman of strength and determination.

In March 1976 Harold Wilson resigned as Prime Minister. He had headed four administrations, a record matched only by Gladstone's in the nineteenth century. He had evolved a strategy for industrial recovery which, though controversial, did indicate an extremely able intellect and an immense knowledge of the economy. His successor as leader of the Labour Party and Prime Minister was James Callaghan. He had been a union official for many years and was one of the few Prime Ministers of the twentieth century who had not gone to university. He continued the policies of his predecessor with tenacity. Callaghan had an avuncular style and had hardly any enemies in politics. He viewed the work of government with measured calm; this inspired confidence among many but was also portrayed as complacency (almost as turgidity) in the election campaign of 1979.

David Steel is leader of the Liberal Party which has a small number of representatives in Parliament. The party claims to suffer from an electoral system geared to encourage only two major parties.

In May 1976 Jeremy Thorpe resigned as leader of the Liberal Party in sad circumstances. He complained that a 'witch hunt' was being conducted against him (principally by the Press) after a male model, Norman Scott, told a court that he had had a homosexual relationship with Thorpe. In August 1978 Thorpe was remanded on a charge of conspiracy to murder Scott but was acquitted in 1979.

Jeremy Thorpe is vivacious and witty. He always enjoyed

the respect of Parliament. He gave the Liberal Party dynamic leadership but could not fulfil the task which had defeated all Liberal leaders, that of making the Liberals a party of government. Thorpe's successor, David Steel, had a pleasing appearance and manner. He was the Member for a Scottish constituency (in the border country) and represented the vigorous strand of Liberalism found in Scotland and in Wales and Cornwall too.

The election in 1979 saw the return of Mrs Thatcher and the Conservatives, with 339 seats against Labour's 267. The elections for the European Assembly (1979) confirmed the swing to the Conservatives, who took the majority of the British seats.

In 1979 Margaret Thatcher became the first woman Prime Minister in Europe. She won the election on the pledge to revive the British economy by tough, Conservative policies. Her stand against Communism has earned her the title of 'the Iron Lady' in the Soviet Union.

197

10

Epilogue

The economic pattern of the sixties and seventies had been one of government planning as opposed to private initiative, and restraint of pay, prices and profits as opposed to their free rise. Underlying Britain's economic performance was the fact that much of Britain's industry was archaic and had to be renewed either through private or government investment. War, some apathy and sometimes too much emphasis on past achievement had brought about this state of affairs. When the realisation came that Britain was economically weak, the British indulged in self-criticism and self-examination which was brutally severe. Foreign viewers tended to see the situation as even worse than it was, though the exploitation of North Sea oil and the curtailment of inflation caused the sharp rise of the pound in 1978 and 1979 – an indication that foreign opinion (or foreign money) had acquired new confidence. In fact, the British economy presented a familiar picture of boom and depression. Oil, chemicals, arms manufacture, specialised electronics, agriculture, tourism and international finance were doing well. Thousands of small industries, from boat building to raincoat manufacture, showed by their export sales that inventiveness and salesmanship were at a high level. The coal industry was booming, and Britain was self-sufficient in natural gas and had large oil reserves. Industrial recession hit the motor industry, shipbuilding, textile manufacture and the steel industry. Britain's motor bicycle production ceased. Some of these industries abroad faced similar problems. Unemployment (1,500,000 in 1979) was the product not wholly of industrial decline but also of industrial renewal. Technological change – the introduction of computers, for example – radically reduced the demand for labour.

There can be few more important decades in British history than the sixties. Those years marked a change in outlook, behaviour and appearance which, for better or worse, made Britain a liberal society. As liberalisation coincided with economic difficulty, critics of liberalisation were able to claim that changing standards brought economic decline. The assumption of economic failure has to be put in context. Though it was apparent that Britain needed to modernise her industry and reassess her role in the world, living standards

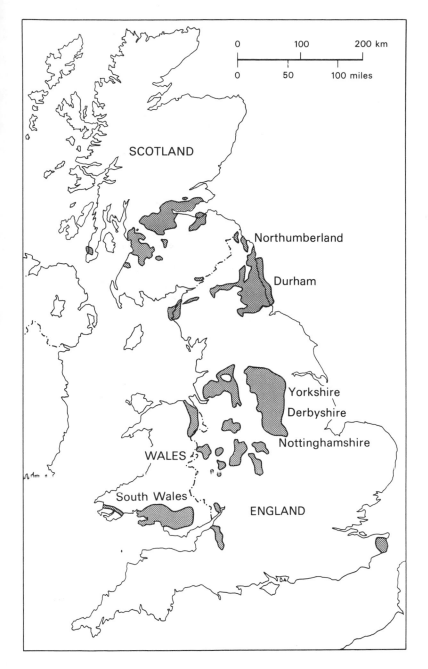

Britain's coal fields

were higher than ever before. The prosperity moreover, gave the working class a freedom it had never enjoyed before and gave the young an extraordinary degree of importance.

Young people were better nourished, clothed and educated than at any time in history. In 1972 the school-leaving age was raised to sixteen. The number of students in full-time

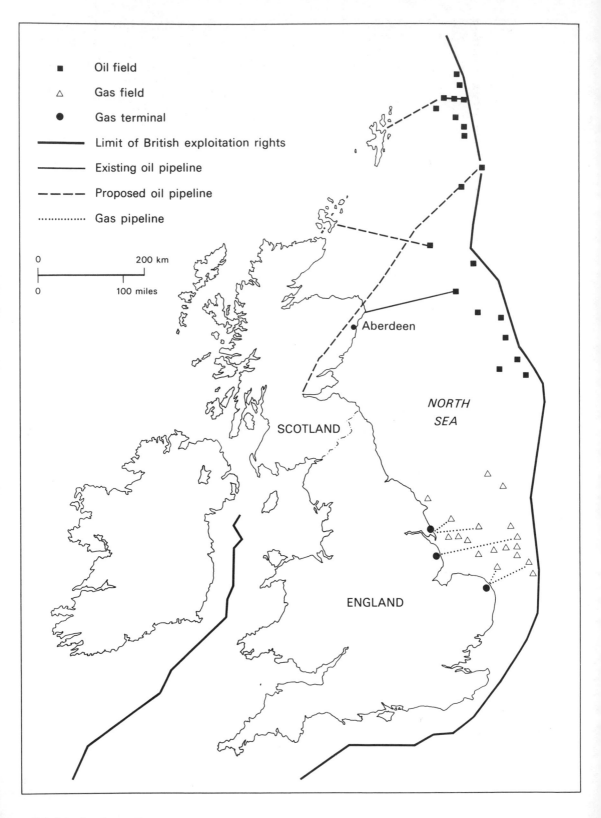

Legend:

- ■ Oil field
- △ Gas field
- ● Gas terminal
- ▬▬ Limit of British exploitation rights
- —— Existing oil pipeline
- – – – Proposed oil pipeline
- ·········· Gas pipeline

0 ———— 200 km

0 ———— 100 miles

Aberdeen

SCOTLAND

NORTH SEA

ENGLAND

Britain's oil and natural gas resources

higher education rose from 170,000 in 1965 to 350,000 in 1975. Though there were severe problems in education in inner urban areas, and though the number of university graduates was a small percentage of the numbers who went through school (7 per cent), the general view must be that education took off in the sixties. Broader-based curricula were introduced throughout the educational system. Social sciences became the most dynamic faculty in universities. Those not attending educational courses could not escape the volume of information which poured from television and radio. The Open University, started in 1971, enabled students to gain a degree by television viewing and correspondence. Somewhat inevitably, the largest occupation group among the Open University students has been teachers (in teaching a degree means more money, and the knowledge gained can be instantly applied in the classroom), but many other people, from dockers to old-age pensioners, have gained degrees.

The initial enthusiasm of the sixties for higher education cooled in the seventies, partly because there were not the jobs for university graduates and other people with qualifications in higher education. In some respects this development has been a healthy one, as instead of acquiring a qualification for its own sake, young people are now trying to gain knowledge which will be relevant in a job.

Society's liberalisation was marked by legislative changes. In 1954 and 1964 the Obscene Publication Acts left opinion to decide what was immoral in literature. In 1965 the death

The highly manoeuvrable Mini became immensely popular in the sixties, while its successor, the Metro, promises to be the car of the eighties with its high performance and low petrol consumption. The photographs show the cars in production: men work on the Mini (left) while the Metro (right) is the result of sophisticated new technology.

201

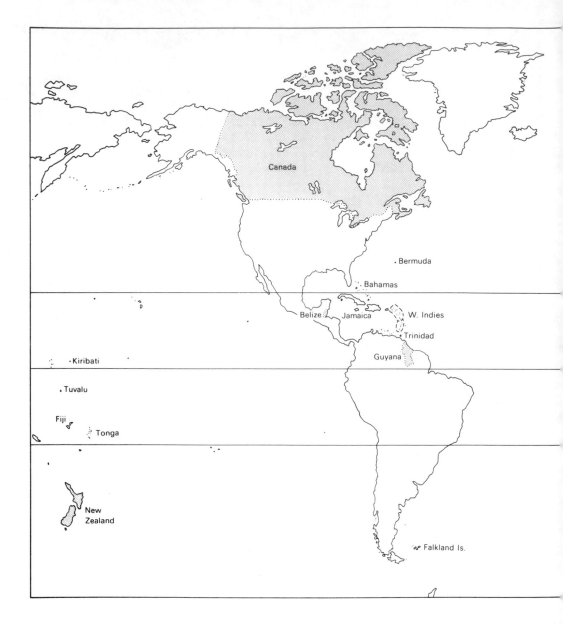

The Commonwealth today

penalty was abolished, and periodic moves to restore capital punishment have not met with success. In 1967 there was a change in the law governing homosexuality, which made legal homosexual practices between consenting adults in private. The change in the law brought to an end a lucrative blackmail trade. The Abortion Act of 1967 legalised abortions conducted

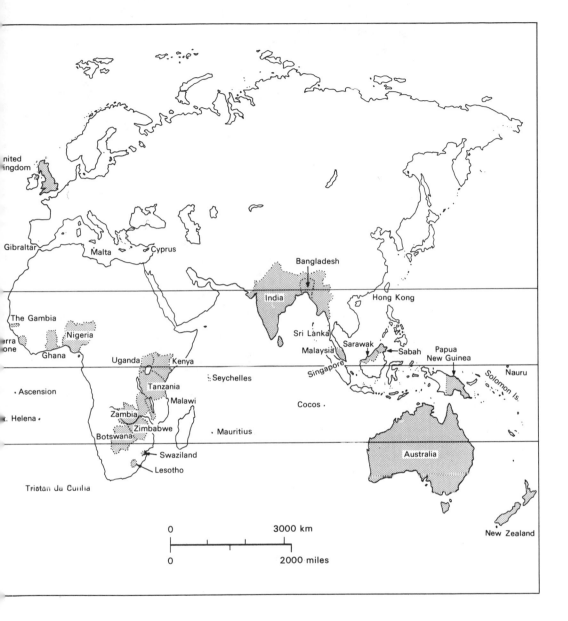

by a doctor after at least two physicians had agreed that the life or mental health of a woman was endangered by continuation of her pregnancy. This law has been attacked by numerous (principally Catholic) critics. The Sex Discrimination Act of 1975 made it illegal to discriminate against either sex (obviously women were in mind when the Act was framed) in

203

Gas and oil from the North Sea have become very important to the British economy. Many politicians hope that the oil revenues will revitalise industry in the eighties.

matters of employment and social activity, though the Act made necessary provisions for the preservation of single-sex activities.

Legislation may respond to demand for change (perhaps from an articulate minority in society) or it may anticipate change of thought in society (sometimes majority opinion does not change, as in the case of capital punishment – according to opinion polls, a majority of Britons want its restoration). Small considerations beyond the scope of parliamentary legislation perhaps indicate a changing public mood more accurately. The sixties made casual clothes acceptable and the bizarre fashionable. There were mini-skirts, and dresses which touched the floor (for ordinary and not evening wear). After a battle, women were able to wear trousers wherever they wished. Men discarded ties. Long hair became fashionable. (Hair became an emotive issue: parents, schools and employers who equated short hair with good values battled, largely in vain, to make young men have short haircuts

The Beatles – heroes of the sixties.

again). The sixties' legacy was that in the seventies flexibility ruled. This was one outward sign of a changed society. Women had more freedom. The institution of marriage was questioned – the number of divorces was 39,000 in 1966 and 126,000 in 1976. Society was more mobile. People travelled abroad. Young people chose increasingly to live away from their homes and families. Some said society was free; some said it was rootless.

The importance of the Beatles cannot be exaggerated. They represented not merely a sound or a form of music, but a concept. They were sometimes cheeky, often irreverent, apparently undisciplined and, on the odd occasion, provocative. They were folk heroes, challenging the values and customs of society – but, more important, they succeeded and became rich. The Beatles and other groups made regional accents not only acceptable but fashionable. There was a growing trend for proper accents to be considered just one type rather than the best, but the media's use of anything but the public school or Oxbridge accent made regional accents or a drawling mid-Atlantic style of speech fashionable. The late seventies was to see a strange supremacy of a Londonish nasal accent linked with the punk movement. Changes in dress, accent and behaviour made it virtually impossible to determine a person's class. The English gentleman could, in fact, turn out

The Queen's Silver Jubilee, marking the first twenty-five years of her reign, brought the crowds on to the streets in celebration in 1977. A 'walkabout' among the people is a relatively recent innovation indicative of the more relaxed style of modern royalty.

to be a smartly dressed working-class man; the casually dressed youngster could be the son of a peer.

The impact of social change on London was very marked. It became a mecca for young people wanting to set up on their own. It became the centre of the pop world and the world of down-market fashion. The decline of the pound helped to make London a focus of mass tourism. It was also a major centre of the arts, with an unrivalled reputation for classical music, the ballet and the number of its art galleries. Though historically England was divided between north and south, the real demarcation seemed to be between London and the provinces.

But throughout Britain the face of towns and cities changed. Supermarkets replaced small shops, and new shopping centres vied with the traditional High Street. Cities like Coventry, which had been blitzed in the Second World War, emerged with a huge pedestrian shopping area. Coventry also gained a handsome modern cathedral. High-rise flats replaced streets of back-to-back houses, although the passing of the old houses was not without regret. The English on the whole did not like flats, and certainly not those in very high blocks (on the other hand, the Scots, particularly Glaswegians, had a long tradition of flat dwelling). People in blocks of flats missed the neighbourliness of streets of terraced houses. The television programme *Coronation Street*, which depicted life in such a street in Greater Manchester, was the most popular programme throughout the sixties and seventies. Was there perhaps nostalgia among viewers for a rapidly passing way of life?

Tradition remains strong in Britain. So much of the past

remains in the form of architecture. Institutions have been adapted rather than radically altered, and colourful ceremony has tended to be retained for the sake of continuity and nostalgia. But the persistence of traditional institutions should not be allowed to mask the change beneath the surface. Oxford and Cambridge universities have beautiful buildings and some quaint customs but also a continuing high academic reputation. The Church of England remains hierarchical, and ceremonious by various degrees, but it has regrouped its parishes to make the best use of its clergy and is deeply involved in the problems of modern society, such as drugs and homelessness. The House of Lords has been revitalised with the inclusion of life peers, though the presence of any hereditary peers at all needs serious examination. Public schools, like all other schools, have been involved in educational change, but it is open to question whether the education of children of (usually) wealthy parents within a different system from that which caters for the vast majority is compatible with the need for greater social cohesion in society.

The oldest institution, and the one which gives Britain part of its unique character, is the monarchy. The monarchy is a success story. It helps to give unity to the Commonwealth. It plays a discreet role in the British constitution; it is not involved in decision making but provides a stable headship of government. Queen Elizabeth and other members of the royal family are first-class representatives of Britain abroad. The fact that the monarchy comprises a family is in itself important: the royal family has the same feelings and problems as millions of others, and it is appreciated that the head of state is a mother and a grandmother rather than a clever politician or a general. The British people's admiration for the Queen was shown in the Jubilee celebrations of 1977. The trend has been to establish a more personal monarchy, with less emphasis on massive display and ceremony. This is the right course in a changing democratic society.

The adaptation of the monarchy to changes in society reflects the emphasis on compromise as opposed to violent change which has run throughout British history. This compromise has produced a stable and effective system of government and law. Britain's economic difficulties have been partly caused by heavy involvement in war and an inability to renew industry. However, the problem is also sociological, the product of distrust between groups in industry. The compromise that has been so marked in British historical development has been lacking in recent industrial relations – and it should be there. The new technology based on microelectronics and computers will make possible another Industrial

Revolution. Labour patterns will have to change, but more leisure and wealth should result. Nevertheless, dialogue and reason are vital if this revolution is to be affected without great disruption.

Britain remains very much involved with the affairs of the Commonwealth. The great triumph of the Lusaka Commonwealth Conference in 1979 was to break the deadlock over Rhodesia. At the conference, Mrs Thatcher and Lord Carrington, the Foreign Secretary, indicated a strategy which ended with the independence of the renamed Zimbabwe under black leadership chosen in free elections.

British society is on the whole tolerant and considerate. There is a highly developed system of social services. The countryside remains unspoilt. Artistic and cultural life is at a high point, and never before have there been so many visitors to the country or so many people learning English. The quality of present-day life in Britain must render worthwhile the efforts required to reach harmony and achieve progress in industrial life and thereby to ensure the continuation of this island civilisation.

Happy and sad faces of the eighties.

(left, top) Prince William and his proud parents, Prince Charles and Princess Diana, on a visit to New Zealand in 1983.

(far left, bottom) Pope John Paul II on his highly successful visit to Britain in 1982 – the first papal visit to the United Kingdom in history.

(left, bottom) An unemployed worker demands a job from the Prime Minister. His poster refers to the Falklands episode of 1982. This brought military success to Britain, but with high costs in terms of money and good will to Britain in South America.

Further Reading

The first part of this brief bibliography gives titles which offer a general introduction to Britain. The second part lists more specialised works. Up to the nineteenth century I have suggested one book for each period. This was no easy task, but the object was to keep the list to a reasonable length.

General Works

For an introduction to the geography, economy and politics of modern Britain:

Brian Nixon, *The British Isles* (University Tutorial Press, 1979)

Peter Bromhead, *Life in Modern Britain* (Longman, 1962)

For general histories of England, Wales, Scotland and Ireland:

Winston S. Churchill, *A History of the English-Speaking Peoples* (4 vols) (Cassell, 1956) Though Churchill stops at the beginning of the twentieth century the volumes he lists towards the end of the second part deal generously with twentieth century England.

David Thomas (ed), *Wales: a New Study* (David and Charles, 1977)

Rosalind Mitchison, *A History of Scotland* (Methuen, 1970)

Edmund Curtis, *A History of Ireland* (Methuen, reprinted 1978)

F. S. L. Lyons, *Ireland since the Famine* (Weidenfeld and Nicolson, 1971)

For an outline of the main developments in English literature:

Waldo Clarke, *A Short History of English Literature* (Evans, 1976)

And a work which, in addition to providing an historical survey, puts authors in their social and regional context:

David Daiches and John Flower, *Literary Landscapes of the British Isles: a Narrative Atlas* (Paddington Press, 1979)

For a book which gives a stimulating view of working-class culture:

Richard Hoggart, *The Uses of Literacy* (Penguin, 1958)

For a quick, sympathetic survey of English architecture:
  John Betjeman, *A Pictorial History of English Architecture* (Penguin, 1974)
For an account of the way the English countryside has developed:
  W. G. Hoskins, *The Making of the English Landscape* (Penguin, 1970)

More Specialised Works

Colin Renfrew (ed), *British Prehistory: a New Outline* (Duckworth, 1974)

H. H. Scullard, *Roman Britain, Outpost of the Empire* (Thames and Hudson, 1979)

Lloyd and Jennifer Laing, *Anglo-Saxon England* (Routledge and Kegan Paul, 1979)

David M. Wilson, *The Vikings and their Origins* (Thames and Hudson, 1970, new ed. 1980)

G. W. S. Barrow, *Feudal Britain* (Arnold, 1956)

M. H. Keen, *England in the Later Middle Ages* (Methuen, 1973)

Colin Platt, *The English Medieval Town* (Secker and Warburg, 1976)

G. R. Elton, *England under the Tudors* (Methuen, 1955)

Christopher Hill, *The Century of Revolution 1603–1714* (Abacus, 1978)

Dorothy Marshall, *Eighteenth Century England* (Longman, 1974)

Asa Briggs, *The Age of Improvement, 1783–1867* (Longman, 1959)

George Rudé, *Wilkes and Liberty: a Social Study of 1763 to 1774* (Clarendon Press, 1962)

E. J. Hobsbawm, *Industry and Empire* (Penguin, 1969)

Gerald S. Graham, *A Concise History of the British Empire* (Thames and Hudson, 1970)

James Morris, *Pax Britannica* (3 vols) (Penguin, 1978)

T. O. Lloyd, *Empire to Welfare State: English History 1906–1967* (Oxford University Press, 1970)

Trevor Wilson, *The Downfall of the Liberal Party 1914–1935* (Collins, 1966)

C. P. Cook and John Stevenson, *The Slump, Society and Politics during the Depression* (Jonathan Cape, 1977)

Henry Pelling, *Winston Churchill* (Macmillan, 1974)

Alan Sked and Chris Cook, *Post-War Britain: A Political History* (Penguin, 1979)

H. Thomas, *The Suez Affair* (Weidenfeld and Nicolson, 1966)

T. Noble, *Modern Britain: Structure and Change* (Batsford, 1975)

Elizabeth Barker, *Britain and a Divided Europe 1945–1970* (Weidenfeld and Nicolson 1971)

L. J. Macfarlane, *Issues in British Politics since 1945* (Longman, 1975)

Genealogy of the Kings and Queens

England

The Normans

William I, duke of Normandy, the Conqueror (1066–87)
William II, 'Rufus' (1087–1100), son of William I
Henry I (1100–35), son of William I
Stephen (1135–54), nephew of Henry I and grandson of William I. His accession to the throne was contested by Matilda, daughter of Henry I

The Plantagenets

Henry II (1154–89), son of Matilda and her second husband, Count Geoffrey of Anjou (Plantagenet)
Richard I, 'Coeur-de-Lion' (1189–99), son of Henry II
John (1199–1216), son of Henry II
Henry III (1216–72), son of John
Edward I (1272–1307), son of Henry III
Edward II (1307–27), son of Edward I
Edward III (1327–77), son of Edward II
Richard II (1377–99, died 1400), son of Edward, the Black Prince and grandson of Edward III

The Houses of York and Lancaster

Henry IV (1399–1413), son of John of Gaunt, duke of Lancaster and grandson of Edward III
Henry V (1413–22), son of Henry IV
Henry VI (born 1421, ascended throne 1433, reigned 1422–61 and 1470–1, died 1471), son of Henry V
Edward IV (reigned 1461–70 and 1471–83), son of Richard, duke of York and great-great grandson of Edward III
Edward V (1483, reigned 2 months), son of Edward IV
Richard III (1483–85), son of Richard, duke of York and brother of Edward IV

Henry VII (1485–1509), son of Edmund Tudor and Lady Margaret Beaufort, great-grand daughter of Edward III

Henry VIII (1509–47), son of Henry VII and Elizabeth of York, daughter of Edward IV and sister of Edward V

Edward VI (1547–53), son of Henry VIII and his third wife, Jane Seymour

Mary I (1553–58), daughter of Henry VIII and his first wife, Katharine of Aragon

Elizabeth I (1558–1603), daughter of Henry VIII and his second wife, Anne Boleyn

Scotland

Malcolm III 'Ceann Mor' (1058–93)

Donald Ban (1093–94, 1094–97), brother of Malcolm III

Duncan II (1094), son of Malcolm III and Ingibiorg

Edgar (1097–1107), son of Malcolm III and Margaret

Alexander I (1107–24), son of Malcolm III and Margaret and brother of Edgar

David I (1124–53), son of Malcolm III and Margaret and brother of Edgar and Alexander I

Malcolm IV, 'the Maiden' (born 1142, ascended the throne 1153, died 1165), son of Henry (died 1152) and grandson of David I

William I, 'The Lion' (1165–1214), son of David I and brother of Malcolm IV

Alexander II (1214–49), son of William I

Alexander III (1249–86), son of Alexander II. He was succeeded by his granddaughter, Margaret, the 'Maid of Norway' (died 1290); the crown was then in dispute between John Balliol and Robert Bruce

John Balliol, 'Toom Tabard' (1292–96), great-grandson of Earl David, brother of William I

The War of Independence against England

Robert Bruce became Robert I on claiming the throne in 1306 (died 1329); he was grandson of Robert Bruce, claimant to the Scottish throne in 1291, who was grandson of Earl David, brother of William I

David II (1329–71), son of Robert I

Robert II, 'the Stewart' (1371–90), son of Walter Stewart and Marjorie, daughter of Robert I; Robert II 'the Stewart' was nephew of David II

Robert III (1390–1406), son of Robert II

James I (1406–37), son of Robert III

James II (1437–60), son of James I

James III (1460–88), son of James II
James IV (1488–1513), son of James III
James V (1513–42), son of James IV
Mary I, Mary Queen of Scots (1542–67), daughter of James
    V and Marie de Guise
James VI (1567–1625), son of Mary and Lord Darnley

England and Scotland

The Stuarts and the Commonwealth

James VI of Scotland ascended the throne of England in 1603
    (died 1625); he became James I of England; his mother,
    Mary Queen of Scots, was the great-granddaughter of
    Henry VII of England
Charles I (1625–49, when he was executed), son of James

The Commonwealth or the Interregnum (1649–60)
    Oliver Cromwell, Lord Protector (1653–58)
    Richard Cromwell, son of Oliver Cromwell, Lord Protector
        (1658–60)

Charles II (1660–85), son of Charles I
James II of England and James VII of Scotland (1685–88), son
    of Charles I and brother of Charles II
William III and Mary II (1688–1702), William was the son of
    William II, Prince of Orange (of Holland) and husband of
    Mary II; Mary was the daughter of James II and VII and
    his first wife Anne Hyde; Mary died 1694
Anne (1702–14), daughter of James II and VII and Anne Hyde,
    sister of Mary II

The House of Hanover and Windsor

George I (1714–27), son of Ernest, Elector of Hanover and
    Sophia, granddaughter of James I and VI
George II (1727–60), son of George I
George III (1760–1820), son of Frederick (died 1751) and
    grandson of George II
George IV (1820–30), son of George III
William IV (1830–37), son of George III and brother of
    George IV
Victoria (1837–1901), daughter of Edward, duke of Kent and
    Princess Victoria of Saxe-Coburg; Edward was the fourth
    son of George III and brother of George IV and William IV;
    Victoria married her cousin, Prince Albert of Saxe-Coburg-
    Gotha in 1840 (died 1861)

Edward VII (1901–10), son of Queen Victoria and Prince Albert

George V (1910–36), son of Edward VII, assumed the family name of Windsor in 1917 Edward VIII (ascended throne 20 January 1936, abdicated 11 December 1936), eldest son of George V
George VI (1936–52), second son of George V and brother of Edward VIII, married the Lady Elizabeth Bowes-Lyon in 1923

Elizabeth II (born 1926, ascended throne 1952), elder daughter of George VI and Queen Elizabeth (the Queen Mother), married Philip Mountbatten, formerly Prince Philip of Schleswig-Holstein-Sonderburg-Glucksburg in 1947
Queen Elizabeth and Prince Philip have four children:
Charles, Prince of Wales (born 1948), Princess Anne (born 1950), Prince Andrew (born 1960) and Prince Edward (born 1964)
Prince Charles married Lady Diana Spencer in 1981 and has one son, Prince William
Princess Anne married Captain Mark Phillips in 1973 and has one son
Princess Margaret, second daughter of George VI, and sister of Elizabeth II married Anthony Armstrong-Jones, Earl of Snowdon and has two children

Index